The Zionist Movement in Palestine and World Politics, 1880-1918

PROBLEMS IN
EUROPEAN CIVILIZATION

Under the editorial direction of
John Ratté
Amherst College

The Zionist Movement in Palestine and World Politics, 1880-1918

Edited and with an introduction by

N. Gordon Levin, Jr.
Amherst College

D. C. HEATH AND COMPANY
Lexington, Massachusetts Toronto London

International Standard Book Number: 0-669-85605-3

Library of Congress Catalog Card Number: 73-9344

CONTENTS

IV EARLY ZIONISM AND THE PALESTINIAN ARABS

INTRODUCTION

The Jews had made considerable progress toward cultural, economic, and political assimilation in France, Germany, and Austria-Hungary between 1789 and 1870. Even in Eastern Europe where the great majority of nineteenth-century Europe's 5 million Jews lived isolated and confined in Russia's Pale of Settlement, the accession to power of the more liberal Czar Alexander II in 1855 established a situation in which modernist Jewish intellectuals, the *maskilim,* could begin to flourish in the environment of a nascent Jewish enlightenment or *Haskalah.* Yet Jewish progress was soon threatened by a rising tide of politicized anti-Semitism which swept continental Europe, East and West, in the era of the "New Imperialism" between 1870 and 1914. It is only in the context of this powerful wave of post-1870 anti-Semitism that one can comprehend fully the emergence, especially in the West, of a Zionist movement which, despite its modernist and socialist dimensions, represented a particularistic Jewish variant of the very antiuniversalist current of late nineteenth-century thought responsible in large part for anti-Semitism itself.

In the post-1870 German Empire anti-Semitism was fueled by racist and imperialist currents of conservative thinking, currents which further eroded the historically weak foundations of German liberalism. Moreover, Germany's lower middle classes, increasingly threatened by an expanding industrial capitalism from above and by an emergent socialist movement from below, proved receptive to appeals from anti-Semitic Christian Socialist politicians who linked the Jews to these threats. Many of the same social phenomena were found in Austria-Hungary, where their anti-Semitic impetus was strengthened by the identification of the Jews as clients and defenders of the pluralistic Austrian Empire which guaranteed their legal rights. This ultra-Austrian status earned Jews the hatred of those national movements, Pan-German and Slavic, which sought the dismemberment of Austria-Hungary. Even the small French Jewish community of about 70,000, a community which had made the greatest strides of any on the continent towards cultural assimilation, was not spared from the new political anti-Semitism. In France after 1880, army- and church-oriented conservative nationalists used anti-Semitism effectively in their antiliberal assault on the Third Republic. This conservative agitation culminated in the Dreyfus Affair which split French politics in the late 1890s over the issue of a pardon for Captain Alfred Dreyfus, an assimilated Jewish army officer from Alsace, who had been wrongly convicted for treason in 1894. One man especially impressed by the meaning for European Jewry of the French reaction to Dreyfus's conviction was Theodor Herzl, an Austrian Jew who was at that time the Paris correspondent for the Vienna *Neue Freie Presse.* Herzl's seminal Zionist pamphlet, *The Jewish State,* appeared within a year of the initial conviction and public humiliation of Dreyfus.

The masses of Jews in Eastern Europe had to face an even worse onslaught of anti-Semitism after 1870 than did the smaller and more assimilated Jewish communities of Western and Central Europe. By 1900, state-sanctioned anti-Semitism had reduced most of Romania's 250,000 Jews to poverty and desperation. In Russia Jews suffered in the political reaction which followed the defeat of the Polish Revolt of 1863 and brought an abrupt end to Czar Alexander II's relatively liberal treatment of Russia's Jews. In late nineteenth-century Russia Jewish separatism was constantly attacked by reactionary Slavophile nationalism, but the opportunity for cultural assimilation was not granted to Russian Jews. Instead, successive czars sought more completely to isolate the Jews legally and territorially in the Pale of Settlement on Russia's western borders. Contained in the Pale, and excluded from educational advancement, Jews faced increasing poverty and a czarist-inspired anti-Semitism which used Jews as a scapegoat to protect the regime from potential revolutionary passions in the masses. Brutal pogroms, government-sanctioned riots against Jewish communities such as those at Kiev in 1881 and Kishinev in 1903, flared periodically in those years.

Thus, throughout continental Europe after 1870 the Jew was increasingly perceived with hostility as alien. Depending on the part of Europe or the social class involved, Jews were attacked for being too anxious to assimilate, for being too committed to maintaining their separation from Christian society, or for successfully developing the characteristics of intellectual and commercial competitiveness in the process of moving from separatism to assimilation. What continental Europe could not offer the Jews, it seemed, was an environment of tolerant pluralism in which Jews could evolve their own particular fusion of assimilation and independence.

European Jewry had several possible lines of defense to fall back upon in the face of late nineteenth-century anti-Semitism. In Western and Central Europe Jews could attempt to insist that their proven loyalty to the nation should guarantee their full rights as citizens. Assimilationist Jews argued the liberal thesis that they were simply Germans, Austrians, or Frenchmen of the Jewish religious faith. In Romania and Russia, however, liberal universalistic traditions were almost nonexistent and Jews had never been permitted even to begin the process of cultural assimilation. Moreover, only a tiny minority of Russian Jews joined the small Russian revolutionary movements of the populist or socialist variety, movements themselves often as anti-Semitic as the Russian people to whom they tried to appeal. By and large, in Eastern Europe the Jewish people were forced to rely on themselves.

One natural form of defensive self-reliance for Eastern Jewry, and the one favored by the conservative Jewish rabbinical elites, was the reaffirmation of traditional Judaism and the effort to find in community and familial ritual an inner serenity based on a consciousness of their favored status in God's eyes and on a feeling of superiority over the Christian oppressor. Another more modernist line of self-defense sought in the independent Jewish Socialist movement, the Jewish Workers Bund, an answer, at once both Jewish and socially progressive, to the hopeless poverty and legal disabilities confronting the Jewish working class in Russia's Pale of Settlement. Or, for hundreds of thousands of Eastern Jews in whom desperation fused with some capacity for hope and mobility, there was the option of emigration to America. In the twenty-five years before World War I over 1.3 million Jews left Eastern Europe for the United States where they sought the economic opportunity and pluralistic tolerance unavailable to Jews in Europe. Unavoidably, however, such a massive migration of Eastern Jews created social and political dilemmas for the more assimilated Jews of Western Europe and the United States who were seeking to counter rising anti-Semitism with the liberal politics of assimilation.

A final Jewish line of defense was Zionism, a movement which enlisted the allegiance of only a small minority of European Jewry at the outset but a movement which proved, as the tragic course of twentieth-century Jewish history unfolded, to be second only to emigration to America as an answer for Europe's persecuted Jews. In one sense, of course, the Zionist vision—the sense of a Palestinian homeland lost, but to be regained—had always been present in the symbolism of traditional Judaism. Communities of devout Sephardic Jews had continued to live in Palestine in the cities of Tiberias, Safed, Hebron, and Jerusalem since Biblical times. Yet, it was not until the nineteenth century that Jewish thought began to consider the return to Palestine to be termed an ascent, or an *Aliyah,* in practical as well as metaphysical terms. Prior to 1880 Russian Jewish modernist intellectuals of the *Haskalah* had developed the idea of a return to Palestine to reestablish a Hebrew-speaking center for Jewish refuge, religion, and culture. In 1882 the Russian Jew Leon Pinsker built on this tradition and responded to a fresh wave of pogroms by publishing his *Auto-Emancipation* which argued for Zionism as an answer to anti-Semitism. By 1900, despite the overwhelming pull of America for the Russian Jewish emigrant, small groups of Russian Jews, members of the first *Aliyah,* or first wave of Zionist immigration, had begun the hard struggle to settle in Turkish-controlled Palestine.

It was only natural that Zionism should first take tentative roots among the Jewry of Eastern Europe. In the closely knit Jewish communities of the Pale of Settlement the experience and awareness of Jewish identity was part of life itself. In the Pale, as we have seen, Jewish traditionalism and Jewish socialism, whatever their mutual hostility, were both lines of self-reliant defense for Russian Jews. For its part, the Zionist impulse also embodied a self-reliant Jewish nationalist thrust, and this Zionist impulse could appeal, paradoxically, both to Jewish tradition and to Jewish socialism. Zionism spoke to the traditional Jewish yearning for a return to the lost Zion and, despite a continuing Jewish conservative opposition to worldly Zionism as sacrilege, the Zionist movement has never been without religious support. Many primarily secular Zionists possessed a socialist vision of social justice in a Jewish homeland, and this enabled

Zionism to speak as well to members of the Jewish Workers Bund. To be sure, the Bund officially rejected Zionism and sought primarily to transform Jewish life in Russia itself. Yet, Bundists and socialist Zionists shared both a common opposition to bourgeois Jews and conservative rabbis and a common rejection of the alien Russian society. After the failure of revolution in 1905 it was natural that some Bundists would move toward the Zionist vision of a Jewish socialism carried beyond the hostile Russian environment to the ancient homeland of Palestine redeemed by a rebirth of Jewish spirit and labor. In this connection, it is interesting to note that prior to 1914 the Russian-Jewish intellectual Leon Trotsky, a strong advocate of universalistic and assimilationist socialism, saw both the Bund and socialist Zionism as hopelessly flawed by the same Jewish particularist failing.

In sum then, tradition, nationalism, and socialism fused in a Zionist movement which would project onto early twentieth-century Palestine a transformed fragment of the larger Russian Jewish community. For Jewish transformation was, finally, at the heart of the Zionist impulse. To some extent Zionists internalized the anti-Semitic criticism of Jewish rootlessness and commercialism and vowed that Zionism would create in Palestine a new Jewish society close to its own soil and committed to the national community. In reality, and this was a point that assimilated Jewish opponents of Zionism have often made then and since, Zionism was involved in a peculiar intellectual and political dialectic both in opposition to and, paradoxically, in alliance with the very anti-Semitism which called it into being. Assimilationist Jewish liberals in the West and Socialists in the East argued from a universalist perspective that Zionism was guilty of creating a self-fulfilling prophecy as to the inevitability of anti-Semitism and a continuing Jewish nationalism. Needless to say such assimilationist criticism did not destroy the Zionist vision of a Jewish national revival in Palestine.

Yet, if Western and Central European Jewry did not supply a potential mass base for Zionism comparable to the Pale of Settlement, it was the case nonetheless that in an era of rising anti-Semitism assimilated Jewry did furnish crucial intellectual and political leadership to Zionism as well as the aid of prominent Jews with influential contacts in finance and world politics. Figures such as Theodor Herzl and Max Nordau, early leaders of the political Zionist movement, are of course prime examples of this. Herzl and Nordau created political order in the Zionist movement by establishing periodic congresses, clear lines of authority, and effective methods to publicize the basic ideas of Zionism. Herzl also skillfully utilized connections and a bold front to bring Zionism onto the stage of world politics.

Theodor Herzl was an assimilated Austrian Jew and whatever his almost mythic personal popularity among the masses of Eastern Jews, he never fully earned the trust of leading Eastern Zionists. Herzl's influential pamphlet *The Jewish State* (1896) tended to base Zionism on a rational response to anti-Semitism rather than on a rooted sense of Jewish national identity. Eastern Zionists were also put off by Herzl's opposition to immediate practical settlement work in Palestine. In 1903 Herzl further alienated the Palestine-oriented Eastern Zionists by urging acceptance of Britain's offer of land in Uganda for a provisional Jewish national home. This project proved stillborn.

Essentially Herzl was convinced that a secure Jewish national home could be created in Palestine only after the legal sanction of one or several of the great powers had been attained. With a legal charter in hand, Herzl reasoned, the Zionists could attract large-scale investment from Jewish financiers and Jewish settlers secure in the knowledge that what they might build today would not be wiped out tomorrow at the caprice of the Ottoman Turkish rulers of Palestine. Herzl's diplomatic efforts were directed, between 1897 and 1904, through contacts primarily with German and Turkish leaders, at the attainment of Constantinople's and/or Berlin's acceptance of a Jewish national home in Palestine. Herzl's diplomatic method combined statements of Jewish national vision with hints of financial and developmental support for Turkey and promises to free Germany or Russia of unwanted Jews and Jewish radicalism. Herzl's diplomacy uneasily fused megalomania, tactfulness, and sheer bluff. Ultimately he failed.

Not only did Herzl lack the solid financial support that might have enabled him to deal more effectively with the debt-ridden Ottoman Empire, but he was up against an increasingly intractable diplomatic environment. The Turkish sultan feared emerging nationalist movements among the non-Turkish peoples of the Ottoman Empire, and he was not about to create another national minority in the form of a Zionist enclave in Palestine. Moreover, the years immediately preceding 1914 saw a growing diplomatic and political closeness develop between Germany and Turkey. In this situation Berlin could be of little help to Herzl with the sultan. Britain and France, increasingly allied with Turkey's natural enemy Russia during these years, had little to say about internal questions in the Ottoman Empire but both would, of course, have opposed anything like a German protectorate over a Zionist Palestine. Paradoxically, Russia prior to 1914 did offer some diplomatic protection to Russian Jews in Palestine. It was as if Jews could become Russians only by leaving Russia.

Yet, if the first major Zionist effort in world politics had largely failed by the time of Herzl's death in 1904, the less publicized but purposeful task of establishing a Jewish presence in Palestine was proceeding ahead under the direction of "practical" Zionists who rejected Herzl's view that productive work in Palestine had to await the achievement of a charter. By 1914 there were approximately 85,000 Jews in Palestine. Of this total about 60,000 had arrived since 1880 and were part of the new *Yishuv,* the Jewish community in Palestine, as distinct from the more traditionalist old *Yishuv* which subsisted on religious donations from Jews abroad. This new *Yishuv* was led increasingly by members of the dynamic and socialistic second wave of Russian Zionist emigrants, the second *Aliyah* of 1904–1914. Future leaders of Israel such as David Ben-Gurion, Levi Eshkol and Yitzhak Ben-Zvi were members of the second *Aliyah.* These Zionist settlers pioneered defense and agricultural institutions, such as the *kibbutz,* which would become basic to the fabric of Israeli life. Under the leadership of men like Arthur Ruppin, they also laid the foundations of Tel Aviv in the barren sand dunes near what was then the predominantly Arab city of Jaffa. Yet even to mention the difference between Palestinian Arab Jaffa and Zionist projections for a Jewish Tel Aviv, is also to raise the larger question of Zionist-Arab relations in Palestine prior to 1914.

Despite some fantasizing based on ignorance, distance, and hope about an empty and desolate Palestine waiting to be redeemed by Jewish settlement, early Zionist leaders and pioneers did not entirely ignore the existence of the approximately 600,000 Arabs in Turkish Palestine. With the exception of the pessimists or realists who predicted inevitable conflict, however, most Zionists tended to be over-optimistic concerning the possibility of avoiding a head on Arab-Jewish clash. Herzl and other Zionist leaders tended to assume that the Palestinian Arabs, along with the Jewish settlers, would benefit from the development of the land and that the two groups could live peacefully together while the Jews, presumably with Arab acquiescence, steadily changed the character of the land and achieved an eventual Jewish majority in the overall population. Some sincere efforts at Arab-Jewish cooperation based on both commitment and prudence did mark Zionist efforts during these early years. But, such Zionist hopes and efforts notwithstanding, the pre-1914 period saw increasing Arab-Jewish tension in the Ottoman Parliament and in Palestine over the sale and control of land, over the issue of Arab peasant displacement from land purchased by the Zionists, and over the question of Jewish immigration into Palestine. Probably the situation was worsened by the immigrants of the socialistic second *Aliyah* who rejected Jewish use of cheap Arab labor, insisted that Jews do all their own work as part of a process of creating a new and more productive Jewish society, and sought, therefore, much to the Arabs' displeasure, to ban Arab labor from Zionist agriculture and construction.

Palestinian Arabs naturally feared the dynamic ascendancy of this new Zionist culture, and it is not surprising that Arab nationalism, developing as it was in the pre–World War I Ottoman Empire, often marked the Zionist as well as the Turk as the Arabs' enemies. The hard fact was that by 1914 two emerging national movements, Arab and Jewish, found themselves on a collision course over the same Palestinian territory. Those who, along with this author, fundamentally sympathize with Zionism might point to European anti-Semitism, to the desperate Jewish need for even a small national home, to the heritage of Jewish religious and cultural ties to Palestine, and to the existence of vast lands where the Moslem Arabs were and are culturally dominant. Zionist sympathizers must also admit, however, that there was no reason to have expected the Palestinian Arabs voluntarily to accept this rationale for the Zionist transformation of Palestine.

With the coming of World War I, and the eventual adherence of the Ottoman Turks to the side of Germany and Austria-Hungary, the world political situation shifted steadily in favor of Zionism. As the Entente allies moved through complex arrangements with Arab nationalism (the Hussein-McMahon correspondence of 1915) and among themselves (the Sykes-Picot Agreement of 1916) to plan the postwar partition of the Ottoman Empire, Zionists found themselves in a position to realize the goal which had eluded Herzl earlier, namely an international guarantee of the right of a Jewish return to recreate a national home in Palestine. Yet despite the diplomatic opportunity opened by the war, the Zionist movement might not have been able to seize the moment but for Chaim Weizmann's strategic presence in Great Britain.

Chaim Weizmann had a Russian Jewish upbringing, was further educated in Germany, had a brief teaching career at Geneva, and then, in the ten years prior to 1914, became in early middle age a naturalized British citizen employed as a reader in chemistry at Manchester University. Weizmann was also a committed Zionist who combined Eastern European Jewish roots and a commitment to practical work in Palestine, characteristics Herzl had lacked, with something approaching Herzl's sense of the importance of influential connections, skillful propaganda, and the manipulation of world politics. Moreover, Weizmann's diplomatic position was further enhanced in 1916 when he became essential to his adopted Britain as a wartime explosives expert.

Anti-Semitism was traditionally much weaker in liberal Britain than on the European continent, although the large influx of Eastern Jewish migrants arriving in the late nineteenth century did begin to arouse a nascent British hostility to Jews and to create anxiety among members of Britain's highly assimilated Anglo-Jewish elite. Zionism was naturally anathema to members of this elite who saw in its insistence on a Jewish national identity a threat to their own hard-won status as Englishmen of the Jewish faith. Weizmann did receive support from Herbert Samuel, an influential Anglo-Jew destined to become the first British high commissioner in Mandatory Palestine, but the general opposition of Anglo-Jewry might have defeated Weizmann nonetheless had the issue remained primarily Jewish and had British statesmen during the war not come increasingly to see a connection between Zionist and British imperialist interests in Palestine. Thus paradoxically it would be Great Britain, the European nation most hospitable to Jewish assimilation, which would make possible through the Balfour Declaration the realization of the hopes of those nationalistic Jews who most despaired of liberal universalism as the answer to the Jewish tragedy in early twentieth-century Europe. Or, viewed another way, it was perhaps Britain's record of tolerance of Jews which permitted Zionists such as Weizmann, a man himself poised between the Jewish and British worlds, to trust a British protectorate of a Jewish national home in Palestine.

But how does one explain the movement of Britain's wartime leaders toward Zionism? Part of the answer lay in the Biblical Protestant conviction of men such as Arthur Balfour and David Lloyd George that the Jews were legitimately rooted historically and religiously in the Holy Land. Part of the answer lay in the vision held by influential Englishmen such as Mark Sykes and Herbert Sidebotham of a Palestine modernized by Jewish settlers under British protection. Also crucial for British statesmen was the hope that a Zionist Palestine supported by Britain could help to legitimate the postwar maintenance of British power in an area strategic to the defense of the Suez Canal. In this manner London could use the Zionists against French claims on Palestine arising out of the Sykes-Picot negotiations. Finally, however, in the fall of 1917, as the forces of General Allenby were defeating the Turks in Palestine and driving on toward Jerusalem, other pressing considerations moved the British leaders toward issuing the Balfour Declaration on November 2. Essentially London hoped that such a gesture to world Jewry might firm up American Jewish support for the war, swing Russian Jews behind the faltering war effort of Kerensky's threatened provisional government, and head off a possible German endorsement of Zionist aims.

The Balfour Declaration was embodied in a letter sent from British Foreign Secretary Arthur Balfour to Lord Rothschild on November 2, 1917, and it read as follows:

> *His Majesty's Government view with favour the establishment in Palestine of a national home for the Jewish people, and will use their best endeavours to facilitate the achievement of this object, it being clearly understood that nothing shall be done which may prejudice the civil and religious rights of the existing non-Jewish communities in Palestine, or the rights and political status enjoyed by Jews in any other country.*

Spokesmen for assimilated Anglo-Jewry had objected to the entire pro-Zionist thrust of the declaration and the last sentence, concerning preservation of the "rights and political status enjoyed by Jews in any other country," was clearly meant as a concession to Anglo-Jewish anxieties. The British promise not to "prejudice the civil and religious rights of the existing non-Jewish communities in Palestine" was directed at Arab concerns, but such vague language did not fully appease the Arab fear and anger which soon evidenced itself over this Zionist victory. Arab nationalists would always insist that the Balfour Declaration was legally and morally illegitimate and that it betrayed earlier British promises to the Arabs, promises which had helped to foster the wartime Arab revolt against the Ottoman Empire.

Thus embodied in the very language of the Balfour Declaration was that paradoxical alliance of Jewish anti-Zionist universalism and outraged Arab nationalist particularism which would oppose Zionist efforts after 1917. Yet these concessions to Zionism's opponents in the declaration, and the fact that the British pledge of a Jewish national home was not quite so forceful as Weizmann had hoped, could not dampen the joy of the Zionists over their first great breakthrough in world politics. Whatever the ambiguities in the declaration and whatever difficulties lay ahead, after 1917 Zionists could believe realistically that their vision of a Jewish return to Palestine was realizable.

By now it must be clear to the reader that any serious historical analysis of the development of early Zionism involves one in the consideration of paradox and contradiction. We have seen that Zionism spoke to the traditional religious sense of Jewish peoplehood with its Biblical connection to Palestine at the same time that it embodied many modernist Jewish hopes for secular progress and social justice. Yet such an uneasy and often creative tension between tradition and modernity is not unique to Zionism as a movement of national liberation. The same tension has been endemic to nationalist and anticolonial movements throughout the Third World. The tragic irony of Zionism, however, is that it emerged on the world scene at a time, and in an area, which brought Jewish and Arab nationalism into conflict. Because of this conflict many of the essential similarities between Zionism and other movements of national liberation, in their efforts to handle the dialectic between tradition and modernity, and between nationalism and socialism, are hidden.

Whatever balance it struck with traditional Judaism, however, we have also seen that Zionism faced other serious contradictions in the form of criticism from assimilationist Jews oriented toward secular universalism of either the liberal or the socialist variants. Against liberal assimilated Jews who saw Zionism as a particularistic denial of the special modern Jewish commitment to universalistic values, the Zionists argued that in a context of European anti-Semitism the universal was attainable for Jews only in and through the achievement of Judaism's own particular self-determination. In other words, the Jewish movement for national liberation, the Zionists believed, would permit Jews to achieve on their own land those universalistic liberal values which Jews could not successfully champion in a European environment of emergent anti-Semitism. Against Jewish Socialists who saw Zionism both as a particularistic denial of class conflict and as a prop for the world imperialist system, the Zionists argued that the Jewish Question transcended the class question because the non-Jewish European masses saw the Jews as alien. Moreover, Zionists believed that they had no choice but to operate within the existing framework of the international politics of imperialism, rather than in terms of the revolutionary socialist vision of imperialism's imminent transformation, not only because the leaders of Zionism were largely middle class, but also because for Zionists the plight of the Jews and the urge for Zion were both too pressing to permit Zionists to wait for revolutionary internationalists to solve the Jewish Question. Put another way, Zionists were not prepared to sacrifice their particularistic utopian vision for a universalistic utopian vision.

As we have seen in the case of Weizmann's activities, this basic opposition of Zionism to revolutionary socialist internationalism brought the Zionists onto the stage of world history at the time of the Russian Revolution as allies of British imperialism against both Leninist revolutionary socialism in Russia and emerging Arab nationalism in Palestine. From the Zionist perspective, however, it was evident in 1917 that only British imperialism, for whatever combination of idealism and self-interest, was prepared to attempt to establish and guarantee a context in the Middle East in which the aims of Arab and Jewish nationalists might possibly be worked out on some basis of compromise. Zionists must have known that there was no place for their dream in the emerging fusion in world politics between Leninist revolutionary socialism and Arab nationalism. Moreover, there was Woodrow Wilson's promise of the self-determination of small nations to come with Allied victory. Might not the

Zionists, as well as the Poles, Czechs, and Arabs, aspire to Allied liberation?

The readings which make up this volume are designed to permit further exploration of the events and issues introduced above. The selection from Howard M. Sachar's *The Course of Modern Jewish History* provides a concise narrative treatment of the origins and the evolution of Zionism from 1880 to 1914. V. D. Segre's analysis, taken from his *Israel: A Society in Transition,* places Zionism in the larger context of Jewish intellectual history since the Enlightenment. Next, the first selection from Alex Bein's *Theodore Herzl* presents Herzl's reaction to the conviction and humiliation of Dreyfus and Herzl's earliest formulation of his Zionist perspective. The thoughtful reconsideration of Herzl's diplomacy in J. L. Talmon's *Israel among the Nations* precedes a second selection from Bein's *Theodore Herzl* describing the Zionist leader's meeting with the German kaiser in Palestine in 1898.

The first reading from Chaim Weizmann's autobiography *Trial and Error* describes his differences with Herzl over practical settlement activities in Palestine and presents Weizmann's perspective on the concrete Zionist gains made in Palestine prior to World War I. The Weizmann reading is followed by a section from Amos Elon's *The Israelis: Founders and Sons.* In this section Elon seeks to capture the spirit of the Russian-Jewish socialist pioneers of the second *Aliyah* and to consider their approach to the Arab question.

The next group of readings deals with the role of Zionist diplomacy in the achievement of the Balfour Declaration. The selection from Doreen Ingrams' *Palestine Papers 1917–1922* presents carefully edited primary sources from British cabinet papers and government office files concerning Britain's Middle Eastern policy during World War I. The selection from Howard M. Sachar's *The Emergence of the Middle East 1914–1924* presents a thorough narrative treatment of the British-Zionist relationship from 1914 to 1918. The second reading from Weizmann's *Trial and Error* is included to convey Weizmann's own interpretation of the crucial events which led up to the issuance of the Balfour Declaration. Finally, the selection from George Antonius's *The Arab Awakening* presents an Arab perspective on British diplomacy in the Middle East during World War I.

The final group of readings deals broadly with the issue of Zionist-Arab relations in Palestine from 1880 to 1918. The chapter reprinted from Walter Laqueur's *A History of Zionism* focuses in depth on the early Zionist perceptions of the Palestinian Arabs and on the evolving relations between the two groups until the issuance of the Balfour Declaration. And finally J. L. Talmon considers the Arab-Zionist conflict in the larger context of the role, at once both tragic and triumphant, of the Jews in modern history.

Note: Until very recently, the transliteration of Hebrew into the Roman alphabet has not been completely standardized. Jews from different parts of the world pronounce Hebrew differently from one another. Certain Hebrew letters and sounds can be transliterated in more than one way. We have not attempted to impose one system of tansliteration on all of the selections included here. However, where confusion could result from several spellings of the same Hebrew word or name, we have standardized those words. Two excellent sources for additional information are the *Encyclopedia Judaica* and the *Encyclopedia of Zionism and Israel.*

I THE EMERGENCE OF ZIONISM: 1880–1914

Howard M. Sachar

THE RISE OF ZIONISM

Howard M. Sachar, professor of modern history at George Washington University, is the author of several studies dealing with modern Jewish history and with the twentieth century diplomatic history of the Middle East. This selection presents a concise narrative and analysis of the history of Zionism from 1880 to 1914.

It is only against [the] background of gestating national sentiment that the revived pogroms of the 1880s can be said to have intensified the urgency of Jewish nationalism. Weizmann put it well: "In the depths of the masses an impulse arose, vague, groping, unformulated, for Jewish self-liberation. It was genuinely of the folk; it was saturated with Jewish tradition; and it was connected with the most ancient memories of the land where Jewish life had first expressed itself in freedom. It was, in short, the birth of modern Zionism." Many young Jews, formerly indifferent to Jewish values, now were spurred by the pogroms to take an interest in the fate and fortune of their people. Jewish self-defense units were established in the leading cities of the Pale. Even the former Russophile Lev Levanda was moved to address a Jewish public prayer meeting, to exhort his brethren to return to their traditions, to begin thinking in terms of national rejuvenation.

The first clear-cut appeal to Jewish nationalism as an answer to the new anti-Semitic terror, rather than as a fulfillment of a "mission," was sounded in 1882. It was contained in a pamphlet written by Dr. Leon Pinsker, a former *maskil* from Odessa, and was entitled *Auto-Emanzipation* ("Self-Emancipation"). Pinsker, a physician, approached the problem of anti-Semitism "scientifically." Concluding that Jew-hatred was a phenomenon lying deep in human psychology, he made this observation:

> *Nations live side by side in a state of relative peace, which is based chiefly on the fundamental equality between them. . . . But it is different*

Reprinted by permission of The World Publishing Company from *The Course of Modern Jewish History* by Howard M. Sachar, pp. 264–282. Copyright © 1958 by Howard M. Sachar.

with the people of Israel. This people is not counted among the nations, because since it was exiled from its land it has lacked the essential attributes of nationality, by which one nation is distinguished from another. . . . True, we have not ceased even in the lands of our exile to be spiritually a distinct nation; but this spiritual nationality, so far from giving us the status of a nation in the eyes of the other nations, is the very cause of their hatred for us as a people. Men are always terrified by a disembodied spirit, a soul wandering about with no physical covering; and terror breeds hatred.

Pinsker, in short, provided a scientific rationale for the growing numbers of Russian Jews who sensed that Jewish nationhood must now be transformed into urgent physical formulation.

As we review the rise of nineteenth-century nationalism, we note that the German, Italian, and Balkan nationalist movements could count upon a priceless asset, an asset perhaps even more important than a sense of history, a common folk music, a common language, or a common memory. That asset was the ancestral land itself: the land with familiar hills, contours, valleys, familiar graves, place names, relics, and markers. When European peoples spoke of "freedom" they spoke of a land to be cleared of alien soldiers, of subjugated provinces to be reunited. One wonders, at first, how revived Jewish nationalism could be taken seriously without the asset of a land. But for the Jews of Eastern Europe there was a land. It was as real for hundreds of thousands of them as if they had actually been living on its soil. When they spoke of it, prayed for it, yearned to be reunited with it, time and space disappeared, and it assumed a tangibility as concrete as anything in their practical experience. The land was Palestine.

The Idea of Palestine

It was a burnt-out and eroded little wedge of soil, and after the last Jewish uprising against the Romans in the second century A.D. its history had little to do with the Jews. Invaded, looted, and despoiled by succeeding waves of Romans, Persians, Byzantines, Crusaders, and Arabs, it fell at last into the hands of the Ottoman Turks in 1517. Brave and savage warriors, the most ruthless conquerors in Near Eastern history, the Ottomans were destined to hold Palestine until 1917. During the four centuries of their rule the Ottoman sultans did nothing to improve the province and much to ravage it; the land which had once flowed "with milk and honey" lay blighted and depopulated. Rains eroded its hillsides; its valleys became malarial gullies. Its forests disappeared and the remaining vegetation was exposed to the goats, which the Bedouin nomads drove unhindered through the land.

Yet always there remained a handful of Jews, dark-skinned, poverty-stricken people, hardly distinguishable from the Arabs who inhabited the country after the seventh century. Their numbers were slightly augmented by refugees from the Spanish Inquisition, and by pious Hasidim who, during the nineteenth century, settled in the four "holy" cities of Jerusalem, Tiberias, Safed, and Hebron. They were abjectly poor, living like Arab slum-squatters, dependent on *Halukkah* (charity from abroad), for which each of the groups among them sent out periodic solicitors. A deadly inertia lay on these relics; if the restoration of Zion had depended upon them alone, Jewish nationalism would indeed have been a forlorn cause.

Zion, however, was not just the chimera of the living dead. It was enshrined in the hearts of Jews in every part of the world. It was never divorced from Jewish thinking and religious experience through all the centuries of dispersion. On the ninth day of the month of Ab, for example, which commemorated the destruction of the Temple by the Romans, Jews of a hundred generations later fasted and mourned as though they had been witnesses and victims of that ancient catastrophe. Maurice Samuel recalls:

> *I have sat on the floor in stockinged feet among fellow-mourners, listened to the sobbing recital of the Lamentations of Jeremiah and, by the light of the commemorative candles, seen the tears run down the cheeks of grown men. This was no mechanical ritual. It came from the heart of a frustrated people. It was real, poignant and terrifying, a Fourth of July in reverse.*

The obsessive presentness of Palestine in their lives was a fact. At Jewish weddings the groom crushed a glass underfoot to commemorate the lost Temple of Jerusalem. Three times a day, and oftener on special occasions, pious Jews prayed for the Restoration. The prayers for timely rains and abundant harvests were inevitably phrased in terms evocative of the Holy Land; morning and evening they called upon God to send them the *yoreh* and the *malkosh,* the "former" and the "latter" rains, in due season. They might have been living in the Arctic where there were no rains, or in the tropics where rain was a disaster; they were, in fact, usually city dwellers to whom rain had little personal meaning. It did not matter; the chronology of a Jew's life was still measured by the calendar of ancient Palestine. Jews living in the slate-gray wastes of northern Lithuania continued to erect the *Sukkah,* the tabernacle of desert foliage, during the season when once the Palestine harvest was due. In the midst of the insupportable sufferings of the medieval period, tens of thousands of piteously credulous Jews were deluded into following false Messiahs—Solomon Molcho, David Reubeni, Sabbatai Zevi—in expectation of imminent return to the Holy Land.

For most Jews, however, the notion of a physical return to Palestine was as farfetched as the arrival of an authentic Messiah. It was the rise of Hebrew literature, of Jewish nationalism, and of czarist persecution which combined to convert the thought of a Return from a pious hope to a dramatic salvation. *Haskalah* literature, for example, from the beginning of its history to the end of the nineteenth century, referred explicitly and repeatedly to Palestine: the land Palestine, not merely the national destiny of the Jewish people. This was most apparent . . . in the lyric and romantic literature of Micah Joseph Lebensohn, Kalman Schulman, and Abraham Mapu. Even before the pogroms, *Haskalah* authors were developing solutions for the Jewish problem that were not merely nationalist but also Zionist—Palestine-oriented—in everything but name. Perez Smolenskin did not formally embrace Zionism before the 1880s; but as early as 1868 he declared that it was not at all inappropriate for the modern Jew to aspire to political independence in a Jewish state in Palestine. After the pogroms, Smolenskin urged that Palestine be considered not only as a refuge for the persecuted Jews of Russia, but also as a territorial and spiritual center for the Jewish people—the kind of center America could never be. "Even if that land were inferior to all other countries," he wrote, "even if much work and effort be required to rebuild its waste lands, we should still choose Palestine, for that land is the symbol of our nationhood."

Smolenskin was joined in his Zionist appeals by Yehiel Michel Pines, Moshe Leib Lilienblum, and, most important of all, by Eliezer Ben-Yehudah, to whom the cultivation of the Hebrew language and literature was not enough. "If I did not believe in the possibility of Israeli's redemption," Ben-Yehudah declared in 1881, "I would discard the Hebrew language as a worthless thing." He issued an appeal for mass emigration to Palestine, for the physical cultivation of its soil, the use of its hallowed shrines as a stimulus for revived Jewish cultural and religious creativity. Thus, by the year 1881, sixteen years before the first Zionist Congress, Ben-Yehudah, Smolenskin, Pines, and Lilienblum had already formulated the basic contours of the Zionist idea.

The Rise of Zionism

It was not as simple, however, to transform an inspiring idea into a viable movement. What responsible Jew would give even momentary consideration to settlement in a land parched and arid, snagged and straitened by the Turkish master? The Jews of Russia may have found sentimental outlets in dreams of Zion, but their immediate haven of refuge was bountiful America. To be sure, such eminent Western Jewish leaders as Moses Montefiore and Charles Netter, the latter representing the *Alliance*, visited Palestine, and established a few schools there for the children of the *Halukkah* mendicants; but this philanthropy was animated by no Jewish national purpose. More specific Zionist contact with the land of Palestine was needed to prime the pump of emigration there. It was to this end of reviving interest in the Holy Land, during the 1880s, that small numbers of nationalist zealots organized Zionist groups in the cities of the Pale.

The *Hovevei Zion*—Lovers of Zion—collected money, conducted courses in the Hebrew language and Jewish history, organized glee clubs. In the classic pattern of all embryonic national groups they pioneered gymnastic and self-defense organizations which they called Maccabee clubs. Of course these meetings had to be conducted secretly, often disguising themselves as wedding parties, for Zionism was an illegal movement in Russia. When the *Hovevei Zion* conducted their national convention, in 1884, they were obliged to meet in the city of Kattowitz in Upper Silesia, then a part of Germany, where they elected Dr. Leon Pinsker as president of the organization. In large part, it was this need for secrecy which centered leadership in the Russian-Jewish students who were registered at German and Austrian universities. They were mobile, unhampered by police investigation, and in intimate contact with the financial and cultural resources of the West. Even as the bourgeois university student was the classical carrier of modern nationalism, so, too, it was the Russian-Jewish student, moving from one German university to another, who carried with him the torch of national revival.

Jewish emigration from Russia after 1881 was unquestionably motivated by the czarist pogroms. But it was principally as a result of *Hibbat Zion* propaganda that some 7,000 Jews departed in 1882 for Palestine. These young zealots were blissfully unpreoccupied with practical considerations. They did not know how long the suspicious Turkish administration would permit them to stay; nor did they know how they would support themselves once they arrived. After they reached Palestine, therefore, many of them drifted aimlessly into the cities of Jerusalem, Jaffa, Haifa, and Hebron. A few opened shops; others were artisans. Most of them lived on what they had brought with them, and a few even found it necessary to fall back on *Halukkah.* But while these early settlers who came to Palestine in the first *Aliyah,* the first wave, did not fulfill the Zionist ideal of creating a virile new agricultural society, they did nevertheless bring into the country human material which served as the indispensable nucleus for further settlement.

They fared better, at least, than the tiny group of three dozen Russian Jews who called themselves *Bilu* (from the Hebrew initials of "House of Jacob, Let Us Go"). The *Biluim,* all of them young men in their teens and early twenties, combined Marxist zeal with Jewish nationalist fervor. They were determined to settle in Palestine as farmers or laborers and to avoid at all costs, on the ancestral soil of Zion, the stereotype of peddlery and petty trade that they identified, perhaps unfairly, with Jewish life in the Pale. Few of these youths had the foggiest notion of Palestinian conditions, climate, soil, or resources. Some of them hoped to receive financial aid from a sympathetic British-Christian writer, Lawrence Oliphant, whose sentimental goodwill was confused with realistic support. This assurance of security vanished when Oliphant failed to raise money from among his friends in the West. It was a serious blow, but the *Biluim* were endowed with the blindest of faith and they refused to be deterred. In 1882, with hardly more than the clothes on their backs and a total common treasury of a few hundred rubles, they departed for Palestine.

On their way to Constantinople the *Biluim* issued a naive and touching document which expressed the hope that "the interests of our glorious nation will rouse our national spirit in rich and power-ful men, and that everyone, rich and poor, will give his best labors to the holy cause. Greetings, dear brothers and sisters,"—and then, combining this passionate nationalism with a very un-Marxian reli-giosity, they added: "Hear, O Israel, the Lord our God, the Lord is One, and our land, Zion, is our only hope." Once arrived in Pales-tine, the real hardship began. Instead of building cooperative colo-nies of their own, as they had planned, they were obliged to hire themselves out as farm hands on a plantation established by the *Alliance*. Exhausting physical labor under the blistering desert sun, years of crop failures and illness, destroyed their illusions. Some of the *Biluim* died of malaria; some returned to Russia; and some severed their contact with their fellows and strayed off into limbo.

There were, however, several hundred *Hovevei* Zionists of the first *Aliyah*, uncommitted to the socialist ideals of the *Bilu*, who founded a thin line of agricultural settlements—Rosh Pinah, Zichron Yaakov, and Petah Tikvah—and who managed to survive as farmers. They had few scruples about hiring Arab labor to do the heavy work for them. Nor were they unwilling to accept subsidies from Baron Ed-mond de Rothschild of Paris. This dilettante philanthropist was no Zionist, but he welcomed any experiment which could produce Jewish agriculturists, and he made the struggling colonies his pet project. His intentions were honorable but in effect he succeeded only in undermining the initiative of the new settlements. For example, the enormous wine cellars he constructed for them produced little in the way of marketable vintage; yet he was never unwilling to buy the wine at prices well above the market.

Nevertheless, these first Jewish farmers, by their very willingness to remain on the soil, to endure the desert heat, the dangers of malaria, and Arab bandits, played an influential role in securing the first modern Jewish settlement in Palestine on nationalist premises. What discouraged them was not the compromises they were obliged to make with the original austere ideals of Zionism. These could be endured. But to what end if they continued to live in the Holy Land without the protection of juridical status; if they were as much at the mercy of venal Turkish officials in Palestine as they had been of czarist bureaucrats in the Pale? Had they come to Palestine, the *Hovevei* Zionists wondered, merely to resume the statuslessness which had cursed their life in Russia? The more they brooded about it, the more they were convinced that mere settlement could not create the homeland; by itself settlement was far too tortuous and precarious. A bolder and more drastic solution was needed. In 1896 such a solution was formulated by an assimilated Western Jew.

Theodor Herzl

On a May day in 1895, Baron Maurice de Hirsch, the eminent Jewish philanthropist, was sitting in the drawing room of his Paris mansion when his valet ushered in a visitor, a rather impressive man, tall, broad-shouldered, with piercing black eyes, a strong, well-shaped brow, and a long, rich "Assyrian" beard. After introducing himself as Theodor Herzl, a Jew from Vienna, the caller plunged into a discussion of the Jewish problem. He denigrated de Hirsch's scheme for transporting Russian Jewry to the Argentine. "You breed beggars," he stated bluntly to de Hirsch. "This philanthropy debases the character of our people." De Hirsch smiled, and asked Herzl what his alternative was. "My alternative," Herzl said, "is to call a congress of Jewish notables to discuss migration to a sovereign Jewish State." De Hirsch stared at his guest incredulously for a moment, and within a matter of minutes succeeded in closing the interview. What manner of man, he wondered later, could utter thoughts so shockingly at variance with the National Affirmation—the Sanhedrin's dominating tradition in Western Jewish life?

History was to prove that Herzl was eminently sane and sensible. He was the son of assimilated Hungarian-Jewish parents. In his early twenties he acquired an excellent legal education at the University of Vienna. Shortly after receiving his doctorate of jurisprudence, however, he decided to abandon the law for a career in writing. His confidence in his literary ability, as well as in the family fortune which assured him security, was justified; within a few years he achieved a reputation as one of the most brilliant feuilletonists in Central Europe. In 1887 he was appointed feuilleton editor of the *Wiener Allgemeine Zeitung*; and within ten years the liberal daily, the *Neue Freie Presse,* the most distinguished paper in the Hapsburg Empire, offered him the enviable position of Paris correspondent.

His professional accomplishments notwithstanding, Herzl was not a happy man. His best friend committed suicide in 1891. His wife, Julie Naschauer, a lovely Bohemian Jewess, lived in a childlike world of personal whims and caprices, and frequent separations between the two ultimately led to permanent estrangement. Perhaps the most decisive factor in Herzl's deepening melancholy was the bitter anti-Semitism he encountered everywhere in Europe. A man of almost morbid sensitivity, he had suffered keenly, while a student in Vienna, from the frigid correctness of his non-Jewish classmates. As a journalist he was obliged to attend political rallies and public conventions at which anti-Jewish epithets and slogans were far from uncommon. It is likely that Herzl was seriously preoccupied with anti-Jewish discrimination long before he encountered the insane Jew-baiting of the anti-Dreyfusards in civilized Paris, or the malevolent political anti-Semitism of Mayor Lueger in Vienna. He first expressed himself on the Jewish problem, in 1894, in a rather superior play, *The New Ghetto*; the drama dealt with the tragedy of modern Jew-hatred in conventionally liberal terms. Shortly thereafter—exactly when we do not know—the idea of a Jewish homeland began to take shape. By early May of 1895, the rough contours of his concept had become sufficiently definite to be boldly presented in the interview with Baron de Hirsch which opened his Jewish political career.

Undaunted by the failure of his mission to de Hirsch, Herzl cast about for new allies. His diary for the year 1895 tells of a vision of "immeasurable greatness" which obsessed him every waking moment. "It has the appearance of a stupendous dream," he wrote, "but for days and weeks it has absorbed me to the point of unconsciousness. It accompanies me wherever I go, it hovers over my ordinary conversation, looks over my shoulder during my ridiculously petty journalistic work, haunts and intoxicates me." In November 1895, he presented his plan for a Jewish State to the celebrated Jewish publicist, Dr. Max Nordau. Apparently the concept moved Nordau deeply; according to Nordau's daughter, he clutched Herzl in his arms. "If you are insane," he cried, "we are insane together. Count on me!" Measurably encouraged by Nordau's support, Herzl hurled himself into the literary formulation of his "solution." The small volume was completed in 1896, and bore the dramatic and unequivocal title, *Der Judenstaat*—"The Jewish State." "The idea which I have developed in this pamphlet is a very old one," Herzl began; "it is the restoration of the Jewish State. The world resounds with outcries against the Jews, and these outcries have awakened the slumbering idea." This last sentence was the clue to Herzl's theme: the

Jewish State was to be created as an answer to anti-Semitism. The deeply rooted facts of Jewish nationalism, of Jewish cultural traditions, of historic Jewish affinity for Zion, had apparently not occurred to him. The book was devoted to the practical physical functions to be performed by a homeland in which Jews would never again be subjected to anti-Semitism.

It was, however, this very insularity which gave the book its strength. For Herzl entered into the most detailed discussion of the needs of the state: the need for a congress of Jewish representatives, for money, for engineers and technicians. Nowhere did he make it clear that Palestine must be the site of this state. At one point he even touched upon Argentina as its possible location. But Herzl's naiveté was overshadowed by his audacity. The Jews of Western Europe may have mocked him. The German and German-Jewish press may have cracked jokes about the "Jewish Jules Verne" and taken him to task for his betrayal of the tradition of the National Affirmation. But for the Jews of Eastern Europe, even for those who were angered by Herzl's transparent ignorance of the depth and roots of Jewish nationalism, the publication of *Der Judenstaat* was an historic event. Chaim Weizmann recalled:

> *I was in my second year in Berlin when, in 1896, Theodore Herzl published his tract, now a classic of Zionism,* Der Judenstaat. . . . *It was an utterance which came like a bolt from the blue. . . . Fundamentally,* The Jewish State *contained not a single new idea for us; that which so startled the Jewish bourgeoisie, and called down the resentment and derision of Western Rabbis, had long been the substance of our Zionist tradition. . . . Not the ideas, but the personality which stood behind them appealed to us. Here was daring, clarity, and energy. The very fact that the Westerner came to us unencumbered by our own preconceptions had its appeal. . . . We were right in our instinctive appreciation that what had emerged from the* Judenstaat *was less a concept than a historic personality.*

It was precisely this instantaneous and enthusiastic Russian-Jewish response which changed the course of Herzl's plans. As an "aristocrat," with an instinctive distrust of the masses, Herzl had initially gravitated for help to the wealthy and distinguished among his people. But when, in 1896, Edmond de Rothschild and several of his banking colleagues turned down his request for funds and moral support, Herzl began to pay closer attention to the crowds of cheering Galician and Russian Jews who met him at railway stations in his travels through the eastern provinces of the Hapsburg Empire. On July 21, 1896, he communicated his decision to Jacob de Haas, the honorary secretary of the Zionist movement in London: "There is only one reply to this situation: let us organize the masses immediately." It was the fateful moment in the rise of modern Zionism.

Diplomatic and Parliamentary Maneuvers

Herzl determined to summon a World Zionist Congress, to provide the movement for a Jewish State with a mass base. It was a daring, certainly a presumptuous move for one man to make. Ninety years earlier Napoleon Bonaparte had summoned an international colloquium of Jews; but Napoleon was the conqueror of Europe, and even then he had restricted his "invitation" to the Jews of France and Italy. Yet Herzl was not without qualifications for the task he had undertaken. He possessed a superbly commanding presence and personality, a sound legal background, and years of journalistic experience covering the workings of Western parliaments. Of course, his decision to summon a Congress met with strenuous opposition. The leaders of Western Jewry, particularly, were horrified by the announced project. Was Herzl mad, they asked, to summon this kind of international gathering in the presence of the whole world, to publish openly the "treasonable" view that the Jews were not simply a religious community, but rather a separate nation? If Herzl was given pause by the violence of this Western Jewish reaction, he received significant reassurance of support from the thousands of followers who sent delegates to the first Zionist Congress. When the Congress opened, on August 29, 1897, in the Swiss city of Basel, some 204 delegates had arrived from all corners of the world, including 80 from Russia and a handful from America. The delegates were young and old, bourgeois and socialist, Orthodox and non-observant—all of them surcharged with a sense of historic mission.

As Nordau opened the first session in the dignified Basel Concert Hall, as the delegates, secretaries, and spectators took their seats, Herzl found it difficult to control his emotions. Here, he recognized, was a dramatic reassertion of the dignity of the Jewish people in the midst of their European degradation, an answer of at least a significant portion of world Jewry to Bonaparte's Sanhedrin of nearly a century earlier. Herzl, unanimously elected President of the Congress,

presented a clear and intelligible program. Emancipation had proved
to be an illusion, he declared; Jews were everywhere the objects of
renewed hatred and contempt. The one, the only intelligible solution
to the Jewish problem was the reestablishment of a Jewish homeland
in Palestine, a homeland which would be *"offentlich, rechtlich"*—
openly recognized and legally secured. Because he did not wish to offend the Turks, with whom he hoped soon to open negotiations, Herzl
did not deem it expedient to speak openly in terms of statehood.
But the delegates sensed the political realism which tempered his
remarks and voted overwhelmingly in favor of the platform he presented. A World Zionist Organization was established, with Herzl
as its president; a Jewish flag and a national anthem, *Hatikvah,* were
adopted; an Actions Committee was set up in Vienna. By the
elevated level of their discussions and the sobriety of their decisions,
the delegates to the first Zionist Congress made it patently clear
to Christians and Jews alike that they were in deadly earnest. It is
difficult today to take issue with the words Herzl penned in his diary:
"In Basel, I created the Jewish State."

After establishing the basic machinery of the Zionist movement,
Herzl determined now to concentrate on diplomatic negotiations.
His goal was nothing less than a charter for his people from the
Turkish government, a charter which, in one fell swoop, would
legalize Jewish settlement in Palestine on a corporate basis. Ever
the aristocrat, the student of international intrigue, Herzl was convinced that a chain of influential contacts was all that was necessary
to win the cooperation of the Sultan. He began by tracking down
the Sultan's friend and ally, Kaiser Wilhelm II of Germany. After
protracted negotiations with the Kaiser's uncle, Count Philipp zu
Eulenburg, and the German ambassador in Vienna, Herzl managed
to obtain his interview with Wilhelm II in Constantinople in October
1898. One must smile today at the solemn faith Herzl placed in these
interviews. He fancied he understood royalty and knew how to deal
with it. Unquestionably Herzl's aristocratic bearing, carefully culti-
vated, made an impression on the Kaiser. During the course of the
hour-long interview the flamboyant German emperor seemed favorably disposed to the Zionist idea. "There are among your people,"
the Kaiser observed, "certain elements whom it would be a good
thing to move to Palestine." Chancellor von Bülow, standing beside
the two men, smiled an anti-Semitic smile of agreement. The inter-

view ended with the Kaiser's promise that he would take up the matter of a "Chartered Company" with the Sultan when the two monarchs next met. In October, Herzl followed the Imperial German cortege to Palestine (where he himself was shadowed by Turkish detectives). He was again greeted by the Kaiser, who still appeared to be sympathetic to the idea of a Jewish homeland in Palestine. And then months went by, and nothing happened. It gradually dawned on Herzl that his request had been politely ignored.

Between 1899 and 1901 Herzl made a concerted effort to reach the ear of the Sultan directly. It was a complicated and expensive project, for baksheesh was the only sure route to the Yildiz Palace, and Herzl had already used up the larger part of his private fortune in organizing the Zionist movement. But eventually he made some headway through the clotted throng of avaricious Turkish officials. By the expeditious use of an influential Jewish apostate, one Armin Vámbéry, Herzl at last obtained his interview with the Sultan in May 1901. The sight of the ugly, hook-nosed little degenerate, the murderer of hundreds of thousands of Armenians, physically revolted Herzl; but he masked his feelings and launched into a two-hour conversation. The Turks were up to their ears in debt, Herzl pointed out. Indeed, the bondholders of Europe had placed a "lien" on Turkey in the form of an Ottoman public debt. In return for a charter of Jewish settlement in Palestine, Herzl shrewdly suggested, perhaps the wealthy Jewish bankers of Europe might be willing to pay off the debt. It was pure bluff: Herzl had no such contacts, but he was convinced that the promise of a charter would produce them. The Sultan was interested. He plied Herzl with cigarettes, the Grand Cordon of the Order of the Medjidje, and the vague promise of a charter; but he also wanted to see the color of Herzl's money. Herzl promised to have an answer for the Sultan soon. He rushed back to Paris, tried desperately to get some kind of a commitment from Rothschild—and failed. In February 1902, he returned to Constantinople and attempted to maneuver the Sultan into making a firm bid. But this time the Sultan was more explicit: the Turkish government would approve Jewish settlement throughout the Ottoman Empire, but not as a corporate group in Palestine. Herzl's heart sank; he recognized that the Sultan had made a fool of him, and was using the threat of a Jewish loan to obtain better interest terms from French creditors. Herzl's morale badly shaken, he gave serious consideration now to resigning from the presidency of the movement.

Had Herzl but known it, the Zionist movement was beginning to make encouraging progress; it was progress which dwarfed in significance the failure of his diplomatic negotiations. In the year which followed the first Zionist Congress, as a direct result of the "Basel Platform," the number of Zionist societies throughout the world increased from 117 to 913. Each subsequent Congress lent new strength and enthusiasm to the movement. In 1901 the Jewish Colonial Trust was established; and while the trust had sold only a million dollars worth of shares by 1904, out of this modest beginning arose the Anglo-Palestine Company, which in years to come was to play a leading role in the development of Palestine. The Jewish National Fund was founded at the behest of an eminent German Zionist, Professor Hermann Shapira. Because its purpose was to purchase land in Palestine as the inalienable property of the Jewish people, the fund ultimately made possible the impressive social experiment of cooperative farm settlement. Each Zionist Congress attracted as its delegates some of the finest minds of the Jewish world, and of the Eastern European Jewish world at that. It was, in fact, the infusion of large numbers of Russian Jews which insured the strength and permanency of the Zionist movement. For these were the zealots, men for whom Zion was not merely a solution to political problems, but rather a fact of the deepest cultural and religious significance, and for whom, therefore, the short-term success or failure of diplomatic negotiations brought neither elation nor dismay.

The Great Crisis

Still unwilling to abandon the "diplomatic" approach altogether, Herzl proceeded to cultivate contacts in England. There was always an outside possibility that London might prove to be a better avenue to Jerusalem than Berlin or even Constantinople had been. It was in London that Herzl won the friendship and admiration of Lord Nathan Rothschild, who in turn secured an interview for him with Joseph Chamberlain, Britain's secretary of state for colonial affairs. Bluff, genial Joe Chamberlain was not without sympathy for the Jews of Russia; but his principal motivation in receiving Herzl was to find a solution to the congestion of London's East End. Like most non-Jews, he was favorably impressed by Herzl's bearing and eloquence, and he offered to help. Herzl suggested that el Arish in the Sinai Peninsula might be a feasible area of settlement. El Arish was adjacent to Palestine, and possessed historic Jewish associations. When Chamberlain countered with the suggestion of some other spot in Egypt, Herzl remarked: "Egypt? No, Mr. Secretary, we will not go there. We have have already been there." Chamberlain grinned appreciatively, and agreed to explore the possibilities of el Arish with Foreign Secretary Lansdowne, with the British agent in Egypt, and with Zionist officials in England. Herzl returned to Vienna to await developments. The el Arish plan, unfortunately, was soon entangled in a Gordian knot of Egyptian and Turkish intrigue and came to nothing. But Chamberlain promised to explore other alternatives and to notify Herzl if a solution presented itself.

One wonders if, at this point, Herzl [was] willing to dismiss Palestine altogether as the site of a Jewish State. Certainly the torment of Romanian and Russian Jewry affected him deeply; he was convinced, in fact, that an immediate asylum for these wretches had become a matter of life or death. More important, Herzl was obsessed with the need to present his followers with a tangible diplomatic coup in the near future, lest—in his opinion—the Zionist movement collapse for lack of hope and inspiration. For that matter, Herzl did not know how many more years of leadership he personally could offer. He had already suffered several heart attacks, the direct result of annoyance and overwork.

One gains insight into Herzl's thinking by reading a short novel he dashed off as a form of therapy during the black days of 1902. It was called *Altneuland* ("Old-New Land"). *Altneuland* dealt with Herzl's vision of a Palestine recreated by Zionist enthusiasts. The mediocre plot and the uninspired character sketches were so thinly contrived that they need hardly preoccupy the reader today. Obviously, he was no novelist. But he was truly prescient in his detailed discussion of the new society. His descriptions of modern trolley cars, of electric turbines, of theaters, commercial enterprises, clinics, research institutions, were unexceptional. Through his protagonist, Friedrich Lowenberg, Herzl repeatedly assured the reader that Altneuland represented the synthesis of the best technology and the ideas of the West. His notions of Altneuland's cultural future, an amalgam and refinement of Jewish linguistic and intellectual accomplishments in Europe, were curiously pedestrian and superficial. Hebrew, to be sure, occupied a place in the new society; but so did French, German, Italian, Spanish, and Yiddish. The sturdy peasants of Altneuland spoke Russian or German, and gave Russian or German names to their model villages and their children. Herzl neither foresaw nor apparently hoped for a Hebrew press, Hebrew assemblies, Hebrew schools, nor did he foresee a life thoroughly rooted in the Hebraic idiom. Altneuland, in sum, was viewed as a political and technological answer to Jewish oppression—little more.

It was in this respect that Herzl was destined to come a cropper in his dealings with the vast hinterland of world Jewry, the Jewish community of Eastern Europe. For the Zionists of Russia and Romania were even then under the spell of one of the most influential personalities in modern Jewish history. He was Asher Ginzberg (1858–1927), a man who refracted and distilled in brilliant literary form the innermost religious and cultural traditions of the Pale. Ginzberg was a Ukrainian Jew who managed, at heavy personal sacrifice, to obtain a modern education at several Western European universities. Like many of his generation, he was caught up in the restless surge of Jewish nationalism, and joined the *Hibbat Zion*. Yet, while not devout, but as a proud and tradition-minded Jew, Ginzberg was disturbed by Zionism's emphasis upon the physical rebuilding of Palestine. In 1881, he published an article in a Hebrew journal over the pen name by which he was henceforth known: *Ahad Haam*—"One of the People." The article was entitled *Lo Zeh Ha-Derech* ("This Is Not the Way") and it attracted wide attention among the Russian-Jewish students of Germany. Virtually overnight Ahad Haam became the spiritual conscience of Jewish nationalism.

There was too much concern in Zionism, Ahad Haam insisted in *Lo Zeh Ha-Derech* and in subsequent writings, for the physical safety of the Jew. Instead, Jewish nationalism ought properly to be concerned with reviving the cultural loyalties and spiritual productivity of the Jewish people. ". . . The whole point of the material settlement [in Palestine] consists, to my mind, in this . . ." he wrote, "that it can be the foundation of that national spiritual center which is destined to be created in our ancestral country in response to a real and insistent national demand. . . . Not twenty agricultural colonies, not even a hundred . . . can automatically effect our spiritual salvation." The mission of Zionism, in Ahad Haam's thesis, was to solve the problem not merely of the Jew, but of Judaism as well. Convinced that Palestine offered little solution to Jewish political disabilities, that most Jews would continue to live in the Diaspora for many generations to come, Ahad Haam urged the Zionists to concentrate their energies on evolving in Israel's historic land a community which would be a "true miniature of the Jewish People." He likened Palestine to a hub and the outer Jewish community to the spokes of the wheel of Judaism. This spiritual revival, of course, depended almost exclusively upon the prophetic and spiritual significance of Palestine, the only land which possessed uniquely Jewish historical associations.

The theory was attractive. And yet Ahad Haam was no mere theorist, dreamily ignoring the routine necessities of Jewish life. In his own career, for example, he was an eminently practical person. The great tea firm of K. W. Wissotzky sent him to London to manage its English branch, and he did this extremely well. It was the clarity of his mind, and the beauty of his Hebrew idiom, which made his arguments irresistible. Weizmann recalled the personal magnetism of this spare little man, with his sunken cheeks, carefully trimmed goatee, and pince-nez—and his remarkable influence over his Zionist colleagues:

> He had the profoundest effect on the Russian-Jewish students in Europe.
> . . . The appearance of one of Ahad Haam's articles was always an event
> of prime importance. He was read and discussed endlessly. . . . He was,
> I might say, what Gandhi had been to many Indians, what Mazzini was to
> Young Italy a century ago.

Ahad Haam's suspicion of Herzl's political Zionism was perhaps overstated. It was little short of ludicrous for him to say, for example: "At the first festive gathering in Basel, I sat like a mourner at a wedding." But he reflected the misgivings of ever larger numbers of Russian Zionists, men like Weizmann, Yehiel Tchlenov, Menahem Ussishkin, Shmarya Levin, who called themselves the "practicals." Strongly influenced by Ahad Haam, they placed little faith in Herzl's diplomatic Zionism—the Zionism of the "politicals"; they preferred to concentrate on the day-to-day construction of a Jewish community in Palestine, and on an equally steady program of Zionist education throughout the Jewish world. Because they represented the masses of devout, impoverished Russian Jewry, the "practicals" had little patience with what they considered to be the aristocratic "pretensions" of Herzl and his German-Jewish colleagues, people who flaunted their contacts with "influential" European statesmen. Weizmann recalled Herzl's attempt to put Sir Francis Montefiore, a nonentity, into the office of vice-president of the World Zionist Organization. "But Dr. Herzl," protested Weizmann, "the man's a fool." To which Herzl replied, with immense solemnity, *"Er öffnet mir königliche pforten"*—"He opens the portals of royalty to me." When Weizmann could not help smiling, Herzl turned white. "He was full of Western dignity," the Russian Jew added, "which did not sit well with our Russian-Jewish realism." It was this dichotomy between the Western-Jewish "aristocratic" approach, seeking a quick political solution to the Jewish problem, and the approach of the Russian-Jewish traditionalists, who sought in Palestine a touchstone for Jewish cultural rejuvenation, which was intensified now by the abortive Uganda project.

In the summer of 1903 Herzl was suddenly called back to London for another interview with Joseph Chamberlain. The colonial secretary had just returned from a trip to Africa. "On my travels," he said, "I saw a country for you: Uganda. On the coast it is hot, but in the interior the climate is excellent for Europeans. You can plant cotton and sugar. I thought to myself: that's just the country for Dr. Herzl. But *he* must have Palestine and will move only in its vicinity." The news of the Kishinev pogrom had just reached Western Europe, and Herzl was no longer certain that he ought to wait for Palestine. He asked Chamberlain for time to consider the proposal. Later in the summer he visited the Pale personally and witnessed at firsthand the desperate conditions of Russian-Jewish life. The sight of the squalor and beggary in the Pale's ghettos horrified him; it was much worse than he had ever imagined. Thus, when the British Foreign Office offered Uganda to him officially, in August 1903, Herzl reluctantly decided to accept it as a temporary asylum, and to present the project for ratification to the sixth Zionist Congress, scheduled to meet in Basel.

Herzl expected opposition from the Russian-Jewish delegates. So, too, did Max Nordau, who presented the plan at the opening session of the Congress. Nordau pointed out, with grave eloquence, that Uganda was not meant to serve as a permanent solution, but rather as a *nachtasyl,* a mere haven for the night. Neither, however, anticipated the heat of Russian-Jewish reaction. A deadly silence followed Nordau's address; he recalled later that hate and fury from the floor of the auditorium seemed to well up toward him in waves. Herzl's personal prestige was such that the Uganda plan was accepted on the first balloting; but the margin of approval was extremely narrow—and when the delegates from Eastern Europe indignantly walked out of the auditorium en bloc it was apparent that the vote itself was of much less consequence than the imminent disruption of the Zionist movement. Herzl watched the departure of the Russian Jews with his mouth agape, and then commented to a friend, with sublime misunderstanding of the kind of Zionism that animated the *Ostjuden*: "These people have a rope around their necks, and still they refuse!"

During the next few days the Zionist movement was threatened by an irrevocable schism. The Russian-Jewish delegates, the "practicals," met in a rump session and hooted down Herzl's efforts to pacify them. The Congress remained in a state of high tension; family bonds and lifelong friendships were shattered. When the proceedings ended, the Russian Zionists departed for Kharkov. There they convened their own conference and committed themselves permanently and exclusively to the idea of Palestine—even issuing a brutal denunciation of Herzl. But it hardly mattered; the Uganda question was soon to become academic. Public opinion in England was running strong against turning "rich" Uganda over to the Jews; and in response to this public clamor, as well as to the evident division on the matter within Zionist ranks, the English government made a graceful withdrawal. The passions and the resentments of the debates died down, and the Zionist movement was not shattered. It was the ideological chasm momentarily revealed by the Uganda issue, however, which made it clear to Herzl for the first time how profound was the yearning for Palestine in the racial memories of his kinsmen east of the Elbe. It was then, too, that Herzl grasped an inescapable portent: it was only a matter of time before the potent reservoir of *Ostjuden* would take over the movement altogether.

The strain of this last battle proved too much for Herzl's weakened heart. In May of 1904 he began spitting blood and was rushed off to Franzensbad for a rest cure. On July 3, at the age of forty-four, he died at Edlach. His body was sent back to Vienna, draped in a Zionist flag, and carried through the streets of the city. An immense procession of 10,000 Jews followed his funeral cortege to the graveside, arousing the wonder and awe of Christian bystanders. Throughout Europe, even as far away as Vilna and Odessa, streets and highways in the Jewish sections of town were packed with mourners. Old acrimonies were forgotten when the giant passed away; only his dedication and devotion to his people were remembered. Perhaps the best epitaph for the man was penned by Herzl himself in a diary entry of January 24, 1902:

> *Zionism was the Sabbath of my life. I believe that my influence as a leader is based on the fact that while as man and writer I had so many faults, and committed so many blunders and mistakes, as a leader in Zionism I have remained pure of heart and quite selfless.*

History has not dimmed the judgment.

The Zionist movement was severely shaken, but not destroyed, by Herzl's death. The accomplishments which had been telescoped into the seven years since the first Congress could not easily be erased: there was the World Zionist Organization, the Congress itself, the Jewish Colonial Trust, and the Jewish National Fund. There were intangible assets, too: vigor, international sympathy, momentum. The new president, David Wolffsohn, was, to be sure, no Herzl; but he was a congenial and diplomatic man. Born in Lithuania and settled in business in Cologne, Germany, he served as the ideal intermediary between Westerners and Easterners, "politicals" and "practicals." It was largely due to Wolffsohn's talents for compromise that the Zionist movement was opened on a federative basis to groups that had formerly avoided Zionism as too relentlessly doctrinaire. Orthodox Jews now entered Zionism through the *Mizrachi* party to stand guard against the impairment of traditional Judaism in the affairs of the movement. Socialist Jews entered through the Labor Zionist *(Poalei Zion)* party to strive for a cooperative commonwealth in Palestine without "exploiters or exploited."

The highest tribute to Wolffsohn's healing leadership was the "official" fusion of "practical" and "political" Zionism at the 1907 Congress. A resolution of the gathering pledged the movement not merely to the quest for a charter, but to the physical settlement of Palestine, to the moral strengthening of Jewish consciousness, and to the revival of the Hebrew language. In that year, too, the Palestine Department of the Zionist Organization was created, and Dr. Arthur

Ruppin was placed in charge of colonization. For the next decade the decisive developments in the Zionist movement were to take place in Zion itself.

Palestine before the First World War

By 1907 there were perhaps 70,000 Jews in Palestine; most of them were city dwellers, and of these at least 60 percent were *Halukkah* mendicants. While there were some 5,000 Jewish agriculturists living on twenty-two farm colonies, the majority of these colonies were still controlled by the paternalistic Palestine Jewish Colonization Association—PICA—of Baron Edmond de Rothschild. A number of excellent citrus crops were undoubtedly produced by these colonies; but most of the settlers were hardly farmers in the classical sense. Indeed, they had grown into a miniature planter aristocracy, supervising large gangs of Arab laborers who did the actual drudging spadework on the soil.

A change in orientation was foreshadowed in 1904, when a new wave of Jewish immigrants, the second *Aliyah,* departed for Palestine. Most of the 15,000 to 20,000 pioneers of this second *Aliyah* were resolved, first and foremost, to be men of the soil. They despised the urbanization of Jewish life in the Pale, and were determined to transform themselves into a race of hardhanded farmers or die in the attempt. The most articulate spokesman for this return-to-the-soil movement was Aharon David Gordon, the "Tolstoi of Palestine." For twenty-seven years Gordon had served as administrator on one of the estates of Baron Günzberg. Then, at the age of fifty, he followed the pattern of Tolstoi's flight to Yasnaya Polyana and he joined the second *Aliyah.* Heroically he worked out, on his own aging body, the painful transformation which he demanded of a whole people. Gordon did not believe in waiting for the improvement of the social order to bring about an improvement of the individual. He insisted that labor, the dedication of one's body to creation, was the proper function of man. "Too long," he observed, "have the hands been the hands of Esau, and the voice the voice of Jacob. It is time for Jacob to use his hands, too." A people compelled by persecution to live by its wits had forgotten the exaltation of manual labor as it was known to the men of the Bible.

While Gordon himself was not a socialist, most of the would-be farmers of the *Aliyah* were. They were influenced to some extent by

the Socialist, or Labor, Zionism of Nachman Syrkin (1867–1924) and
Ber Borochov (1881–1917)—although neither of these men ever
settled in Palestine. Syrkin was an evolutionary socialist, the founder
of the *Poalei Zion* party; Borochov was a Marxist, the founder of the
radical *Hapoel Hatzair* party. The ideological points of difference between them, and the partisan rivalry of their adherents in Palestine,
were less important, however, than their points of agreement. In fact,
the two groups ultimately merged in the *Mapai* party in 1930. Both
Syrkin and Borochov held that Zionism and socialism, far from being
incompatible, were actually complementary. Zionism was needed to
liberate the stateless Jewish people; the Jewish state could be created only on socialist principles. The settlers of the second *Aliyah*
believed, moreover, that a return to the soil was a tangible fulfull-
ment of socialist ideology. From Marx to Lenin, socialist thinkers
had cited the absence of a Jewish peasant class as evidence that
the Jews were not a nation, but rather a peculiar racial or func-
tional entity. Many of these young Jews were determined to disprove
the charge.

Syrkin and Borochov stirred the minds and shaped the spirit of
the second *Aliyah;* they channeled into the Zionist movement, and
into Palestine proper, thousands of formerly intransigent Bundists.
. . . Yet the labor ideology of the second *Aliyah* was less the creation
of these two men than of the collective experience of the early
settlers themselves. Indeed, those who came in the 1904–1914 period
were destined to be the most influential pioneers in the history of
the Zionist movement. Included in the second *Aliyah,* for example,
were the brothers Lavee of Plonsk, Berl Katznelson of Bobruisk,
Yitzhak Ben-Zvi of Poltava, David Remez of Mogilev, Aharon David
Gordon, Joseph Baratz—the founding fathers of what was to be a
new age in Palestine. One of the recruits was a tough-minded young
man, David Green, from Plonsk, Poland, who changed his name,
shortly after arriving in Palestine in 1906, to David Ben-Gurion. Ben-
Gurion's career in Palestine was quite typical of the second *Aliyah.*
Like the others, he was imbued with the agriculturist ideals of A. D.
Gordon and with the socialist aspirations of Labor Zionism. He wrote
later of his first night in Palestine:

> *It was sealed in my heart with the joy of victory. I did not sleep. I was
> among the rich smell of corn, I heard the braying of donkeys and the*

rustle of leaves in the orchards. Above were massed clusters of stars clear against the deep blue firmament. My heart overflowed with happiness, as if I had entered the realm of legend. My dream had become a reality!

But it had not. As Ben-Gurion and his colleagues encountered the planter aristocracies at Petah Tikvah, Rishon le-Zion, Zichron Yaakov, and Rehovoth, as they were compelled to work as Judean farm hands for a few piasters a day, often collapsing from the blistering heat of the sun, or from malaria or hunger, they recognized that the ideals of socialist agriculture would have to be won painfully. They organized into unions, under *Poalei Zion* or *Hapoel Hatzair* auspices, edited their own newspapers, made desperate attempts to begin their own collective settlements. Ben-Gurion himself took the lead in these efforts. When his father begged him to return, he wrote back furiously: "These mummified Diaspora Jews wouldn't emerge from their bog even if they heard the streets here were paved with gold. But the new Jew is proud and full of fight. He won't turn back. I only feel sorry for those petty-minded people who have fled the battleground and then try to foist the blame on bad conditions here." Ben-Gurion, Ben-Zvi, and those who came with them did not retreat.

It would have been profoundly difficult, however, if not impossible, for these courageous zealots of the second *Aliyah* to realize their goal, had it not been for the sympathetic support of Ruppin and the Palestine Department. With money from the Jewish National Fund, Ruppin purchased for them the Kinneret tract lying on the eastern side of the Jordan River. It was on this tract that the collective settlements of Daganyah A and Daganyah B were founded, and the nucleus laid for others to be established later. When the First World War began there were forty-three Jewish farm colonies, of which only fourteen stood to the credit of the Zionist Organization. But a wave of hope swept over the land. Jews took heart at last in the knowledge that they could work in the fields in a productive way, without "exploiting" others. While the discipline and dedication of Ben-Gurion and his friends brought no immediate fulfillment, their efforts were destined to shape the economy—indeed, the entire social philosophy—of Jewish Palestine.

Another towering accomplishment of the embryonic settlement in Palestine was the transformation of the Hebrew language into a living vernacular. It was a transformation which took place only after a bitter Kulturkampf. The struggle resulted partly from the fact that Hebrew was, for most of the settlers, an alien tongue. Accordingly, the German and French Jews, who administered the best-equipped schools in Palestine, argued that it was necessary for youngsters to be taught a practical language. German or French—even Yiddish— were practical languages; Hebrew was not, for it could not be used in business or professional life. Why, therefore, must children be compelled to study a language which was valuable only for reading the Bible or the Talmud? There was another factor, too. As the Ottoman Empire continued its steady decline, the various European powers began using their hospices and monasteries, their schools and hospitals in Palestine as the cultural advance guard for their imperialist designs. Perhaps the French-Jewish administrators of the *Alliance's* network of schools, or the German-Jewish administrators of the *Hilfsverein's* school system, were not conscious imperialists; but as patriotic citizens of their lands they felt it their duty to encourage the use of their native tongue on Palestinian soil.

The Zionist educational system established by the colonists had little in the way of physical or financial resources to match the powerful institutions of the *Alliance* and *Hilfsverein.* But the settlers, particularly those of the second *Aliyah*, were grimly determined to create a Hebraic culture for Palestine, and they resolutely placed their children in Hebrew-language schools. Moreover, they made every effort to use Hebrew as their daily idiom in the home and field. It was an excruciating discipline for Yiddish-speaking immigrants, but they submitted to it willingly. They received effective assistance from the Zionist intellectuals. The philologist and philosopher Ben-Yehudah spent the last three decades of his life tracking down the root of every Hebrew word, and creating a monumental Hebrew dictionary which became the basis for the modern Hebrew language. Ahad Haam, Reuben Brainin, and Chaim Nachman Bialik gave the language extraordinary literary and practical suppleness. Above all, it was the settlers themselves, by their iron self-control and devotion to the most deeply felt ideals of cultural Zionism, who transformed Hebrew into a living tongue. By the First World War Hebrew had taken precedence over all other languages as the vernacular of Palestine.

How far, then, had the Jewish awakening to the Return developed? So far, indeed, that by 1917, on the eve of the Balfour Declaration, the Jews were sufficiently advanced by preparation and effort to make the offer of a Jewish Homeland reasonable. The awakening was made possible not merely by the organization of the World Zionist Organization, and by the instruments of that Organization, the Jewish National Fund and the Anglo-Palestine Bank; it was made possible, too, by the presence of 90,000 Jews in Palestine, nearly 10 percent of them on the soil—many of them speaking Hebrew, their hands on their own plows and their own guns. Had the policy of extending Jewish holdings in Palestine not been followed, there is little doubt that the Zionist movement throughout the world, waiting breathlessly for some miracle of statecraft, would have died of inanition. It was between 1907 and 1914, therefore, that the foundations of the Jewish Homeland were laid. "Above all," reflected Weizmann, "we got the feel of things so that we did not approach our task after the Balfour Declaration like complete beginners."

V. D. Segre

FROM ENLIGHTENMENT TO SOCIALISM

V. D. Segre is associate professor of political science at Haifa University in Israel. Born in Italy in 1922, he settled on a kibbutz in Palestine in 1939 and later served both in the British and Israeli armies. Before entering academic life he was a member of the Israeli Foreign Service. In this selection from his Israel: A Society in Transition *Segre seeks to interpret Zionism as a particular Jewish fusion of tradition and modernism.*

We must digress a moment to look into the conditions of the Jews in 1880. Although many European countries had emancipated their Jewish citizens—following the revolutionary events of 1848—the total number of Jews who benefited from these liberal measures was still very limited.

From V. D. Segre, *Israel: A Society in Transition,* pp. 24–34, 58–60, published by Oxford University Press. Reprinted by permission of the publisher. (Footnotes omitted.)

No statistics exist for the total number of Jews living in the various countries of the world by the end of the century. Those living in the Islamic countries aroused the interest of their Western coreligionists only in time of misfortune, such as that . . . which befell the Jews of Damascus in 1840, following the charge of ritual murder brought against them by the Franciscan friars. But on the whole their existence was considerably more secure and comfortable than that of most of their European brethren.

In Western Europe a fraction of the Jewish people was engaged in the intense battle for modernization. There were those who fought for complete assimilation; those who felt with Moses Mendelssohn that a new *Jüdische Wissenschaft* (Jewish learning) should replace the old rabbinical learning of the ghetto, thus giving a new cohesive identity to modern Judaism. And finally there were the Orthodox who fought a losing battle to maintain the old Jewish way of life and traditional code of ethics in a changing world, which was becoming more and more alienated from the "godly Society."

The situation in Eastern Europe was totally different. In this part of the Continent, particularly in the fifteen provinces of western and southern Russia called the Pale of Settlement, lived the majority of Jews. By their very number—not less than 2 million by the end of the century—they constituted a compact, homogenous, culturally self-sufficient society, practically untouched by modernism.

It was, paradoxically, an oppressed minority society which socially stood well above the Gentile population among which it lived.

Catherine II, in establishing the Pale of Settlement, had not only reversed her previously favorable policy towards the Jews, but sought by this to restrict the movements of the hated Jewish minority, which the partition of Poland had suddenly increased by at least 1 million souls in the largest ghetto there has ever been. But she intended also to make sure that the Russian Jews should not enjoy the relative autonomy which the Polish Jews used to have under their communal organization, the *Kahal,* and a kind of national ruling body, called the Council of the Four Lands. Her successor, Alexander I, transformed the *Kahal* into an organization for collecting Jewish taxes and at the same time issued, in 1804, a set of comprehensive regulations for the Jews, known by the name of "The Constitution of the Jews" and under which the Jews were to live in fear for the next fifty years. It was a paradoxical piece of legislation which on the one hand created a "New Judea" and on the other hand tried to destroy it. In the Pale of Settlement the Jews seldom came into contact with outside civilization. They wrote and prayed in Hebrew, spoke Yiddish among themselves and local Slavonic dialects with their neighbors. They could not intellectually "Russify" themselves because the Russian culture of the time consisted of ideas imported from the West. They were asked to become farmers, but only in the most inhospitable parts of the empire; they were allowed to go to universities, but on the condition that they should take compulsory courses in Christian religion.

The life of the Russian Jews became an inferno under Alexander's brother and successor, Nicholas I, who decided that the Jewish question would be best solved by forcibly enrolling them into the army, after a "preparatory" educational period starting at the age of twelve. To obtain the necessary "quotas" of boys the czarist officials used the community leaders who were thus forced to become instruments of their own people's oppression. Nicholas's reign was a period of expulsions and pogroms for the Jewish population of Russia, who became dejected and miserable beyond imagination. No wonder that the liberalizing measures of Nicholas I's son, Alexander II, appeared to the Jews to be a miracle and a sign that Russian society was finally choosing the path of liberalism. After 1855 the Jews were no longer obliged to part with their young sons by compulsory conscription into the army; they began to enjoy a measure of autonomy in the Pale of Settlement while the richest among them were even allowed to live outside the restricted areas.

A new Jewish "intelligentsia" was thus created. Its members spoke Russian, it was full of hope in future collaboration with the Russians, and it took a great interest in Russian thought, culture, and political ideology. It was, however, a very limited even if important group, and the Jewish masses remained faithful to their traditional religious culture.

In the Pale of Settlement where 95 percent of Russian Jews resided, they represented 12 percent of the total population but controlled 30 percent of the textile industry and 70 percent of the commerce. Fifty-one percent of the Jewish population was concentrated in the towns, as against 12 percent of the non-Jewish population. At the age of 10, Jewish children were one and a half times more literate than the non-Jewish children. In monetary terms, the

Jewish population disposed of a liquidity superior to that both of the landed aristocracy and of the farmers. Thus, they were the natural financiers of both. The situation was not fundamentally different in Romania and the Austro-Hungarian Empire, and it was similar in some respects to that of the Asian minority in contemporary East Africa. The situation of the Jews in Russia was a perfect example of social superiority linked with ethnic inferiority, thus inviting inter-professional, interclass, intercommunal strife. When the government allowed this strife to break out in 1881, it produced a catastrophe and a shock of unexpected magnitude and consequence.

The pretext for the 1881 pogroms, which shattered more than 150 Jewish communities (as a diversionary measure of Russian internal policy), was the assassination of Alexander II.

His successor, Alexander III, was less responsible for the tragic events which befell the Jews than his reactionary courtiers, espe-cially Constantine Petrovich Pobyedonostzev, the main instigator of the new anti-Semitic policy, who aimed at driving "one-third of the Jews out of Russia, one-third to apostasy, and one-third to death," and at making them the scapegoats of the government's antiliberal policy.

In 1882 the "Temporary Rules" issued by the commission investi-gating the causes of the pogroms, under the direction of Count Ignatiev, became the rules according to which the Jews of Russia were afterwards forced to live. Jews were forced out of the agri-cultural areas of the Pale of Settlement; they were submitted to a strict *numerus clausus* in the schools and universities; their trade was hindered, so that many Jewish artisans found themselves fi-nancially ruined. With the approach of the Russo-Japanese War more violence, culminating in the Kishinev pogrom in 1903, was openly instigated by the authorities as a way of distracting the Russian population from the hardships imposed by the government's policy.

Three Jewish movements were—in time—born out of these drama-tic events: Jewish Socialism, Americanism, and Zionism. I shall not discuss the first movement, the "Bund," that anti-Zionist and yet national Jewish workers' organization of Eastern Europe, which Johnpoll has so well described in his book *The Politics of Futility*. I shall recall only that the Bund was born in the same year as the Zionist Organization—1897—and that it played a role in shaping, through bitter opposition, the conscience of the Zionist workers' groups.

The second, far more important Jewish movement created by Russian anti-Semitism is what I call Americanism, namely mass emigration to the United States, and in more limited numbers to South America.

The fact that 2 million Eastern European Jews, mainly from the Russian Empire, crossed the Atlantic between 1881 and 1914 to America is a phenomenon of particular importance for Zionism. It raises the question why so few Jews from Eastern Europe went to Palestine in the same period and what the Jewish American community means to the rest of the Jewish Diaspora in political and philosophical terms.

The problem is a fascinating one. . . . Here I shall limit myself to underlining two facts. The first, that the same shock of anti-Jewish events—the pogroms of 1881—was what sent the Jews to Palestine and the United States. The second, that the same eighteenth-century Enlightenment ideals which served as a catalyst in the Zionist utopia also served as philosophical justification for the East European Jews establishing a new Diaspora in the New World.

This does not mean that the Jewish immigrants to America were motivated by any ideal other than the one of finding a haven from persecution. But in the United States the new immigrants also found themselves politically and ideologically conditioned by the small but influential Jewish community which had preceded them across the Atlantic. This community enjoyed a level of equality and freedom unsurpassed by any other Jewish community of the world; it had taken an active part in the American Revolution and now saw its status fully recognized by the new republic's constitution.

To give an idea of the difference in status between the Jews in the U.S.A. and the Jews in Europe, it is sufficient to recall that in 1789, three years before the Jews were considered citizens in France and eighty-five years before they were emancipated in Switzerland, kosher food was provided for them at the garden party given by the City of Philadelphia in honor of the new American Constitution. At the time there were only 3,000 Jews in the Union. They not only played an active role in American politics, but were conscious of that fundamental distinction between an American and a non-American Jew, namely that to be a Jew in America was one accepted way of being American, whereas to be a Jew in Egypt or in France was —and still is—to be considered somehow a foreigner by the respective nation.

The new immigrants in America found themselves confronted with a society which, for the first time since the destruction of the Temple of Jerusalem, considered the Jews not only equal but cofounders of the American commonwealth. They were willing to believe that at last they were not exiles in a foreign land, but partners in a "New Jerusalem" totally different from the "Old World." It was purest Enlightenment utopia, a start *ex nihilo.* It is thus not difficult to understand why Zionism made so little impact on American Jewry, in spite of the passionate interest shown by the East European American Jews for the national home which their Eastern European Zionist brethren were building in Palestine.

Zionism was the third movement set in motion by the dramatic events of 1881. I have already shown how deeply these events shattered the faith of the Russian Jewish intelligentsia in the liberal evolution of Russian society. "Close your eyes and hide your heads, ostrich fashion, as much as you like; if we do not take advantage of the fleeting moments of repose [of the pogrom] and devise remedies more fundamental than those palliatives with which the incompetents have for centuries vainly tried to relieve our unhappy nation, lasting peace is impossible for you," wrote L. S. Pinsker, a distinguished doctor in Odessa, addressing himself to his fellow Jews. At the time, he did not dare, or at least did not think it advisable, to sign his pamphlets with his own name, and just described himself as "A Russian Jew." But his pamphlet *Auto-Emancipation,* published in Odessa in 1882, was to become the inspiration for the first organized movement for the Jewish return to the homeland.

The movement, which had originally started in Romania, was the *Hibbat Zion* (Love of Zion) and its members called themselves the *Hovevei Zion* (Lovers of Zion). They were a mixed group: some religious, others not; some very simple people, and others young, idealistic university students, too educated to accept a return to ghetto culture, too clear-sighted to trust the forces of Russian liberalism, especially after the significant silence of men like Tolstoi over the 1881 massacres (although later, in 1903, he strongly protested against the Kishinev pogrom, in a famous pamphlet called "I Cannot Keep Silent"). They were also too proud to embark on the road of a new West European or American exile. So they decided to go to Turkish Palestine where they were to be supported by committees organized on their behalf all over Russia and, later, by the French Baron Edmond de Rothschild.

In the year in which Pinsker's *Auto-Emancipation* was published, 1882, the first Jewish colony in Palestine, Rishon Ie-Zion (First to Zion), was founded south of Jaffa. The young Jewish students from Russia who set it up had been moved by the writings of thinkers as different as Smolenskin, A. D. Gordon, and Lilienblum, who had little in common apart from the intellectual malaise brought on by the frustrations of assimilation and anti-Semitism. Significantly, they called themselves by the name *Bilu,* an acrostic of the biblical verse: *Beith Yaakov lehu veneelcha* (House of Jacob, let us rise and go). With this motto they established, in a romantic and unplanned agricultural crusade, the villages of Zichron Yaakov in Samaria, Rosh Pinah in Lower Galilee, and Wadi Hanin, south of Jaffa; they reinforced the colony of Petah Tikvah, founded in 1878 by Jews from Jerusalem, and in 1883 they founded Yesod Hamaalah in Galilee. Strangely enough, these were the boundaries the Jews were prepared to accept in 1937, when the partition of Palestine was first envisaged by the British government.

The *Hovevei Zion* were idealists who set the ball of the return to Zion rolling but who still lacked a clear-cut program. It took thirteen more years for the program to mature in the mind of an assimilated Austro-Hungarian Jew, Theodor Herzl, and one more shock, the Dreyfus trial in Paris, to determine its final elaboration and almost immediate success.

Theodor Herzl was born in Budapest on May 2, 1860, the son of a rich merchant. It would be interesting to have a detailed psychological study of his relationship with his mother, who remained until his death, on July 3, 1904, the dominant influence in his life. It was she who raised him in the Nietzschean dream of Promethean realization. He was a realist with a romantic streak, German-speaking, alienated by assimilation and milieu both from Judaism and Hungarian patriotism. But one should not underestimate the influence of his grandfather, Simon Loeb, who had been a personal friend of Rabbi Alkalai, the forgotten precursor of the Jewish risorgimento, on his early spiritual formation. Herzl's first brush with anti-Semitism at the University of Vienna did not shake his faith in the ultimate success of liberalism and rationalism over the existing obscurantism. Later he went to Paris as a correspondent of the *Neue Freie Presse* of Vienna, convinced that France was still the main hope for human progress and civilization and Russia the last bastion of obscurantism. His covering of the noisy anti-Semitic activities of Edouard Drumont, author of the best seller *La France juive,* led him to the conclusion that anti-Semitism was a "lightning conductor" universally used for drawing the "revolutionary ire of the masses away from the real woes of society." As a result of this revelation he wrote a play, *The New Ghetto,* in which, for the first time, the Jewish problem became a major theme in his work. The underlying idea of the play was, in fact, that a Jew, even the most assimilated one, lives in an invisible ghetto in the Gentile world. This idea still remains fundamental to the ideology and mythology of the modern Zionist movement.

For Herzl the moment of truth came, however, only two years later, with Captain Dreyfus's arrest and trial in 1894.

The Jewish State, that booklet which set political Zionism in motion, was historically the outcome of the emotional crisis suffered by Herzl when he witnessed the shattering of his hopes in democratic France. It was in fact the elaboration of a long letter sent to Baron Maurice de Hirsch on June 3, 1895 (after an interview in which Herzl discussed the possibility of a political solution to the Jewish question) and of a much longer memorandum prepared for the Rothschild family on the same subject.

The refusal of both leading oligarchic and philanthropic Jewish families to take the Viennese journalist seriously made him the founder and the first leader of Jewish political risorgimento.

Subsequent events in the history of Zionism are well known, documented, and studied in the many analyses of Zionism. We shall not, therefore, delve into them, but rather look briefly at the extraordinary figure of Theodor Herzl.

Hertzberg says that Herzl was a man of the West, a journalist of European reputation whose stature among his East European Jewish brethren was enhanced by his standing in the Western Gentile world. I would accept this description and I would also agree with Hertzberg that, although Herzl wrote his book "in the presence of the two gods of the *fin-de-siècle* (progressive) intellectual, Marx and Nietzsche," he did not follow either of them. He was too Marxist to allow himself to be labelled utopian and too Nietzschean to renounce his eighteenth-century belief in the ability of men to change the world. Hertzberg is also right when he explains Herzl's political Zionism as the dialectical synthesis of the inevitable clash between the omnipresent anti-Semitism (thesis) and malaise of the Gentile world regarding the persisting Jewish problem (antithesis). Where I think his analysis falls short is on the evaluation of the role of anti-Semitism—a positive force "which made sense—the visa to the Jews' passport into the world of modernity."

Herzl certainly had an optimistic view of anti-Semitism and his "official" visits to the arch-Jew-baiters, the leaders of czarist Russia, were motivated by political realism and by his belief that the Russian government was as fed up with the Jewish question as the Jews were with the Russian regime.

Such an analysis was probably correct and it holds good not only for czarist Russia but, in more recent times, for East European Communist regimes. They seem, in fact, as relieved as Israel to see their Jews out of East European apartments and jobs, now coveted by the new Gentile Communists.

The guiding principle behind Herzl's Zionist strategy seems to me to have been the idea of honor. Herzl, contrary to most of the assimilated, modernist Jews of his time, was a true aristocrat and, in this sense, he was more traditionally Jewish than many of the rabbis of his generation.

The president of the World Jewish Congress, Nahum Goldmann, in a speech in Basel on October 18, 1957, gave a very clear definition of what Jewish aristocracy meant up to the eighteenth century.

The notion of the "Chosen People," which in the Old Testament possessed a considerable metaphysical and ethical value, became for the ghetto's Jew an ever renewed Messianic hope. The Jewish people reacted to attack, to persecution, to humiliation as a man reacts to a dog's barking. One takes cover from a dog; one runs away from a dog. But one is not offended by a dog. The ghetto's Jews considered his persecutors with the detachment due to a barbarian or to a heathen. He suffered physically, never morally. It sounds paradoxical but never a people felt so proud as the Jews of the ghetto: persecuted in this world they were conscious of being the chosen ones in the world to come; slaves of the barbarians, they felt they were the privileged of the Almighty.

It was this Jewish pride that Enlightenment and assimilation were destroying in the nineteenth century, as an inevitable price for Jewish equality within the Gentile society. For an assimilated Jew like Herzl, who apparently kept intact his inborn sense of dignity (he had significantly resigned from a fashionable students' association in Vienna because of their participation in a Wagnerian meeting which turned out to be anti-Semitic), honor became a bridge on which modern ideas could travel back into the Jewish soul and culture without destroying it.

Herzl did not build or invent a new road between modernism and traditionalism. He started by formulating a simplified slogan, expressing in a nutshell the complex and often contradictory Jewish national aspirations in his time: "A nation without land must go to a land without nation." When he saw his idea enthusiastically received, he refused to go into the details of the national goods which he promised to deliver: he loaded the whole Jewish question, complete with anti-Semitism, on to the fast-moving vehicle of honor and national dignity, and without being asked by anyone, sat at the driver's seat, with anti-Semitism and Jewish nationalism as his, often recalcitrant, horses.

He, indeed, possessed the necessary qualities for such a feat. He had a royal bearing and a charismatic personality. He impressed people with his mixture of greatness and humility. His early death, at the age of forty-four, after a short meteoric career as the uncontested leader of nationalist Jews, crowned him with immediate legend. He was not a man of learning and was almost totally ignorant of Judaism, but he was deeply civilized and honest. A religious agnostic, he was—paradoxically—an unshakable believer.

> *Before him [said Nakum Goldmann in the same speech], the Jewish people, as a political factor, as an active fighting group capable of taking decisions, did not exist. The Jews who had died heroically at the stake had never been able to present themselves as a unit in order to negotiate instead of begging. Herzl was the first Jewish statesman in 2,000 years. . . . He spoke in the name of the people as if this people already existed, as if it was already organised. All this was fiction but it is through this fiction that a people was created.*

The president of the World Zionist Organization omitted to say that this was also pure utopia and that Herzl made the greatest contribution towards the realization of utopia in a century of hate of and of disbelief in utopia.

This alone should be sufficient to explain Herzl's difficulties in putting his ideas across, within and without the Jewish community. But he possessed and used skillfully another powerful ingredient from his alchemistic laboratory of Jewish risorgimento, an ingredient which was to remain a particular source of antagonism and dissent within the Zionist movement itself and inside the Jewish Diaspora: the ingredient of honor.

"Honor," said Montesquieu, "is the foundation of monarchy, the binding force of aristocracy." In his way, Herzl, who of course lacked any sort of institutional control over the Jewish people, proved this to be singularly true in modern times and of the Jewish people. His movement enjoyed much support among the masses of the European Jewish population but remained, for better or for worse, an elite movement. By the very fact of being a select society within a select society—the chosen people of the Bible—Zionism opened an aristocratic rift, a battle of legitimacy, the intensity of which reminds one, somehow, of the older Jewish-Christian rift for the control of *verus Israel.* This time it was of course no longer a question of being faithful to the Father or to the Father and Son together. Still, the rift was again closely connected with the legitimacy of God's presence and role in God's own people.

Who was in fact to be the new legitimate ruler of reunited and independent Judaism in Palestine? The Almighty, who established his Covenant with the Patriarchs and renewed it with the fugitives from Egypt? Or the new gods of the world, State, Nation, Historical Determinism, and so on? More than sixty years after Herzl's death the question is still unanswered and as far from solution as it was during his lifetime, especially in Israel where the new state created by Zionism has been unable to define its own nature to the point of being unable to give itself a constitution. . . . The stubborn refusal of the minority religious parties to recognize any constitution except the Divine Law of Mount Sinai succeeded in crystallizing an opposition which transcended the borders of affiliation to particular political parties.

The question of the control of the source of legitimacy raised by Herzlian Zionism remained closely connected with the monopolization of power in Judaism, a problem derived from legitimacy itself. It expressed itself throughout the years in a triangular fight of elites for exclusive influence over the modern national version of *verus*

Israel. On one side there was the confrontation between Zionism and assimilation, expressed especially in Reform Judaism. Moses Hess had predicted the inevitable clash between those who were proud of being Jews and those whose attempts to disguise themselves in the Gentile world was given away by "their Jewish noses." This was only to be expected, since the central argument of the Jewish assimilationists was the need to dissociate religion and nationality and insist on the universality of Judaism. This is still the main argument of the "progressive Left" against "tribal Zionism." Lucien Wolf, the British Jewish leader who so strongly opposed the idea of Britain offering a Jewish state to the Jews, defended, more than half a century ago in an article significantly entitled "The Zionist Peril," the idea that the Jews were "not the nation of a kept principality but the holy nation of a kingdom of priests." Claude Montefiore, another leading British Jew, wanted not Zionism but Jewish "self-purification and brave endurance to await the better time that civilization will shortly bring." But bound up with these lofty ideas was the fear of successful Jews that Zionism might endanger the position they had attained in Gentile society. "The Zionists," wrote Laurie Magnus, "are part-authors of the anti-Semitism they profess to slay." . . .

When in 1906 the *Poalei Zion* emerged from the mosaic of Russian-Jewish Marxist factions, Ber Borochov wrote together with Yitzhak Ben-Zvi, the future president of Israel, the first attempt at an ideological "platform" for the new movement. It was the first serious attempt to accommodate Marxism and Zionism and it is interesting to see how near Borochov came with his solution to the thesis defended seventeen years later by Sultan Galiev, the vice-commissar for the nationalities in Soviet Russia, at the famous Baku Conference for the Liberation of Oriental Peoples. Like Galiev, Borochov equated the situation of the oppressed nations with the status of the proletariat. It was a bold idea which contained the grain of the future Marxist "colonial" revolution of conquered minorities against Russian imperialism, even of the Soviet brand. Galiev paid for it with his life. Borochov's Socialist Zionism remains to this day a monstrous Jewish aberration of Marxism, equated by communists with Social Democratic heresy.

Ber Borochov in fact believed that the Jewish national struggle was waged, unlike the class struggle, not only for material advantages, but for values and possessions shared by all classes, namely political unity, political institutions, culture, and language, and for the achievement of nationhood. For the Jewish people, the struggle to achieve nationhood, through the return to its historical homeland, was thus a prerequisite of the class struggle. Once Jewish nationhood was assured, each of its component parts could go its own way and the class struggle begin, not vice versa.

But how could the Jewish occupation of Palestine be justified? Ber Borochov realized that this could not easily be explained and that "this country will provide the line of greatest resistance." But Palestine was also a derelict country. So derelict and poor, in fact, that "big capital will hardly find use for itself there, while Jewish petty and middle capital will find a market for its products in both this country and in its environment." Thus the land forgotten by capitalism could be left to the most "proletarian" people of the world, the Jewish nation.

It was a Jew, Karl Marx, who proclaimed, in *The Communist Manifesto* in 1848, that the worker had no fatherland. It was another Socialist Jew, Moses Hess, who proclaimed the right of the Jew, Socialist or not, to a fatherland. Jews were prominent at all stages of the development of Marxism. Singer and Bernstein, Rosa Luxemburg and Lassalle, Trotsky and Ana Pauker were Jews, but this did not make them or their fellow socialists and communists any more sympathetic to the Jewish cause. Many of the Jews killed in Russia were workers, but the British Socialists refused to join the Hyde Park demonstrations against the Kishinev pogroms of 1905, just as the Russian workers refused to make common cause with their Jewish compatriots. Almost everywhere anti-Semitism was stronger than socialist brotherhood, and this remains true to this day in Russia, Poland, and Romania after decades of Marxist rule and the physical destruction of large sections of the Jewish communities there. No wonder, then, that classical Marxism never struck root in Palestine, although Marxist techniques were enthusiastically adopted. Franz Oppenheimer and his plan for cooperative settlements, rather than Lenin's Bolshevism, seemed to the Palestinian Jews to offer a practical solution to the integration of socialist ideals and national needs in Palestine.

Another important trend in Jewish socialism was represented by A. D. Gordon. Gordon was born in Russian Ukraine in 1856, became an early supporter of the *Hovevei Zion* movement, emigrated to Palestine in 1904, and died there in 1922, the uncontested prophet of the "back-to-the-land" Zionist religion.

Gordon was not a socialist theoretician. In fact he can hardly be called a socialist. He represented "pure soul," animated by a belief in total morality. His basic philosophy can be defined as the fight of man against alienation from nature. To him manual labor was the only way of returning to nature, and it could also be the ultimate expression of human fulfillment, a true religion of redemption.

By giving the labor movement in the Holy Land a spiritual significance, Gordon bridged, in his own Tolstoian way, the gap between the mystical call of the religion of labor and the mystical call of the religion of messianism. He gave a new universal meaning and dimension to the "back-to-the-land" call of Zionism, especially when expressed through kibbutz collectivism.

Borochov, by the end of his short life (he died in 1917, returning from the United States to serve under Kerensky in Russia), had already become aware of the inconsistency of his own Marxist Zionist theories. Unlike Gordon, who remained to the end a prophet of international religious atheism, he made his appeal more and more to simple Jewish nationalism, deliberately forgetting to use in his speeches and articles the unbiblical noun of Palestine in favor of the more passionate one of *Eretz Yisrael* (Land of Israel).

Another socialist, Nachman Syrkin (1867–1924), tried to go further than this. He believed that through socialism the world could be freed of anti-Semitism as well as of any other social and political strife. But he saw that the process would take a long time, so he said that the Jews should fight for survival through a national state. Syrkin thus pleaded for the establishment of a Jewish state as the only way to solve the Jewish problem, but insisted that such a state should be conceived, from the beginning, in terms of socialism. This is what indeed happened in Palestine, and from this point of view one can say that Syrkin was the most successful prophet of Socialist Zionism. But, to complete the picture, one should not forget another important, apparently self-contradictory, trend in the movement: socialist traditionalism.

Jewish nationalism being an integral part of Jewish religion, no nationalist Jewish group could avoid facing the challenge of tradition. Moses Hess had grasped the importance of the problem and hoped for a gradual evolution of Orthodoxy through a Jewish risorgimento. The Socialist Zionists went a step further. They took upon themselves the task of preserving traditionalism, not as a religious way of life, but as a national culture.

For Berl Katznelson (1887–1944), one of the central figures of Socialist Zionism in Palestine, the founder of the organ of the Jewish Workers' Federation, *Davar,* and of *Am Oved* (the workers' publishing house), Jewish revolution could not be dissociated from Jewish tradition.

> We like to call ourselves rebels, but may I ask, What are we rebelling against? Is it only against the tradition of our fathers? If so, we are carrying coals to Newcastle. Too many of our predecessors did just that. Our rebellion is also a revolt against many rebellions that preceded ours. . . . Primitive revolutionism which believes that ruthless destruction is the perfect cure for all social ills reminds one, in many of its manifestations, of the grownig child who demonstrates his mastery of things and curiosity about their structure by breaking his toys. In opposition to this primitive revolutionism, our movement, by its very nature, must uphold the principle of revolutionary constructivism.

For Katznelson, true Socialist Zionism could thus realize its aims only by becoming the carrier, not the destroyer, of national tradition.

From Jewish traditionalism to socialist traditionalism, via Enlightenment, assimilation, nationalism, and Marxism, the ideological circle of Zionism was completed. None of these trends could, however, have materialized without the emotional, antirational, anti-Enlightenment, nationalist, and racial obscurantism of European anti-Semitism.

It was this negative force, not ideology, which pushed the Jews in their millions across the Atlantic and, when immigration to America was restricted after the First World War, to Palestine and later to Israel in their thousands. With them to Palestine came the new national institutions of Zionism, originally conceived in the context of the hopes and utopias of the eighteenth century—those hopes and utopias which first gave equality to the Jews through the American and French Revolutions—and later slowly matured in the tense atmosphere of uncompromising strife between Jewish and Arab nationalism.

*   *   *

Historically, there was one long, uninterrupted flow of immigrants —combined with an equally uninterrupted flow of emigrants; in perspective, however, this trend appears as a succession of human waves, each one characterized by the country of origin of its members, their motives for coming, the rate of their arrival, and so on. In the history of Jewish Palestine, each wave of immigrants became a milestone in the development of the "national home." They were called *Aliyot,* plural of *Aliyah*—ascent—since a Jew "goes up" to the Holy Land.

Two of the waves of immigration had taken place before the British conquest of Palestine.

The first *Aliyah* lasted from 1882 to 1903. It was an heroic, political, pre-Zionist *Aliyah,* which brought some 25,000 Jews, most of them Russian, who, fleeing from the pogroms of 1881, chose to go to one of the most unhospitable districts of the Turkish Middle East.

The newcomers' energies were quickly blunted by the harsh conditions in Palestine. Those who did not die of malaria quickly adapted to a colonial European way of life. In the twelve villages which they managed to establish with the help of Baron Edmond de Rothschild there were 473 Jewish workers in 1900. It is interesting that the Jews were not the only immigrants in Turkish Palestine at the time. Members of German Protestant sects established at the same time wealthier agricultural colonies at various points in Palestine, such as Jaffa, Jerusalem, and Haifa. An agricultural German village north of Jaffa, Sarona, now in the heart of Tel Aviv, was later to become the main center of Nazi anti-Jewish activities in Palestine between the two world wars.

It is also interesting to recall that the first *Aliyah* reached Palestine partly as a result of the capitulation rights held by the European powers—including Russia—in the Turkish Empire. The immediate reaction of the Ottoman authorities to the increasing numbers of Jews fleeing from Russia into Palestine was a negative one. It took the form of a publication of an Imperial Ordinance, displayed in April 1881 in the offices of Turkish consulates abroad, especially in Odessa, according to which all Jews were informed that they could settle in any part of the Ottoman Empire, but not in Palestine. If Jews managed to do so, in spite of Turkish opposition, this was due to two factors: bribery, the usual way of overcoming administrative obstacles in the Ottoman Empire, and, as I have already mentioned, the fact that, as Russian citizens, they could claim capitulation rights. The first Arab and Turkish accusations of Jewish colonialism date back to this time.

The second *Aliyah* extended from 1904 to 1913, ending on the eve of the First World War. It coincided with the beginning of organized political Zionism. Only 40,000 Jews out of the 2.5 million which moved out of Eastern Europe in that period came to Palestine; and of those who came, more than half reemigrated. But it was a wave which held the highest political potential for the future. Almost all the founding fathers of Israel: Ben-Gurion, Levi Eshkol, Yitzhak Ben-Zvi, the second president of Israel, were among these immigrants. More important, they gave Jewish Palestine three ingredients vital for its future independence: the kibbutz; the first Jewish defence organization, the *Hashomer* (Watchman); and the first entirely Jewish town in the world, Tel Aviv, established in 1909 as a separate Jewish quarter of Arab Jaffa. Most important, this *Aliyah* brought with it to Palestine the idea of the *halutz,* the pioneer, that combination of the Jewish man of action and the nationalist, socialist ascetic. It emphasized the importance of manual work and it revived the Hebrew language. It was characterized by the ideological (Marxist) sectarianism of its members and by their will to create a new, larger framework of thought and action for the whole nation. It put new life into the political press with the appearance of *Hapoel Hatzair* (1907) and *Ahdut* (1910). It laid the foundations of the future labor exchanges, labor federation, and social services, and of the future political parties.

Yet, the second *Aliyah* gave rise to persistent Islamic and Arab objections, and brought about the first tentative Jewish-Arab discussions on the possibility of collaboration. The little-known story of Arab-Jewish relations in this period has been studied in detail by a British scholar—Neville Mandel—in the light of the changing Turkish policy towards the two nationalities and of the internal problems of modernizing Turkey. Here I shall mention only one of his conclusions which seems to me to be of particular interest. Contrary to common belief, the two main trends of Jewish-Arab relations in Palestine—the trend in favor of collaboration and the trend in favor of open hostility—coexisted well before the British publication of the Balfour Declaration. For many years one of the mainstays of the political programs of Arab politicians in the Ottoman Empire, used by them to win seats in local authorities or in the Turkish Parliament, was anti-Zionism. Other Arab nationalists well before the First World War saw the confrontation between Jewish and Arab nationalism as crucial for Arab revival. But at the same time contacts on both a personal and a communal basis existed. Unfortunately, when one community was ready to talk, the other no longer wanted to—and vice versa. The permanent stumbling block was, of course, the question of Jewish immigration—to which the Jews were passionately attached and the Arabs fiercely opposed. But one should not overlook the effects of the interference of the powers which then—as today—had a direct interest in the Palestine question.

Alex Bein

HERZL ON DREYFUS AND ZIONISM

Educated in Germany, Alex Bein arrived in Palestine in 1933 where he began work in the Zionist Archives. He has been the state archivist of Israel since 1956. In his biography of Herzl, Bein draws heavily upon Herzl's diaries. In this selection he describes Herzl's response to the humiliation of Captain Alfred Dreyfus and his earliest formulations of Zionist theories. Bein contrasts Herzl's vision with the programs of earlier Jewish philanthropists, notably Baron de Hirsch.

It called for a frightful effort to descend from the intoxicating heights of creativity to the ordinary round of work. For weeks now his regular employment had filled Herzl with revulsion. The first reports of the Dreyfus trial, which appeared while he was working on his *New Ghetto,* therefore made no particular impression on him. It looked like a sordid espionage affair in which a foreign power—before long it was revealed that the foreign power was Germany, acting through Major von Schwartzkoppen—had been buying up through its agent secret documents of the French general staff. An officer by the name of Alfred Dreyfus was named as the culprit, and no one

From Alex Bein, *Theodore Herzl, A Biography* (Philadelphia: The Jewish Publication Society of America, 1940), pp. 108–120, 123–124. Reprinted with the permission of the publisher.

had reason to doubt that he was guilty, even though Drumont's *Libre Parole* was exploiting the fact of the man's Jewishness.

In November the death of Alexander III, Emperor of Russia, took up more space in the newspapers than the Dreyfus case. Then the latter gradually forged to the front. Herzl himself sent in several reports, and like the rumors which then filled the air, they were contradictory. On December 6 he wired his paper the final results of the preliminary investigation. Dreyfus denied having written the note on which the prosecution was basing its case. The handwriting experts were not unanimous as to the authorship of the note. Public excitement mounted from day to day. An atmosphere of mystery had begun to envelop the case, which was taking on international significance. The actual trial, following on the preliminary investigation, began on December 19, 1894.

Herzl was present in his capacity as representative of the *Neue Freie Presse*. He wrote: "Today this affects more than the army, this question whether Dreyfus betrayed his fatherland, or whether it was possible to arrest him on the most frightful charges without sufficient evidence, and then to disgrace him publicly. At the beginning the vast majority demanded the head of the accused without delay, but soon after a great deal of doubt was expressed as to his guilt." Herzl then goes on to describe in detail the actual scenes of the trial.

A few moments pass. Deathly silence in the hall. All eyes are turned toward the little door, and suddenly the accused man appears before the public. There is an extraordinary tenseness in the looks which are directed at him. A trim, erect figure, somewhat above the average height, clad in the elegant dark uniform of an officer of artillery, the three gold stripes of the captain's rank on his sleeves. With lowered head Dreyfus passes through the crowd of onlookers, mounts the three steps to the prisoner's bench, draws himself up before the court, and makes a brief, stiff bow. Then he sits down, and I have a chance to get a good look at his face. He looks ten years older than he really is. It is said that this change came over him in prison. The short hair is tinged with grey, the forehead runs up into a bald patch, the nose is sharply curved, the ears stand away from his head, cheeks and chin are clean-shaven, the thick moustache is close-cropped, the mouth painfully drawn. He wears a pince-nez. Dreyfus's bearing is calm and firm.

The court debates the question whether the proceedings shall be secret or public. Demange, the attorney for the defense, clashes again and again with the presiding judge. The court withdraws to consider. "Dreyfus stands up and looks round the room without a trace of embarrassment. Then he sits down at his ease, fingers his moustache, and exchanges a few words with the lieutenant at his side."

The court returns. It has decided that the proceedings shall be secret. The room is cleared of spectators and journalists. Even the witnesses may be present only when they are on the stand. The trial goes on behind closed doors.

Thus, during the next few days, Herzl can write only about the general impression produced by the trial, and about the particular impression the prisoner has made on him. He observes Dreyfus as the latter marches, in uniform and white gloves, from the guard-house to the courtroom. "His bearing is calm, his features more relaxed than yesterday." The interest and excitement among all elements of the population reach new levels; nearly everyone is convinced that he will be condemned; there are rumors that additional evidence of his guilt has been uncovered.

The public proclamation of the verdict came as the relaxation of a tension which had become almost unbearable. Here is Herzl's description:

> *The public was admitted to the courtroom at six o'clock in the eve-ning, after the attorney for the defense had made his last plea. The room was jammed, and the spectators were gripped by a nameless and breath-less excitement. At seven the judges entered, to the cry of "Attention!" The silence became deeper. In a firm, clear voice Colonel Maurel an-nounced that the court-martial had unanimously declared Dreyfus guilty (a deep "Ah!" from the audience). Maurel went on to pronounce the sentence of the court: military degradation and deportation for life. Some-one in the courtroom cried out "Vive la Patrie!" but already there was a rush for the doors on the part of those who wanted to be first to spread the news.*

The nation received the verdict with satisfaction; the general belief was that the man was guilty. No one knew as yet what was to be revealed by years of courageous investigation, namely, that the verdict had been based on a forged document which neither the accused man nor his attorney was permitted even to look at. Nor did it as yet occur to anyone that "the foreign power" to which Dreyfus was supposed to have sold his country's secrets would permit an innocent man to be condemned without declaring openly that it had had absolutely no relations with him. When however, such a declaration was actually made—later—it found no credence. Only his family expected him to be set free, and on the day of the verdict his place was set at home for the family dinner. Dreyfus himself at once appealed the case. Shortly before the trial, wrote Herzl on December 27, the accused man had told the noncommissioned officer on guard that he was the victim of a personal plot and of private vengeance, and that the case against him would collapse at the trial like a house of cards. "I am being persecuted because I am a Jew," were his words.

Such was the report. But it is improbable that Dreyfus whose bearing throughout had been proud and confident, and who was moreover an assimilated Jew, should have expressed himself thus to his guard. What is interesting is the fact that Herzl should have written this report. It indicates the direction his mind had taken, and is the first mention of the Jewishness of the prisoner appearing in Herzl's articles on the Dreyfus affair.

At about this time Herzl wrote for his newspaper a review of the internal situation in France in the year 1894. "Anyone who has lived in France during this period," he observed, "has been the witness of important events." He was referring to the struggle of the French Republic against anarchism and socialism, those two movements which stand in diametric opposition to each other. The red flag of the Socialists was countered by the old cocarde of the tricolor. The national idea took on new life and penetrated into the most diverse sections of society. At the same time socialism was making practical progress, as was evidenced by the introduction of the income tax. This did not mean, however, that the French bourgeoisie had given up. "The forces of the French Republic are not yet exhausted, and the world may still rivet its attention on this land, where all-human matters are being dealt with. It is the land of experimentation. It is a great honor to fulfil this function—an honor which must be earned. France is the great pot in which new political preparations for the entire civilized world are simmering."

In this same France, "where all-human matters were being dealt with," there took place on Saturday, January 5, 1895, the public degradation of Captain Dreyfus. Herzl's description of the event appeared in the evening edition of the *Neue Freie Presse* of the same date:

> On this dismal winter's day the degradation of Captain Dreyfus, which was carried out in the grounds of the Military Academy, drew large numbers of the curious to the vicinity. Many officers were present, not a few of them accompanied by ladies. Entry into the grounds of the Ecole Militaire was permitted only to army officers and some journalists. Outside the grounds swarmed the morbid crowds which are always attracted by executions. A considerable number of police were on duty. At nine o'clock the great open court was filled with a detachment of troops in square formation: five thousand men in all. In the centre a general sat on horseback. A few minutes after nine Dreyfus was led forth. He was dressed in his captain's uniform. Four men conducted him before the general. The latter said: "Alfred Dreyfus, you are unworthy to bear arms. In the name of the French Republic I degrade you from your rank. Let the sentence be carried out." Here Dreyfus lifted his right arm and called out: "I declare and solemnly swear that you are degrading an innocent man. Vive la France!" At that instant the drums were beaten. The officer in charge began to tear from the condemned man's uniform the buttons and cords, which had already been loosened. Dreyfus retained his calm bearing. Within a few minutes this part of the ceremony was over.
>
> Then began the parade of the condemned before the troops. Dreyfus marched along the sides of the square like a man who knows himself to be innocent. He passed by a group of officers, who cried: "Judas! Traitor!" Dreyfus cried back: "I forbid you to insult me!" At twenty minutes past nine the parade was over. Dreyfus was then handcuffed and given into the custody of the gendarmes. From that point on he was to be considered a civilian prisoner and treated as such. When he had been led away the troops defiled off the grounds. But the crowd surged toward the gates to watch the condemned man being led away. There were passionate shouts. "Bring him out here, and we'll tear him to pieces!" But the crowd waited in vain. There was a curious excitement amongst those who had been able to witness the ceremony of the degradation. The strange, firm bearing of the prisoner had made a profound impression on some of them.

Later in the day Herzl sent off a supplementary report which appeared in the Sunday edition of his paper:

> To complete the picture of the ceremony it should be added that as Dreyfus was being paraded before the troops, among whom there were numbers of recruits, he kept calling out: "I am innocent!" When he passed near a group of journalists he stopped for a moment and said: "Tell all France that I am innocent!" Some of the journalists retorted with insults.

Part of the crowd outside, which was able to catch a glimpse of the ceremony, shouted again and again: "Death to the traitor!"

It was indeed in a state "of curious excitement" that Herzl left the scene. What was it that moved him so? He was—as the tone of his report showed—becoming more and more convinced of the innocence of the condemned man. He had not the slightest external evidence on which to base this feeling; it was an insight born of his new understanding of the problem of the emancipated Jew. He did not believe that a Jewish officer was capable of committing an act of national treachery. "A Jew who, as an officer on the general staff, has before him an honorable career, cannot commit such a crime. . . . The Jews, who have so long been condemned to a state of civic dishonor, have, as a result, developed an almost pathological hunger for honor, and a Jewish officer is in this respect specifically Jewish." That Captain Dreyfus, a well-to-do Jew who had been prompted to a military career by pure ambition, should have committed such a crime therefore seemed to Herzl a psychological impossibility. This was the view expressed in a conversation with the Italian military attaché Panizzardi, who was later to play an important role in the breaking of the case. At that time, however, the Italian was convinced of Dreyfus's guilt, for to this honest soldier it seemed impossible that seven officers should have condemned a comrade without overwhelming proof of his guilt. But just this happened to be the problem which lifted the case out of the ordinary class of judicial error.

For even if we grant, on insufficient grounds, that it was really a traitor who was being condemned and degraded, the attitude of the crowd was—according to the printed report—a strange one. We read, in the *Neue Freie Presse,* that the crowd shouted: "Death to the traitor." This is quite comprehensible—but there is something incomplete about it. We cannot avoid the impression that Herzl's telegrams were edited before they were printed, and it was fear that motivated the excisions. It is unlikely that Herzl, in the condition in which he then was, had himself colored the report. Four years afterwards there still rang in his ears the shouts of the crowd, which left him shattered: *"A mort! A mort les juifs!"* What! he asked himself. Death to *all* the Jews because *one* of them is a traitor? "The Dreyfus case," he wrote in 1899, "embodies more than a judicial error; it embodies the desire of the vast majority of the French to condemn a Jew, and to condemn all Jews in this one Jew. Death to the Jews! howled the mob, as the decorations were being ripped from the captain's coat. . . . Where? In France. In republican, modern, civilized France, a hundred years after the Declaration of the Rights of Man. The French people, or at any rate the greater part of the French people, does not want to extend the rights of man to Jews. The edict of the great Revolution has been revoked."

Illumined thus in retrospect, the "curious excitement" which gripped Herzl on that occasion takes on a special significance. "Until that time most of us believed that the solution of the Jewish question was to be patiently waited for as part of the general development of mankind. But when a people which in every other respect is so progressive and so highly civilized can take such a turn, what are we to expect from other peoples, which have not even attained the level which France attained a hundred years ago?"

We need Herzl's formulation of the situation as set down in 1899 in order to put his impressions of January 1895 in the proper light. In that fateful moment, when he heard the howling of the mob outside the gates of the *Ecole Militaire,* the realization flashed upon Herzl that Jew-hatred was deep-rooted in the heart of the people— so deep, indeed, that it was impossible to hope for its disappearance within a measurable period of time. Precisely because he was so sensitive to his honor as a Jew, precisely because he had proclaimed, in *The New Ghetto,* the ideal of human reconciliation, and had taken the ultimate decision to stand by his Jewishness, the ghastly spectacle of that winter morning must have shaken him to the depths of his being. It was as if the ground had been cut away from under his feet. In this sense Herzl could say later that the Dreyfus affair had made him a Zionist.

But only in this limited sense. For a new question mark had risen before him, and the answer was not clear: how was he to feel and what was to be his reaction? His play, which was to set things in motion by putting the Jewish question before the public, was rejected by the leading German theaters. What was he to do?

He was overcome by a feeling of the forlorn and abandoned; an impenetrable loneliness descended on him. He tried to flee from it. "Why have I heard nothing about your play? Why don't you send it to me? Haven't I come close enough to you during these recent

FIGURE 1. Theodor Herzl. *(Courtesy, The Central Zionist Archives)*

months of conspiratorial secrecy?" Thus he wrote bitterly about mid-
February to Schnitzler, he who as a rule was so proudly reticent.
"Really, I almost feel like putting an ad in the papers: 'Man in prime
of life seeks friend to whom he can confide without fear all his
weaknesses and absurdities . . .' I really don't know, am I too shy,
or too distrustful, or am I seeing too well: I don't find any such friend
among my acquaintances here."

But while he sought a friend frantically, while he felt himself
drowned in loneliness, he saw all about him the ever fiercer light of
a blazing anti-Semitism. In the French Chamber of Deputies the
deputy Denis made an interpellation on the influence of the Jews
in the political administration of the country. In Vienna a Jewish
member of the City Council rose to speak and was howled down.
On April 2, 1895, were held the municipal elections of Vienna, and
there was such an enormous increase in the number of anti-Semitic
aldermen, all of them followers of Lueger, that the majority held
until that time by the Liberal party was reduced to ten. "One little
step more," wrote the *Neue Freie Presse,* "and Herr Lueger will be
the head of the municipality of Vienna and of the only great metrop-
olis to be branded with the shameful mark of an anti-Semitic administration."

Herzl had lived through these elections, for he had made a short
visit to Vienna, and was in the city on March 22. It was as if the
lonely man, whose faith in mankind had suffered an almost fatal
diminution through the Dreyfus affair, had fled to his nearest and
dearest, and to the place in which he had passed his early manhood,
in order to find strength again. But we cannot be clear as to the
mysterious processes then at work in him. Herzl himself could not
have given a picture of them even a few weeks later. We do know
that there was awakening in him a rebellion against the importance
of the Word. "Aren't they inclined to overrate the value of the Word
in the Palais Bourbon?" he asked on March 2, 1895, and the question might very well have been directed toward himself. He wanted
to burst out beyond the Word. There was in him a fierce urge to the
Act. For the first time he went to the religious services in the temple
on the Rue de la Victoire. "Once again I found them moving and
solemn." There was much to remind him of his youth and of the
temple on the Tabakgasse in Pest. Changing plans passed tumul-
tuously through his mind. He wanted to write a book on "The Con-

dition of the Jews," consisting of reports on all the important areas of Jewish settlement in Russia, Galicia, Hungary, Bohemia, the Orient—and the recently founded colonies in Palestine, about which he had heard from his relative Löbl on his brief visit to Vienna.

There was a conversation between Herzl and Alphonse Daudet, for whom Herzl had translated an article, and the Jewish question inevitably crept into it. Herzl said: "Out of all these faithful and accurate descriptions of Jewish life, there will emerge the proof that the Jews have not merited the misfortunes which are visited on them, that they are men and women who are attacked without being known." Daudet was known as an anti-Semite, but Herzl unfolded to him his views on the Jewish question, and was confirmed in his outlook when he marked what a deep impression they produced on Daudet. Daudet felt that Herzl ought to write a novel; it would carry farther. "Look at *Uncle Tom's Cabin.*"

That was enough to throw into confusion Herzl's idea of a sociological report. He returned to his former plan of a Jewish novel which he had abandoned when he was called to his assignment on the *Neue Freie Presse* in Paris. Friend Kana, the suicide, was no longer to be the central figure. He was instead to be "the weaker one, the beloved friend of the hero," and would take his own life after a series of misfortunes, while the Promised Land was being discovered or rather founded. When the hero on board the ship which was taking him to the Promised Land would receive the moving farewell letter of his friend, his first reaction after his horror would be one of rage: "Idiot! Fool! Miserable hopeless weakling! A life lost which belonged to us!"

We can see the Zionist idea arising. Its outlines are still indefinite, but the decisive idea is clearly visible: only by migration can this upright human type be given its chance to emerge. In *The New Ghetto* Jacob Samuel is a hero because he knows how to choose an honorable death. Now the death of a useful man is criminally wasteful. For there are great tasks to be undertaken. Life! Life is needed!

In essence it is the Act and not the Word that confronts us. What last impulse it was that actually carried Herzl from the Word to the Act it will be difficult to tell—he himself could not have given the answer. Little things may play a dramatic role not less effectively than great ones when a man is so charged with purpose as Herzl then was.

It is possible that something apparently irrelevant was the immediate efficient cause. On April 29 Herzl reported in great detail a
catastrophe which had occurred near Epinal: a dam had collapsed,
a great flood had burst over the countryside and more than a hundred human beings had been swept to their deaths.

This incident, coming at this moment, appears like a liberating
symbol for his own life. In him too a dam collapsed. In him too
great floods were released to carry him away.

In the early days of May, Herzl addressed to Baron de Hirsch the
letter which opens his Jewish political career.

"Honored Sir:

When may I have the privilege of visiting you? I wish to discuss
the Jewish problem with you. It is not a question of an interview,
still less a direct or indirect money matter. I want to discuss with
you a Jewish political plan the effects of which will perhaps extend
to days when you and I are no longer here."

This is the opening paragraph of the letter to Baron de Hirsch
which Herzl drafted in the early days of May 1895. He let the draft
lie on his desk for fourteen days; his family, which was living with
him, returned to Vienna and he, following his usual custom for that
period of the year, moved to the Hotel Castille in the Rue de Cambon.
Toward the middle of the month he sent the letter off. He asked the
Baron to set a day on which he could spare him an hour or two
without interruption. The tone of the letter is proud and cool, almost
condescending; he wanted to make it absolutely clear from the outset that this was not a journalistic device which was to lead up
to a request for money. "It is evident," wrote Herzl, "that there are
so many demands being constantly made on you that one cannot
be too hasty in anticipating and disarming any suspicion of ulterior
intentions."

Baron Maurice de Hirsch, freiherr von Gereuth, was one of the
richest men of his time, and the foremost symbol of Jewish philanthropy. In 1891 he had founded the Jewish Colonization Association
(ICA) with a capital of £2 million. Its purpose was to solve the
problem of depressed Russian Jewry by the systematic, planned
transference of some millions of Jews to the Argentine. In that
country Hirsch had purchased large areas for colonization. Hirsch

had considered the question of Palestine, a country which he had learned to know well at first-hand when he carried through the extension of the first railroad from the Balkans to Constantinople; he had come to the conclusion that for political and economic reasons Palestine was not suited for a permanent and well-secured Jewish colonization. He had been in contact with the *Hovevei Zion,* the pre-Herzlian Zionists, who had tried to win him over to the idea of Palestinian colonization. He had acknowledged the deep traditions, worthy of all reverence, which bound the Jew to Palestine. Nevertheless, as he stated in a letter of August 1891, he did not consider these traditions a solid enough basis for the security of the new fatherland and as a protection against a repetition of Jewish misfortunes. However, he soon discovered (in 1891) that the Argentine, too, presented no easy task. When the actual colonization began he was confronted with vast difficulties rising in part from the unsuitability of the human material, in part from the nature of the soil, and in part from the clumsiness and inexperience of the directing personnel. Of what significance, in the light of his original, grandiose intentions, were the four colonies which he had managed to create by 1894, with their total population of 3,000—especially when one bears in mind that 800 of the original colonists had to be resettled in the United States? And what a disproportion between the sums expended and the results obtained! Perhaps, thought Herzl, the willpower and energies of this man, who had been so obviously and so deeply moved by the plight of his people, were now ready to be diverted toward the great plan which had fired the imagination of Herzl and which seemed to him to promise swifter results: the founding of a new, publicly secured Jewish community.

He received from Hirsch a request to submit his plan in writing. On May 24 he wrote to him: "What you have undertaken till now was as magnificent in conception as it has proved futile in actuality; it is as costly as it is hopeless. Until now you have been only a philanthropist, a Peabody. I want to show you the way to become something more."

A week later, at half past eleven on the morning of June 2, 1895, the interview took place in the palace of Baron de Hirsch. Herzl had prepared notes which took up twenty-two quarto pages. He knew that he, the intellectually superior mocking spirit, the ready *causeur,* was always handicapped by a preliminary shyness when he confronted a personality of high rank or standing, and the copious notes were intended as a safeguard and as a help to his memory.

In these outlines—they were the first written expression of his new idea—Herzl offered the great philanthropist two alternatives: solution of the Jewish question without migration, and solution by migration. Either solution presupposed a preliminary process of education of the Jewish masses. What Herzl sought first was to win Hirsch over to this idea of the education of the Jewish masses in self-sacrifice, moral bearing, and capacity for great enterprises. The solution of the Jewish question without migration (i.e., by complete absorption in the surrounding population) would, if at all possible, call for a long period of time.

> But, [the notes continue,] "if the Jews are to be transformed into men of character in a reasonable period of time, say ten or twenty years, or even forty—the interval needed by Moses—it cannot be done without migration. Who is going to decide whether conditions are bad enough today to warrant our migration? And whether the situation is hopeless? The Congress which you [i.e., Hirsch] have convened for the first of August in a hotel in Switzerland. You will preside over this Congress of notables. Your call will be heard and answered in every part of the world."
>
> And what will be the message given to the men assembled? "You are pariahs! You must forever tremble at the thought that you are about to be deprived of your rights and stripped of your possessions. You will be insulted when you walk in the street. If you are poor, you suffer doubly. If you are rich, you must conceal the fact. You are not admitted to any honorable calling, and if you deal in money you are made the special focus of contempt. . . . The situation will not change for the better, but rather for the worse. . . . There is only one way out: into the promised land."

In the actual discussion Herzl did not manage to reach these, the central points of his thesis. For at the very outset of the conversation, in his basic presentation, he came into sharp conflict with Hirsch's views and practical measures. Herzl began the talk thus:

"Some of the things I have to say you will find too simple, others too fantastic. But it is the simple and the fantastic which leads men." He then leaps into the center of the problem, and outlines the basis in a few words. It is the logical extension of the thoughts with which he was occupied in *The New Ghetto*. History was responsible for the condition of the Jews, and for the torments which were inflicted on them. "Throughout the two thousand years of our dispersion," he said now, "we have lacked unified political leadership. I consider this our greatest misfortune. It has done us more harm than all the persecutions. It is this that is responsible for our inner decay. For there was no one, not even a king inspired by selfish motives, to educate us as men. . . . If we only had a unified political leadership . . . we could initiate the solution of the Jewish question." It is clear now: for Herzl the problem has been transformed from something social into something purely human, taking on for that reason a political character; and its solution could be effected only by political means.

The first thing to be created, therefore, was a political center, from which could issue the leadership of the people in its totality. This was the fundamental prerequisite now insisted on by Herzl. This center would also direct the national reeducation, whether or not migration was proposed. For the process of reeducation new methods would be called for from the outset. First would have to come total repudiation of the principle of philanthropy: this was the second basic principle involved in the new concept. "You breed beggars," he told the great humanitarian. "It is characteristic of the situation that among no other people is there so much philanthropy and so much mendicancy as among the Jews. It is impossible to escape the conclusion that there must be an organic connection between these two phenomena. This philanthropy debases the character of our people." With this observation Hirsch was in agreement. Then Herzl went on to criticize the Argentinian colonization, which had also been conducted on false principles—false because they were of a philanthropic character—and which was therefore bound to end in failure.

"You transport these Jews as plough-hands. They naturally feel that henceforth they have a claim on you, and this certainly does not promote the will to work. Whatever such an exported Jew costs you, he is not worth it. And how many individual samples can you transplant in any case? Fifteen thousand, twenty thousand. There are more Jews in one street in the Leopold district of Vienna."

The direct method, he went on, was altogether unsuited for a mass movement. Only indirect methods could be effective. Great aims, daring and attractive enterprises, were alone capable of driving masses of men toward higher objectives.

Along these lines, the first task was to improve the mass character among Jews wherever they happened to be already. "They
must be made strong as for war, filled with the joy of work, penetrated by high virtues." How was Hirsch to set the change in motion?
By offering prizes for achievements in science and art, for distinguished moral actions, etc. "The annual prizes will themselves be of
little importance. What is of importance is the wide-spread effort
which will be made to be among the prize-winners; through this
the general moral level will be raised."

Here Hirsch interrupted him impatiently: "No, no, no. I don't want
to raise the general level. All our misfortunes come from the fact
that the Jews aim too high. We have too many intellectuals. My aim
is to discourage this pushfulness among the Jews. They mustn't make
such great progress. All the hatred of us comes from this." In the
Argentine, to which bad elements had come at first, things were
already going better. After a few years he would prove to the world
that the Jews made good agricultural workers. One of the consequences might be that the Russian government would then give its
Jews access to the land.

After these remarks of Hirsch's, Herzl said he considered it useless to unfold his ideas any further. "You do not know," he said,
"what fantasy means, and you do not realize that it is only from a
certain height that one can perceive the great outlines of men."

Herzl reports further:

*Hirsch said that migration was the only way. "There is land enough
to be purchased . . ."*

*I almost shouted at him: "Certainly! Who told you that I'm against
emigration. Here it is, in these notes. I will go to the German Kaiser;
he will understand me, for he has been educated to the reception of
great ideas. . . . I will say to the German Kaiser: Let us go forth.
We are aliens here, they do not let us dissolve into the population,
and if they let us we would not do it. Let us go forth! I will show you
the means and methods whereby this migration can be carried out without
causing an economic upset, without leaving a gap behind us."*

*Hirsch said: "Where will you get the money? Rothschild will donate
five hundred francs."*

*"The money?" I said, smiling scornfully. "I will create a national loan
of ten million marks."*

*"Fantastic," smiled the Baron. "The rich Jews will give you nothing.
The rich Jews are bad, they display no interest in the sufferings of the
poor."*

"You speak like a Socialist, Baron Hirsch," I said.
"This won't be our last conversation," the Baron suggested. "The moment I return from London you shall hear from me."

This was the end of that dramatic conversation, as Herzl recorded it. These two men, representing two different worlds, parted, feeling a certain sympathy for each other, respecting each other, but without reaching common ground. Herzl's first attempt to win this great power over by storm had failed. Had he set about it in the right way? Had it been wise of him to try and compel this man to new ways of thought? We can, without presumption, assert that he had not set about it in the right way; he had not approached him from the practical angle, he had not given due weight to Hirsch's positive achievements. He should have come to this cool, practical man with a more specific plan of action, on which they could have united. The larger theoretical aspect could have been introduced later, and by degrees. As it was, he began by bringing to focus their theoretical divergence, with the result that Hirsch felt he was dealing with an interesting dreamer, but a dreamer nevertheless, and Herzl did not get further than the sixth page in his voluminous notes. Thus it was, too, that he left Hirsch, who for years had seen the necessity of emigration as part of the solution of the Jewish problem, with the impression that he, Herzl, was opposed to it, and wanted to solve the Jewish problem by training and reeducation on the spot.

An objective observer who reviews the incident after this lapse of years must further conclude that Herzl had approached Hirsch too soon, before his own vision of the plan had clarified. His dream of the new Jew, of the new Jewish political movement, overshadowed the question of program.

On the day of his conversation with Hirsch, Herzl wrote him a long letter in which he sought to supplement the information and impressions which had been the result of the meeting. How much better he could do it in writing! He outlined the steps connected with the carrying out of the emigration plans. First as to money: "I will launch a Jewish national loan. There's always plenty of Jewish money for Chinese loans, for Negro railroad enterprises in Africa, for the most extravagantly adventurous ideas—and will we be unable to find money for the deepest, most immediate, and most tormenting need of the Jews themselves?" With this loan, which was to be "the main fund of the migration plan," the migration itself was to be organized, "cities are to be built and the new land is to be made so fruitful that it shall become the Promised Land."

Where the Promised Land was to be located, how it was to be acquired, is not yet mentioned. Herzl does not seem to have thought this question of decisive significance; it was a scientific matter, as he later intimated. It was the organization of the migration which held his attention, the political preparations among the Powers, the preliminary changes to be brought about among the masses by training, by "tremendous propaganda, the popularization of the idea through newspapers, books, pamphlets, lectures, pictures, songs." All these works

are to be directed purposively and farsightedly, from a single center. But then I should have had to speak to you finally about the flag which had to be unrolled and under which the movement was to march. And then you would have asked me mockingly: "A flag—what is that? A stick with a rag at the end of it." No, Monsieur le Baron, a flag is a great deal more. It is with a flag that people are led whithersoever one desires, even to the Promised Land. For a flag men live and die; indeed, it is the only thing for which they are prepared to die in masses if they have been brought up to it.

Please believe me, the political life of an entire people—particularly when that people is scattered throughout the entire world—can be set in motion only with imponderables floating high in the air. Do you know what the German Reich sprang from? From dreams, songs, fantasies, and gold-black bands worn by students. And that in a brief period of time.

What? You do not understand imponderables? And what is religion? Bethink yourself what the Jews have endured for two thousand years for the sake of this fantasy. . . .

Certainly this national fantasy must rest on practical foundations. But whence have you the impression that I have no practical ideas for the details?

The exodus to the Promised Land presents itself as a tremendous enterprise in transportation, unparalleled in the modern world. What, transportation? It is a complex of all human enterprises which we shall fit into each other like cog-wheels. And in the very first stages of the enterprise we shall find employment for the ambitious younger masses of our people; all the engineers, architects, technologists, chemists, doctors, and lawyers, those who have emerged in the last thirty years from the ghetto and who have been moved by the faith that they can win their bread and a little honor outside the framework of our Jewish business futilities. Today they must be filled with despair, they constitute the foundation of a frightful over-educated proletariat. But it is to these that all my love belongs, and I am just as set on increasing their number as you are set on diminishing it. It is in them that I perceive the latent power of the Jewish people. In brief, my kind.

Their withdrawal will in itself suffice to lighten the pressure among the middle classes in anti-Semitic countries.

These were the concepts and methods which distinguished him from the Baron. "You are the great money Jew, I am the Jew of the spirit, hence the differences in our outlooks and methods." Hirsch had indeed tried to do much for the Jews. But his methods, which aimed at keeping the Jews on the lowest possible level, contradicted all the laws of human development and were therefore impractical.

Do you know that you have adopted a frightfully reactionary policy— worse than that of the most absolute autocrats? Fortunately your powers are not great enough to carry it out. You mean well, parbleu, je le sais bien. That is why I want to direct your will to the right channel. Do not permit yourself to be prejudiced by the fact that I am still fairly young. At thirty-five men become cabinet ministers in France, and Napoleon was Emperor at that age.

He closes the letter by declaring that he is ready to continue the conversation as soon as Hirsch desires. But he makes it clear that the movement does not depend on the consent of the Baron. "Very definitely I should like to find, through you, an existing and recognized force, the short-cut to my plans. But you would only be the beginning. There are others. And finally, and above all, there is the mass of the Jews, to which I shall know how to find my way."

In this letter of June 3, 1895, Herzl for the first time imparted his new Jewish policy to a stranger. The writing down of his views, as well as his conversation on the subject, had had a stronger effect on himself than on Hirsch. He had obtained a clear vision of the new and revolutionary character of his proposals. On the same day or shortly thereafter he began a diary under the title of *The Jewish Question.*

II EARLY ZIONISM IN WORLD POLITICS AND IN PALESTINE: 1880–1914

J. L. Talmon

HERZL RECONSIDERED

J. L. Talmon is professor of modern history at the Hebrew University of Jerusalem. His earlier works include The Origins of Totalitarian Democracy *and* The Unique and the Universal. *In this section from his most recent book,* Israel among the Nations, *Talmon reassesses Herzl's approach to world politics.*

The lack of full clarity and consistency in Herzl's view of anti-Semitism is very meaningful. The wounded pride is the beginning of everything. But beyond that Herzl does not seem to be sure, no more than Freud in regard to the problem of evil, whether anti-Semitism was a relic, an excrescence that could be removed, only it would take too much time, and the Jews have had more than their fill of humiliation in the West and are driven by pogroms and hunger in the East; or an incurable disease, one of those perversions inseparable from the human condition. At times Herzl seems to reduce it all to a social problem—Jewish competition in the free professions. He appears to believe in the possibility of a kind of deal with the anti-Semites: you say there are too many Jews in your country, and granted the circumstances and your mentality the Jews are too numerous for you to bear them, let us therefore agree: we help you in taking out the superfluous Jews, and you help us to get a place for them, and a state of their own. Alas, time was to show that no bargain was possible with real anti-Semites. But this Theodor Herzl, deeply steeped in European fair-play liberalism, could not even contemplate.

As I have said, there are quite a few inconsistencies in Herzl's attitude, but they are easily explicable.

The Jewish predicament revealed to Herzl something of the abyss, of the ultimate intractable unreasonableness and horrible beastliness of man, yet in his vision of the solution of the Jewish question there is nothing apocalyptic or catastrophic, no war, no clash of rights, no human sacrifices, no gnashing of teeth, no dreadful breakthrough. It is a commercial transaction as far as the preparations are concerned. The passage to Palestine is a pleasure trip, without as much as seasickness. Settlement in the country is depicted as almost a Fourierist Arcadia, with congenial company of *Landsmannschaften,* fine airy dwellings, wonderful technology and gadgets, and not much physical effort. That killjoy Ahad Haam was quick to seize upon the reference in *Altneuland* to the Jews' experience in their new country as a possible lesson to the American Negroes, once they decide to return to Africa and establish themselves there as an independent nation. The Herzlian recipe was as suited to Jews as it was to Negroes: a wholly abstract utopia, not so much based on principles of morality as upon labor-saving devices and enlightened self-interest.

There is the other inconsistency. Herzl never tired of insisting that the misfortunes and humiliations of the Jews were due to their political weakness. Rich and powerful as they were as individuals, they counted for nothing politically, because they were atomised, unorganised, and represented no power, and in this world of power politics pleas for justice and appeals to conscience had no effect. We had nothing to offer in return. In all his dealings with monarchs and potentates Herzl was always deeply conscious of the need of a quid pro quo: Jews would offer money, support, services, etc. At the same time, the Jewish state of the future is depicted in *Altneuland* as a neutral state, hardly a state at all, just "a Jewish Society," internationally guaranteed like Switzerland, with no army and no foreign policy. And the Arabs, unmentioned in *The Jewish State,* barely noticed in his diaries, appear in *Altneuland* as willing and eager to join the "Jewish Society," because of the material benefits accruing to them. And of course the idea of the charter was based upon the hope of international endorsement by all the powers. This conscious wish of Herzl's to lift the Jewish-state issue out of international politics and the rivalries of the powers, baffling as it is, can only be explained as the liberal recoiling from the facts of irreducible conflict and from the specter of force as the ultimately decisive factor in politics. Have not most of us behaved like this for decades in regard to the Arab issue? And surely this is Herzl's version of the messianic faith in the ultimate and inevitable triumph of good, which had propelled Lassalle and Hess, and indeed all Jewish liberals and Socialists, for so long.

At this juncture we may ask how Herzl looks from the vantage point of seventy years after. A utopian? A prophet? A child of his time?

People are inclined to dismiss as fantastic the three main points of Herzl's practical program. He hoped to buy from the sultan the "Charter" for Palestine. He believed he could get the rich Jews—then, when he had learned his lesson, Jewish subscribers in general—to foot the bill. He envisaged a mighty Jewish effort to transport within the shortest possible time all the willing immigrants and settle them in Palestine—under the aegis of the two national Jewish organs, the political—the Society of Jews—and the financial or economic—the Company of Jews. On a closer look at the realities of the late nineteenth century, Herzl appears less a utopian in regard to his international orientation than in his evaluation of the Jewish people.

There was nothing fantastic in the idea of obtaining a concession from the autocrat of Turkey, and, as events were to show, from the powers that were to divide up the dead corpse of the empire. Turkey had a cord around her neck in the form of her international debt. Her main sources of revenue were not merely pawned, but actually supervised and run by representatives of foreign creditors, backed by their respective powerful governments. The expression, "the Public Debt of Turkey," was never absent from the newspaper columns of the day and constituted an international issue for many decades. In a sense, Turkey could call nothing her own. That state of affairs at the end of a long process of internal decay, utterly cruel harassment by foreign powers, and continuing secession of one Balkan nationality after another at the end of bloody revolt and with the help of European powers, made the corruption at the top utterly hopeless. The North African domains of the caliph—Egypt, Tunis, and then Tripoli—were lost in a manner as injurious to Ottoman interests and pride as possible. In each case state bankruptcy invited European loans, and of course interference. Unhonored promissory notes, impediments placed in the way of the foreign creditors, and finally bloody incidents paved the way for foreign occupation—by the British in Egypt, the French in Tunis, the Italians rather belatedly in Tripoli. The idea of the Jews' offer to redeem Turkey's international debt in exchange for a concession of

Palestine, under some form of Turkish suzerainty—provided the money could be raised—was not at all fantastic. No one, least of all Turkey, bothered at that time about the rights of natives to self-determination in Asia and Africa. Palestine was held by the Turks by the right of conquest. And then, if Turkey had been prepared in the 1830s to cling, as the sultan put it, to a serpent for fear of being drowned (by Mehmet Ali), and to invite the Russian navy and troops to the Bosphorus, why should she refuse aid from a politically innocuous factor? And if mighty Britain could put a premium upon the good will of world Jewry, and even Wilhelm II in his letter on Zionism to the grand duke of Baden, such sympathy was surely not less important to the tottering Porte. Owing to fair treatment throughout the centuries, Jews were well disposed towards Turkey. At the time of the Bulgarian uprising against the Sultan, British anti-Turks and anti-Semites, like the historian Freeman, publicly accused Disraeli of pro-Turkish sentiments and anti-Russian bias owing to his Jewish prejudices.

Neither were Herzl's ideas on colonization absurd in the context of colonial history, especially in the age of imperialism.

British and Dutch rule in India and in Southeast Asia began and was carried on well into the nineteenth century by state-supported chartered trade companies, enjoying the widest political, administrative, judicial and fiscal, and indeed military powers. All North American colonies were established by royal charters granted to a group of settlers or individual entrepreneurs. The race for and partition of Africa was carried out by individuals, sometimes single-handedly, sometimes at the head of tiny bands of followers, some of them idealistic explorers, others nationalist visionaries, some of them adventurers, others men of greed. Cecil Rhodes, whom Herzl tried in vain to contact through his many Jewish associates, is only the most famous example of an empire builder. He had his counterparts in other nations, in men who came to Africa with deep sympathetic understanding, like Savorgnan de Brazza, Auguste Pavie, Karl Peters, and above all that amazing German-Jewish adventurer Emin Pasha (his real name Eduard Schnitzer), companion of General Gordon of Khartoum, the only officer to fight his way through with a small detachment, while Gordon and all his soldiers were massacred by the Mahdi. Emin went on to become the ruler of an entirely isolated Equatoria and to be then "rescued" by Stanley. White settlement in Kenya and the lands of South Africa had provided some lessons in organized and planned colonization on a half-private, half-state basis; the international agreement on the Congo, which handed over the administration of that unhappy country to the king of the Belgians in his private capacity, must have been known and remembered by Herzl.

It would be quite anachronistic to mistake the attitude to colonialism in the mid-1960s for the attitude most people had seventy years ago. The anti-imperialist ideology had as yet hardly made itself heard. J. A. Hobson's *Imperialism* appeared only in 1902, and his disciples, Lenin, Rosa Luxemburg, Hilferding, and others, had hardly started writing on the subject, when Herzl died.

Where Herzl showed himself a complete utopian was in his belief that he could get a few dozen Jewish plutocrats to put up all the money, and, after obtaining the charter, to put the Jews on the boats, arrangements for the sale of property left behind and settlement in the new homes having been happily and easily concluded. The amazing thing then is not so much that Herzl could have nourished such sanguine expectations and could so badly underrate the factor of Jewish inertia, but that with all that, he did not give up after his high hopes had been so cruelly and humiliatingly disappointed. His tenacity of purpose commands the deepest veneration. It was sheer greatness. Where did the feuilletonist, who had been gliding through life, with that light touch, so easily bored, and always in need of new impressions, get his steel?

In his admirable *Life of Herzl* Dr. Alex Bein quotes a letter written by Herzl in 1901 to his faithful follower and friend Dr. Mandelstamm:

> *I have run myself ragged and I haven't obtained a hearing from the wretched crew which controls the money. Fire and brimstone must rain from heaven before those stones are softened. It is something utterly unheard of, and 50 years from now people will spit on the graves of these men for the fact that I should have been almost through with the question of the Sultan, and that I should have been held up because I could not get the miserable money. But of course we can't make a display of our rage and pain, because then the Sultan would become aware of our weakness, and I must do my best to hold him off, to gain time, trying meanwhile to squeeze water out of stones and scrape gold from the mud. Yes, it should be the easiest thing for me now to drop the whole business and to issue a proclamation: "Thus it is, Jewish people; in five years I, a*

*poor, helpless journalist, have reached the point where I could conduct
business with the Sultan himself. But you've left me in the lurch; you are
nothing but a rabble—the devil take you! I'm through with worrying
about you."*

To the comfortably established and rationally analytical people
of his day, Herzl must have looked like one of those *"simplificateurs
terribles"* who reduce highly complex issues to a few crude theo-
rems, and are, if not crazy quacks, dangerous demagogues. Those
ardent Zionists who believed in gradualism and organic growth and
cultural work were simply angered by Herzl's insistence that there
should be no piecemeal colonization, without and prior to the charter.
They could hardly hide their opinion that there was a certain charla-
tanism in Herzl's magic wand approach.

Adolf Böhm, whose history of Zionism, available only in the
German original and not going beyond 1924, to our shame still
the only Zionist history of academic standing, has already compared Herzl's idea of a sudden breakthrough—through diplomatic
action—with the early Socialist vision of a violent revolution that
would make a clean sweep and enable men to start all over from
scratch. Did not some Socialists in the early days object to taking
part in the elections to a national parliament, and still more to sitting
in coalition governments with bourgeois parties? Was not Lenin opposed to philanthropic activity among the workers, and did he not
fight the "economists" and trade unionists in czarist Russia because,
in his opinion, they were weakening the revolutionary resolve of the
proletariat, and postponing the Day of Judgment *sine die*?

The dignity of the Jewish people mattered to Herzl most. The
charter was to be the signal of recognition on the part of the nations of the Jews as a people, and not a motley of beggars. The
charter was to serve as a tremendous inspiration to the Jewish
masses. It was to raise their self-respect, offer them a sense of
purpose, indeed a myth—in Herzl's words a flag, which when lacking
the aura of myth was only a rag. It may well be that Herzl, who had
no spiritual-cultural Jewishness to fall back upon, needed all that
more than men like Ahad Haam, Weizmann, and Ussishkin who could
be proud and full-blooded Jews without such a tonic, and who did
not share the fundamentally non-Jewish dependence of Herzl on external symbols. It may well be that a Herzl weighed down by the
consciousness of difficulties, given to analyzing carefully all the pros

and cons, would never have taken off at all. Ahad Haam's carping and caviling were sufficient to make one give up.

But there was another reason for Herzl's refusal to allow for slow infiltration into Palestine without international guarantees and a clear definition of the ultimate goal. In those very days when he was knocking at the gates of the sultan and making his way through the labyrinths of Ildiz Kiosk, the world press was full of stories of the ghastly atrocities committed by the Turks on the Armenians. Herzl was mortally afraid that a defenseless Jewish minority, which had settled there in the teeth of Turkish prohibition, could be wiped out overnight. He may have underrated the power of concrete though piecemeal and gradual achievement. In his pride he felt a deep aversion for the old Jewish methods of oiling the palms of officials, arranging things behind the counter, sneaking in when unobserved, and bowing the head before or pretending not to perceive brutal insult.

There is an ironical and tragic paradox in the fact that while resolved to treat with the leaders of the world, emperors and kings, princes and ministers, on terms of equality and in the light of the day, in his capacity of representative of the Jewish people, Herzl was at bottom compelled to resort to the very, very old Jewish methods of backstairs diplomacy. Reverend Hechler, who managed to obtain for Herzl access to the grand duke of Baden and then Wilhelm II himself, was a religious crank. Nevlinsky, who enabled Herzl to establish contact with the unspeakable ministers of Abdul Hamid, was a shady figure, half-blackmailer, half-spy. And then the man who eventually arranged for Herzl the audience with the sultan, the famous Professor Vámbéry of Budapest, was "a seventy-year-old Hungarian Jew who didn't know whether he was more Turk than Englishman, who wrote books in German, spoke twelve languages with equal mastery, and had professed five religions, in two of which he served as a priest . . ." and "through these many religious intimacies . . . has naturally become an atheist." Wherever he went, Herzl had to oil palms. His reports on his dealings with the fantastic blackguards and thieves in the Turkish government are delightful vignettes, little masterpieces. While feeling out of breath on reading about the infinite crookedness of these viziers, diplomats, and courtiers, the reader is filled with incredulous admiration for the upright and fastidious man's skill in managing and indeed outwitting the thieves.

The Middle East at the Outbreak of World War I

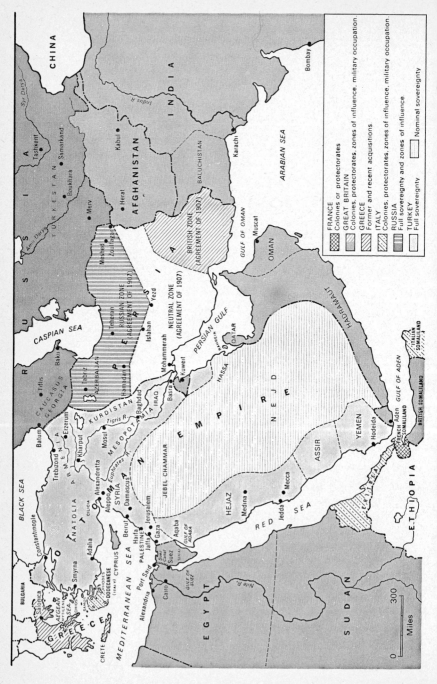

In perspective, Herzl's efforts with Jewish millionaires and the rulers of nations appear quixotic indeed. But if Herzl was chasing after mirages, the princes of the world themselves do not strike one as models of responsible conduct, and their acts as the result of well-thought-out plans and solid assessment of data: the initial enthusiasm of a Wilhelm II, the most powerful man of his time, evaporating so quickly; the sultan calling in Herzl to negotiate with him, while he had in fact already concluded a deal with a French group of bankers, and wanted to use Herzl as a scarecrow; and Herzl deep at heart afraid that after all Abdul Hamid may agree to grant the charter, and he, Herzl, will not be able to raise the millions to pay for it.

But this was not what the masses saw or wanted to see. Starved for leadership, yearning for majesty, not having had either, and having had to put up for almost 2,000 years with rabbis, *rebbes*, and *shtadlanim* as a substitute, they responded with a thrill to the new Moses, who looked every inch a prince, possessed a perfect sense of decorum and a dignity that was as royal as it was charming, and who —as they fondly believed—could hobnob with emperors and kings, and had magical powers at his command. Insofar as it had not given itself up to the universal revolutionary ideal, the Eastern European Jewish intelligentsia had for the most part by then not only renounced any hope of becoming integrated into the majority nation, but had developed an intense national pride. The masses on their part found themselves in that inflammable state which is created by the discrepancy between the growth of a sense of dignity and the realities of worsening conditions of existence, with religion no more a prop or consolation: a situation which at all time engenders revolution. While the Jews had become so conscious of the rights of men, their position was more and more threatened by the competition of millions of peasants and dispossessed gentry flocking into the towns and by rampant chauvinism; and the amateurishness of the *Hovevei Zion* was hardly an answer to the situation.

And so it happened that almost against his own wishes, Herzl, no democrat, and certainly no socialist, who started out with the idea of doing everything for the people, but not with and by the people, became, when rebuffed by the Hirschs and Rothschilds, the founder of a mass movement and a mass mystique. The diplomat ended up by creating in the first place an organization. It was then given to the man who had no interest in the cultural side of Zionism to release tremendous creative energies in the spiritual field. The technocrat, whose social ideas did not go beyond mutualism and cooperativism, inspired after his death a labor movement which in idealism, intellectual daring, social experimenting, practical ability, and sheer success had hardly been equaled by any other labor movement in the world. It was all due to the power of a great idea.

From the vantage point of 1966 in Israel and in the Jewish Diaspora Herzl stands both vindicated and repudiated. The Balfour Declaration, the Palestine Mandate, and the UN decision in 1947 were all Herzlian realizations in content and in spirit. They would not have been achieved without that mighty instrument Herzl had forged, the Zionist Organization, eternally vigilant, most resourceful, and always there to take advantage of every opportunity to further the Zionist aims. And of course, there would have been no UN decision had there been no 600,000 Jews in Palestine in 1947, with hundreds of settlements, a closely knit institutional framework, cadres of armed men, all brought to Palestine or created there in a gradual dogged, practical effort, it is only fair to say—under the protection of the power which first came forward with the offer of a kind of charter, when Herzl was still alive—the Uganda Plan—and then in 1917 gave its pledge of support for the Jewish national home.

Hardly a Zionist leader felt so acutely the ground burning under the Jewish feet as Herzl did in his last few years: witness his readiness, under the impact of the Kishinev pogrom, to accept Uganda. Yet, intensely conscious as he may have been of the progressive deterioration of the Jewish position in Eastern Europe, the author of the *Judenstaat,* the plea to humanitarian sentiment and enlightened self-interest, and of the idyllic utopia *Altneuland,* never envisaged the Jewish state as coming into existence through blood and iron, against a background of a catastrophe without parallel. Nor was Herzl able to visualize a Jewish state as a besieged city, an armed camp, surrounded by implacable hostility. When speaking of the "Jewish Question," a term never mentioned these days, Herzl and other Zionist prophets had in mind the Jews of Central and Eastern Europe, certainly not the Jews of the Oriental countries or for that matter of the West. Not one of them in their worst dreams could have foreseen that there would be no Eastern European Jews to settle in the Jewish state, once established.

Alex Bein

HERZL AND THE KAISER IN PALESTINE

This second selection from Bein's biography explores Herzl's diplomatic negotiations with the mercurial German Kaiser in 1898. Herzl was working behind the scenes with Count Philipp zu Eulenburg. They managed to interest the Kaiser, on the eve of his visit to the Ottoman Empire, with the Zionist vision of a transformed Palestine. Herzl's hopes for support were, however, doomed to disappointment as the Kaiser's temporary enthusiasm was cooled by Turkish opposition to Zionism, by his own hard-headed advisers, and perhaps by his changing moods. Bein documents Herzl's diplomatic technique and the extent to which it depended on the subtle manipulation of the anti-Semitic and antirevolutionary tendencies, as well as the presumed national interests, of Europe's rulers.

Letter from the German Kaiser to Friedrich, Grand Duke of Baden

> Hunting Lodge
> Rominten
> September 29, 1898

My most venerated Uncle,

A brief pause in the amorous concerts of my stags permits me to devote a few lines to you. You had the kindness, during the latter part of this summer, to send me a rather voluminous and very interesting file, the contents of which concerned the Zionists and their movement. I have examined the material and worked through it in conjunction with Count Phil. Eulenburg. The result of my investigations is the following: To begin with, I must extend to you my most sincere thanks for your gracious suggestion and insight in this mat-

From Alex Bein, *Theodore Herzl, A Biography* (Philadelphia: The Jewish Publication Society of America, 1940), pp. 529–530, 290–309. Reprinted with the permission of the publisher.

ter, which I had hitherto been able to follow only superficially, through newspapers and pamphlets, which had been provided chiefly by the notorious, widely known Baron Hirsch. Through the study of your gracious consignment I have, however, now become convinced that we are dealing here with a question of the most far reaching importance. I have, therefore, in a discreet manner, permitted contacts to be made with the promoters of this idea and have thereby been able to establish that the emigration to Palestine of the Israelites who are ready for this has been excellently prepared and even securely based, in every respect, from the financial point of view. I have therefore ordered a reply to be given to Zionist inquiry as to whether I was prepared to grant an audience to a delegation of theirs that I would readily receive a deputation in Jerusalem on the occasion of our presence there. I am convinced that the settlement of the Holy Land by the wealthy and industrious people of Israel will soon confer upon the former unexpected prosperity and blessing, which through further spreading may develop into an important revival and opening up of Asia Minor. This, however, means millions into the pockets of the Turks—also of the Grand Seigneur (Effendimis)—and therewith the gradual healing of the so-called sick man, through which the disagreeable "Eastern Question" would, quite unnoticed at least, be diverted from the Mediterranean and solved step by step. Then the Turk will again recover, that is, will get money in a natural way *without borrowing,* he will no longer be sick, he will build his roads and railways himself without foreign companies, and he will not be able to be partitioned so easily. Q.E.D. Moreover, the energy, creativity, and practical ability of the tribe of Shem would be diverted into more honorable channels than battening on the Christians, and many a Semite, fomenting the opposition and adhering to Soc[ial] Dem[ocracy], will move eastwards where more rewarding work is to be found, the end of which is not—as in the above case—the penitentiary. Now I know well enough that nine-tenths of all Germans would shun me with horror, if they were to learn later that I sympathize with the Zionists and that I might even take them under my protection, as I would do if asked by them. However, here I beg to observe that the Jews have killed the Saviour; this God knows even better than we do, and He has punished them accordingly. But neither the Anti-Semites, nor others, nor I have been charged and authorized by Him to harry these people *in majorem Dei Gloriam.* I think that here one is also permitted to say: He who is free of sin shall cast the first stone on them. To this I would also add: "Love your enemies." And this point we must also not ignore from the secular, *Realpolitik* point of view, namely, that what with the immense power that international Jewish capital, as a matter of fact, represents in all its dangerous implications, it would be an enormous gain for Germany if the world of the Hebrews looked up to it with gratitude! Everywhere the Hydra of the most vulgar and most hideous Anti-Semitism is raising its gruesome head, and fearfully the Jews—ready to leave the countries where danger threatens them—look for a protector. Well, those returning to the Holy Land shall enjoy protection and security, and I shall intercede for them with the Sultan, for the scriptures say make friends even with unjust Mammon; be ye wise as serpents and harmless as doves.

Your nephew who loves you with all his heart,

Wilhelm.

He [Herzl] stayed only a few days in Vienna. There were again scenes with his publishers which caused him more heartache than his interview with [Foreign Minister] Bülow and [Reich Chancellor] Hohenlohe. He met with difficulties in picking his deputation. Finally it was so constituted as to be able to furnish information on the widest possible range of subjects: Wolffsohn, the prospective director of the Colonial Bank, was a merchant; Bodenheimer, president of the Zionist Federation of Germany, was a lawyer; Seidener, the only one with a first-hand knowledge of Palestine, was an engineer; Schnirer, vice-president of the Actions Committee, was a physician. The parting was hard for Herzl. Ben-Yehudah, the Hebrew writer and lexicographer, had warned him specifically that the journey was not without its dangers. Would he return in good health? And with what results?

On October 13 [1898] he took the Orient Express, without letting even his nearest friends know his destination. He discussed with Bodenheimer the formulation of his demands. Bodenheimer made detailed suggestions on the development and management of the land, and Herzl agreed. But on his arrival in Constantinople the next day he bethought himself that it would be unwise to submit detailed and far-reaching proposals which might at this stage lead only to refusals. His original idea of the Jewish Company fused in his mind with the suggestion made by Seligman in London. "We can ask only for permission to create an organic, initial cell: a Jewish Land Company for Syria (with a charter of rights); this is as much as we can expect, if we are lucky."

His very first step in Constantinople brought him up against bitter disillusionment. While Herzl was delivering Nevlinski's letters of introduction to the assistant secretary for foreign affairs, Djewad Bey, and the major domo, Munir Pasha, he had sent Bodenheimer to the German ambassador, Freiherr von Marschall, to ask when he could be received. Marschall replied that he did not know Dr. Herzl, and that since he had to leave in half an hour for the Dardanelles to greet the Kaiser, he could not receive him at the moment. The grand duke's statement about Marschall's report had been wrong, no doubt an old man's error of memory; apparently Marschall was as cool as von Bülow, if, indeed, he knew anything about it at all. The situation was therefore much darker than he had anticipated, the road to the Kaiser more difficult. The next day passed without any activity. On October 17, Herzl decided to request an audience with the Kaiser via the Court Marshal August zu Eulenburg.

"The Imperial reception of the Zionist deputation in the Holy Land," he wrote, along the lines of Philipp zu Eulenburg's ideas, "will undoubtedly precipitate much discussion in Europe. Should our demonstration be regarded as evidence of a *fait accompli*—even if its full implications are not revealed—then it will be too late for any hostile intervention that might have been contemplated. . . . Everything depends on the form which this *fait accompli* is made to take. Consent to the formation of a 'Jewish Land Company for Syria and Palestine' would, in my humble opinion, suffice for the time being. . . . The acknowledgment of the general political situation would ensue when more emphasis would be laid for public purposes on the German protectorate." The last ship which Herzl could still catch for Palestine and arrive in time was leaving the next morning. He therefore requested the Court Marshal to take immediate action. He also wrote in the same vein to Bülow.

At half past one Wolffsohn returned from the Ildiz Kiosk, the Turkish seat of government. Thanks to his ingenuity he had managed to get past the guards and to reach August zu Eulenburg, who had given him a friendly reception. Bülow had been ill-humored and brusque. Less than three hours later a messenger appeared at the hotel with instructions to Herzl to present himself at half past four at the little palace which had been specially erected for the Kaiser. Five minutes before the appointed time Herzl and Wolffsohn were at the gates. Wolffsohn waited outside, Herzl entered. Not a single one of the German court attendants was to be seen. Herzl stood in the corridor, no one paying any attention to him. After a short interval he asked one of the Turkish adjutants for the Kaiser and was told that the latter was expected any moment. Then he was led into a waiting room—and a guard set over him. Finally, at half past six, he heard the command given to the guard of honor outside to present arms: the Kaiser had come. Five minutes later Herzl was called. Count Eulenburg pointed upstairs. Count Kessel led him past the Empress and von Bülow into the Emperor's working room. Bülow entered behind him. The Kaiser, in dark Hussar uniform, came forward to receive him. Herzl, dressed in a dark frock coat, stood still and made a deep bow. The Kaiser came closer and put out his hand. He was happy to see Dr. Herzl, he said. "Your Imperial Majesty, I am very happy at the honor conferred on me." The Kaiser then went round the table, pushed a chair round to Herzl, himself sat down with his back to the table and crossed his booted legs. Herzl and Bülow sat down, and throughout the interview held their silk hats between their knees, in accordance with form. The Kaiser asked Herzl to speak.

The long awaited moment had come for Herzl. Ever since he had first seen the Kaiser at the maneuvers in September 1896, he had considered the man and the method of approach. He had observed, in particular, the crippled left arm, a decisive physical characteristic which, strangely enough, very few people noticed. Herzl had then written in his diary (anticipating Emil Ludwig by more than a quarter of a century): "I believe that his condition as a cripple explains his entire character. This supreme war lord would be rejected by the medical officer if he were an ordinary recruit. Hence perhaps his pathological preference for all things military. Nor can he ever carry himself freely, for he must always bear his defect in mind. The truth is that he deceives the majority by the way he holds the reins with his short left hand. Also he loves magnificent, dazzling uniforms, shining helmets which attract and divert the eye. But he seems to me to be a likable man; or, in a single word, a man."

He came closer to the man through his defect. Herzl could feel in him the impulse to exaggeration, the desire to overwhelm; but in this more intimate contact he also was aware of something winning about him—in brief, the entire mixture which captivated those who were admitted to his presence. Herzl considered the Kaiser gifted to the point of genius, and somehow felt a relationship to him: in the love of the theatrical gesture, in the emphasis on the idea of leadership, in the coining of brief, telling slogans, and above all in the high evaluation of technology. Like many of his contemporaries Herzl saw in the Kaiser the prototype of the modern-minded prince: how few there were who could discern, behind these undeniable virtues, the essential weakness and hesitancy of his nature, his susceptibility to external influence, the lack of seriousness behind his multifarious activities, and the self-regard which the flattery of his courtiers had intensified into delusions of grandeur. Herzl barely noted these negative elements. He was greatly impressed by Wilhelm's great, sea-blue eyes: "I have never seen such eyes. They express a remarkable, daring, and searching soul." The entire personality of the Kaiser moved him enormously.

And against this the Kaiser was strongly impressed by Herzl's personality, "one which awakens confidence" as he expressed himself to the grand duke of Baden, and as the latter in turn reported to Herzl in December of that year. The impression was confirmed at the meeting in Palestine.

Herzl had expected that the Kaiser would open the conversation. The request that he speak first embarrassed him somewhat. He began by repeating the contents of his letter. The Kaiser soon broke in and explained why the Zionist movement attracted him. The considerations were, as Herzl immediately observed, essentially anti-Semitic.

"There are among your people," said the Kaiser, approximately, "certain elements whom it would be a good thing to move to Palestine. I am thinking, for instance, of the province of Hesse, where usurers are active among the farmers. If these were to take their capital and settle in the colonies, they would be more useful."

Herzl was angered by this identification of the Jewish people with a few usurers; he recovered his coolness, and delivered a speech against anti-Semitism, which, he said, happened to fall most heavily on the best Jews. Bülow parried by speaking of the ingratitude of the Jews; the House of Hohenzollern had always been gracious toward them, and now they were joining the revolutionary party. This gave Herzl his opening for his favorite argument, that Zionism would dissolve the revolutionary parties in the Jewish peo-

ple. The Kaiser expressed himself as convinced that the Jews would
go in for the colonization of Palestine if they knew that he would
take them under his protection, so that in a sense they would not
really be leaving Germany.

Bülow then adverted to the fact that the rich Jews and the powerful newspapers, among them Herzl's own, were hostile to Zionism.
It was evident that he wanted the Kaiser to infer that there was no
power back of Herzl. He did not contradict the Kaiser openly—that
was not the manner of a court politician. But except that he did not
use the word No, he opposed every conceivable negative to the idea.
" 'Yes, of course, but'—'yes, if only'—all masked 'No's,' " as Herzl
observed in his diary.

There followed a detailed discussion of the French situation;
Herzl felt that the inner weakness of that country would make opposition to the plan impossible. The Kaiser spoke openly of the Dreyfus
affair. Herzl expressed no opinion, "but it soon became clear that
everyone present considered Dreyfus innocent. It was something
utterly astounding."

By this detour Herzl came back to the Jewish question, and unfolded his plan in all its details, and with all the essential arguments
regarding the advantages which would accrue to Germany and
Turkey. The Kaiser listened, and nodded repeatedly.

"I do not know," said Herzl, "whether I've lost my sense of pro-
portion, but the whole thing appeals to me as being quite natural."

The Kaiser answered: "To me, too."

Bülow objected: "Yes, yes, if they'll only let you, here. You ought
perhaps to see the ministers . . ." he rubbed his forefinger and thumb
together significantly. "They all take it here."

The Kaiser threw the suggestion off with a light gesture and said:
"It certainly won't fail to make an impression if the German Kaiser
shows his concern in the matter. . . . After all, I am the only one who
still sticks by the sultan. I mean something to him."

The Emperor looked at his watch for the second time, and rose
to his feet. "Have you another question?" he asked. Herzl brought
up the details of the audience in Palestine, the address, or memorial,
to be prepared for the Kaiser, and so on. The Kaiser said: "Write
your address out and give it to Bülow. I will then work it out with
him. . . . Only tell me in brief what you want me to ask of the sultan."

"A Chartered Company—under German protection."

" 'Good, a Chartered Company,' and therewith he gave me his hand, which is powerful enough for two, pressed mine vigorously, and strode out before us through the middle door."

The secret audience had lasted a full hour. As Herzl went out with Bülow, the latter said: "That is a man of genius!" He advised Herzl to consult with Marschall, and to get full information from him. Herzl promised to do so, and then, immediately after, to work out the address and send it over.

He went at once to the German Embassy, but Marschall had left. Exhausted by the sheer physical strain of the day Herzl returned to his hotel. His heart was rebelling. While Wolffsohn packed the bags he tried to work on the address. At eleven o'clock he gave it up and lay down in his bed. At four in the morning (October 19) he woke, worked for half an hour, and broke off, exhausted. At six o'clock he got up again and worked till half past eight. He sent what he had done, with a covering letter, to Bülow, promising to forward the remainder to Palestine. Then he rushed to the harbor, where Wolffsohn had made all the necessary preparations. At eleven in the morning, under a cloudless sky, the steamship *Emperor Nicholas II* left Constantinople.

A week later, on October 26, 1898, Herzl, somewhat rested and recovered, arrived in the gaily bedecked harbor of Jaffa. As the party mounted the steps of the Hotel Kamenetz they heard the sound of saluting guns. The Kaiser had arrived in Jaffa from the landward side.

Herzl had not come to Palestine for a tour of inspection, but he was naturally anxious to take in whatever he could before the audience. His first visit was to Mikveh Israel, where he was accorded a festive reception by the directors of the agricultural school. Herzl conversed with the pupils, visited the grave of Charles Netter, the founder of Mikveh Israel, and then continued on his way to the Rothschild colony of Rishon le-Zion.

The news of his approach traveled before him. No one knew for what purpose he was coming. Some believed that he had merely been sent by his newspaper; others read a much deeper significance into his visit. All the circumstances hinted at great, imminent events, and every colony was excited by his visit. There was the fact that he was coming first to one of the Rothschild colonies, and his negative attitude toward the work of the baron was of course widely known: that he arrived in the country at the same time as the German emperor; that the messianic enthusiast Hechler had preceded him, and had woven a mystery, full of vague hints and promises, round his voyage. And there was, on top of all this, the halo which had gathered round the name of Herzl. The young colonists were on fire with enthusiasm, and the flame communicated itself even to the officials of the colonies. The director of Rishon le-Zion was both friendly and distant, keeping a double eye on the colonists and on Paris. Herzl made a thorough inspection of the famous wine cellars. A deputation then led him to the decorated community house, which was packed with an expectant crowd. A thunder of *Hedad!* greeted him, accompanied by well-meant music. The oldest settler saluted him in the name of the colony. Herzl was visibly affected; this was the first Jewish colony he had set eyes on. In his brief speech of response he expressed his happy astonishment at the work that had been accomplished, and praised the "magnificent generosity" of the baron. The aim of Zionism was, to be sure, a greater one, the Jewish people was to find refuge here. But it was far from the intention of the Zionists to undertake anything in opposition to the rulers of the country or the direction of the colonies. The colonists only had to go on preparing the soil for the future, no other Zionist work was demanded or expected of them.

Then Herzl visited the individual houses, and was depressed by the wretched condition of the workers. He listened to a report from Dr. Mazie on the fever which raged in the vicinity, and discussed with him the necessity of large-scale drainage of the swamps. On the whole, the colony made a bad impression on him. He had never doubted that with money industrial enterprises could be created. But the amounts that had been spent should have shown better results. But what he, whose Zionism was grounded in the feeling for human dignity and freedom, marked with the greatest distress was the relations between the settlers and the management. "Over all broods the fear of the Baron in Paris. The poor colonists have exchanged one dread for another."

The next morning he traveled on in the carriage of the Rothschild managers. In Ness Zionah (Wadi Hanin), then a tiny settlement, he was received by the entire population, children sang songs, an old colonist came out with bread, wine, and salt—the bread and wine grown on his own piece of land. Herzl was compelled to visit almost every house.

They traveled on—preceded always by the breathless announcement of their approach. Outside Rehovoth he was encountered by a stormy calvacade of sixteen young riders, who galloped in wild circles about his advancing carriage, sang Hebrew songs, and shouted *Hedad!* and *Hoch Herzl!* Herzl stopped his carriage and stepped out. His eyes were filled with tears. He was thinking: when would these high-spirited Jewish lads cease to be lonely symbols? In Rehovoth itself the whole population was drawn up in two lines, and the songs of the children rose to the skies. Here Herzl saw no bowing and scraping, no fearsome glances, no repression. He remembered this when he wrote, a year later: "There are in Palestine other colonies than those of Rothschild. They cost less and yet they have become self-supporting sooner, and in these freer settlements there grows a sturdier generation. I need only mention the colony of Rehovoth which must be regarded, by everyone who has seen it, as superior to, for instance, the more costly Rishon le-Zion."

Herzl returned in the evening to Jaffa, exhausted by the heat and the multitude of impressions. Soon after he received a visit from Hechler, whom he now encountered for the first time in Palestine. Through him he sent a message to Count Eulenburg that he would wait for the Kaiser on the road that ran by Mikveh Israel.

The next morning—it was a Friday—Herzl set out at an early hour for Mikveh Israel. He was not feeling well, and he had to make an effort to remain erect in the intense heat. The thermometer showed thirty-one degrees centigrade in the shade, forty-one in the sun (eighty-eight and a hundred and six Fahrenheit). In front of the school the pupils were assembled, and many colonists had come from outlying points to join in the greeting. At nine o'clock the imperial cortege approached. First came grim Turkish horsemen, then the Kaiser's outriders and finally, among a gray group of ladies, the Kaiser himself. Herzl gave the signal to the young choir, which broke into the imperial hymn. Then he stationed himself near a plough and took off his tropical helmet. The Kaiser recognized him from a distance. To the amazement of the assembled he suddenly pulled up his horse, and the entire procession halted. He rode up to Herzl, held out his hand to him, and called, "How are you?"

"I thank Your Majesty. I am taking a look at the country. How has Your Majesty's journey been till now?"

"Very hot! But the land has a future."

"For the moment it is still sick," said Herzl.

"It needs water," answered the Kaiser, "plenty of water."

"Yes, Your Majesty, large scale irrigation."

"It is a land with a future," repeated the Kaiser. He extended his hand again to Herzl and, while the children sang the imperial hymn again, rode off with his suite.

The scene made the profoundest impression on the assembled, and on Herzl no less. He regarded it as a good omen for the forthcoming reception of the deputation. He returned with his companions to Jaffa. In the fearful heat of midday they set out by train for Jerusalem. The compartment was crowded. Herzl began to feel feverish, and the attack became stronger as the hours passed. He was greatly weakened. The train was late, and so, to Wolffsohn's utter despair, they were still on the train when the Sabbath set in. Moonlight lay over Jerusalem when they arrived. Feverish, supporting himself with a stick, his free arm given alternately to Schub and Wolffsohn, Herzl staggered rather than walked into the Hotel Kamenetz. In spite of his exhaustion, the sight of old Jerusalem stretched out in the moonlight made a mighty impression on him. Within the hotel he felt sick, took quinine, retched, and became very weak. Schnirer, as a doctor, attended on him. Wolffsohn was beside himself with distress, and feared the worst. The next morning Herzl woke feeling better, though still weak; Wolffsohn had nothing to fear for the present.

That morning the Kaiser rode into the city, which had made great preparations for his reception. A new entrance had been broken through the Jaffa gate, so that the Kaiser would not have to dismount. The Jews, like the Turks, had put up a triumphal arch. Herzl would have liked greatly to greet the Kaiser under this arch; but the opposition of the hostile orthodox Jews, and the well-grounded fears of responsible Jewish leaders regarding the reaction of the Turkish authorities, made this impossible. So he sat alone in his little hotel room, outlined the conclusion of his address to the Kaiser, entered into his diary his impressions of the visit to Rishon le-Zion, and from his window watched the Kaiser passing first under the Jewish and then under the Turkish arches. In the evening he sent a clean copy of the address, with a covering letter, to Eulenburg, via

Wolffsohn, and asked to be informed when he and his delegation would be received.

After the close of the Sabbath Herzl moved to a private house in the Mammillah Street, where an entire floor was reserved for him and his entourage. Thither, on the next day, flowed a ceaseless stream of visitors—Zionists, admirers, curiosity hunters, people of the most diverse views and attitudes. Herzl listened attentively to their reports and recitals, and whatever he thought of importance he entered into a little notebook which he kept at hand. In the evening the party made a tour of the old city, under Schub's guidance. At the Wailing Wall, which he visited again the next morning, he was repelled by the sight of "the ugly, miserable, competing beggary," so that his deeper emotions were untouched. When he stood on the Tower of David, which they mounted that evening, he was entranced by the panorama of "the city covered with the first faint twilight of evening." On October 31 he again visited the Old City, and was careful to avoid the imperial train, which was making its way to the dedication of the Church of the Redeemer. He also inspected a Jewish hospital, and from the gallery of the old synagogue looked out upon the panorama of the Temple site, the Mount of Olives, and the city. The Old City, with its oriental filth, left him depressed. He was haunted by constructive ideas. He thought of cleaning out the Old City, and of retaining it simply as an area of religious sanctities. Round about this area would rise, upon the encircling hills, "a glorious New Jerusalem," airy, clean, gracious, in a modern architectural style deriving from the ancient. He returned to this idea over and over again.

Above all these thoughts lay always the shadow of the fear that the delegation might after all not be received. There was as yet no reply from Eulenburg. There were rumors that the Kaiser was breaking off his journey and returning direct to Berlin; France had declared war on England. Those were the days of the Fashoda incident. Herzl sent Wolffsohn and Hechler to the imperial encampment; at half past seven Wolffsohn and Schnirer reported that Eulenburg had given Hechler the answer: the delegation would be received "tomorrow or the day after." Meanwhile the ship on which Herzl had planned to return left for Europe. On November 1 Herzl hit upon the idea of compiling a photographic album of the Jewish colonies and of sending it to the Kaiser, reminding him at the same time of the audience.

Then at last, while Seidener and Schnirer were busy looking for the album, the message came from the German consulate: he was to report to Legation Councillor Kemeth in the imperial encampment with regard to the address.

The Councillor received him somewhat condescendingly, and handed him back the address with some of the passages crossed out in pencil. This, that, and the other he could not permit Herzl to say to the Kaiser. Herzl was to prepare a new address and to submit it again for the Councillor's approval. Herzl ignored the man's impertinence and in the evening sent him the new fair copy via Bodenheimer. Commenting on a question raised by Herzl, Kemeth remarked that the German government expected no publicity to be given to the audience for the time being.

Extraordinarily enough Herzl was not staggered by the corrections; at least he gives no evidence of it in his diary. Actually all those passages had been deleted which referred specifically to the aim of the Zionist movement, to the desperate need of the Jewish people, and to the petition for the Kaiser's protection of the projected "Jewish Land Company for Syria and Palestine." The address was thereby robbed of a great deal of its character. Herzl seems to have looked upon these changes as intended for public consumption only. He was soon to learn that they meant a great deal more.

On Monday, November 2, the exact date on which the Balfour Declaration was to be issued nineteen years later, the audience took place in the palatial imperial tent.

The Kaiser was wearing a gray uniform, a turban, and gray gloves. In one hand he carried a riding whip, the other he extended in a friendly gesture. Herzl presented the delegation. Then he read out the address, while Bülow followed him in his manuscript. Herzl spoke first of the historic tie between the Jews and Palestine and of the aims of the Zionist movement, without however being permitted to allude to the official program; then he went on to speak of modern technology which made possible rapid colonization, and of the blessing for all humanity which would issue from this enterprise. "This is the land of our fathers," read the main passage, "a land suited to colonization and cultivation. Your Majesty has seen the land. It cries out for men to come and build it. And we have among our brothers a tragic proletariat. These men cry out for a land to build. Now these two crying needs—that of a land and that of a people—may be brought together for the alleviation of both. We believe this enterprise to be such an excellent one, so worthy of the participation of the most magnanimous spirits, that we bespeak for it the high help of Your Imperial Majesty."

The Kaiser in his answer thanked Herzl for the address, which he said had interested him extremely. "In any case," he added, "the enterprise must be made the subject of further investigation and conversation." He then made some observations on such colonization as had already been achieved. "What the land needs above all is water and shade." It was the Kaiser's opinion that the soil was culti-vable. "The settlements which I have seen, the German no less than the Jewish, may serve as samples of what can be done with the land. There is room here for all. Only provide the water and the shade. For the native population, too, the colonization will serve as an example of initiative. Your movement, with which I am thoroughly familiar, is based on a sound idea." With the assurance of his sus-tained interest he closed the official reply, held out his hand to Herzl, and opened a less formal conversation. He referred to the frightful heat. Bülow, whom he had drawn into the circle, repeated the Kaiser's phrase about the great need of water.

"That we can supply," said Herzl. "It will cost billions, but it will bring in billions, too."

The Kaiser: "Well, you certainly have enough money, more than all of us."

Bülow: "Yes, when it comes to money, which is such a problem for us, you certainly don't suffer from a shortage."

The conversation passed to the harnessing of the water power of the Jordan, the hygienic condition of the country, and Herzl's plans for a "New Jerusalem." Then the Kaiser closed the audience by again holding out his hand to Herzl.

This audience was shorter than the one granted in Constantinople. It was also more vague. Certain influences or obstacles must have intervened during that period. The Kaiser assured Herzl of his interest and stated that further investigation was necessary. With regard to the projected protectorate nothing more was said; whether from caution, or to indicate refusal, remained an open question. "He said neither yes nor no." This was how Herzl summarized his im-pressions in his diary.

That evening Herzl and his friends packed their bags, and to escape observation, left by the early morning train for Jaffa. Herzl was for leaving the city and the country at once, before the news of the audience got abroad and produced dangerous repercussions. He did not feel safe on Turkish soil. It was not only Ben-Yehudah's warning that disturbed him; he had received various intimations of the hostile attitude of Turkish officials. In Jaffa and Jerusalem he had observed that he was being followed by the secret service agent, Mendel Krämer; the latter did in fact let it be known afterwards that he had carried about with him an order for Herzl's arrest, to be used in case the visitor behaved suspiciously. Herzl was constantly thinking of the fate of Sabbatai Zevi [a false Messiah of the seventeenth century], with whom he was often compared. On the ship which took him to Palestine he spoke of "the high point of the tragic enterprise" which he was approaching. When he mounted the Tower of David in Jerusalem he said to his friends: "It would be an excellent move for the Sultan to have me taken prisoner here." And when, after waiting a day and a half, he boarded the English orange freighter, the *Dundee,* on the evening of November 4—this after some unpleasant incidents in Jaffa, and over the protests of his companions (Wolffsohn excepted) who found the boat too small—he wrote in his diary: "Now at last I consider our expedition ended, with, I believe, fairly good results. Palestine was a bit too hot for me, in more than one sense. If the Turkish government were possessed of a grain of political foresight, it would have finished the job there and then."

In Alexandria they abandoned the cockle-shell of a boat, on which all except Herzl and Schnirer had been sick, and transferred to the Italian luxury liner, *Regina Margheritta.* Herzl brooded without letup on the possible causes of the Kaiser's change of attitude. Had external difficulties intruded or had there been a change of feeling in the Kaiser himself? In reply to a cable inquiry, he received from his father the news that the audience had become public. But it was only when they debarked in Naples that they read the official German communiqué, which hid the audience in a closing paragraph among a score of unimportant political announcements, and deprived it of all significance. The communiqué reported first the Kaiser's visits to the Mosque of Omar and to the Roman Catholic and Greek patriarchs, who received him surrounded by their respective hierarchies. "Later the Kaiser received the French Consul, also a Jewish deputation, which presented him with an album of pictures of the Jewish Colonies in Palestine. In reply to an address by the leader of the deputation, His Majesty remarked that he viewed with benevolent interest all efforts directed toward the improvement of agriculture in Palestine as long as these accorded with the welfare of the Turkish Empire, and were conducted in a spirit of complete respect for the sovereignty of the Sultan."

It was a frightful and sudden descent from the summit of hope into the empty abyss. Everyone was utterly dispirited. Herzl, the hardest hit, kept his head up. He would know what version of the affair to offer to the public. And in this manner of encountering defeat, he also felt himself the leader. "I am neither cleverer nor better than any one of you. But I am undiscouraged, and that is why the leadership belongs to me." And as his first reaction to the news, he wrote in his diary: "The fact that the Kaiser has not taken over the protectorate is of course excellent for the later development of our enterprise. . . . For the protectorate would have been a clear immediate advantage, but not a long range one. We should later have had to pay the most usurious interest for this protectorate."

The later student of events cannot but agree with this appraisal. The successive alienation of Germany from the Western Powers and Russia would have turned a German protectorate into a serious obstacle. The rivalry round Palestine would not have been mitigated; on the contrary, it would have been exacerbated. It would have been impossible to create a peaceful basis for Jewish colonization. Other difficulties of an internal Jewish character would also have arisen; there would have been a clash of patriotisms, and the funds on whose cooperation Herzl counted would, in such circumstances, hardly have been placed at his disposal.

But complications and difficulties would in all likelihood have arisen also within the sphere of German politics. Herzl himself admitted, after the audience at Constantinople, that from this point of view Bülow was perfectly right in behaving coolly toward the plan. As a responsible German statesman he foresaw that, even under the most favorable external circumstances, the practical realization of the plan was endangered by the negative attitude of the rich Jews. Besides, there was the sultan's dislike of the Zionist policy. It had manifested itself so vigorously when the Kaiser first raised the subject that the latter, as the sultan's guest, simply could not return to it again. Such was the account given later by Philipp Eulenburg; and the grand duke of Baden told a Zionist deputation in 1902 that on this visit the Kaiser made two unsuccessful attempts to broach the subject. It is quite certain that the German ambassador to Turkey, who accompanied the Kaiser on the return journey, influenced his master in the same direction. The whole thing had from the beginning been a personal affair of the Kaiser's, who had been won over by the grand duke and Philipp Eulenburg. What Eulenburg's motives were remains unclear; they can hardly have been benevolent like the grand duke's. The most obvious assumption is that he wanted to put a skillful and prominent journalist under obligation to him. The Kaiser was wildly enthusiastic about the idea, and the reception of the deputation in Jerusalem must have been due to his personal initiative; it was thoroughly in keeping with his passion for theatrical gestures. Bülow, Marschall, Turkish influence, and anticipated difficulties with France, England, and Russia gradually cooled his enthusiasm; to these must be added the bad impression which the Jews of Jerusalem made on him and which the grand duke and Eulenburg blamed primarily for his change of heart. He cooled off as swiftly as he had fired up. No one then is to be blamed for the collapse of the protectorate idea; if any blame attaches it is to the Machiavellianism and court flunkeyism of Bülow, who permitted the Kaiser to make promises which were later to be broken. But this was the man all over. As far as he was concerned, the whole business was settled with the communiqué. What did it matter to him that he had landed Herzl in a most difficult situation?

Chaim Weizmann

A RETURN TO REALITIES IN ZIONISM

Chaim Weizmann was born in 1874 in Motol near Pinsk in Russia. He died in 1952 in Rehovoth, Israel, while serving as the first president of the State of Israel. Weizmann had a distinguished and dedicated career of leadership in Zionism. His role in the attainment of the Balfour Declaration has been briefly described in the Introduction. In 1920 Weizmann was elected president of the World Zionist Organization, a post he held until 1931 and again from 1935 until 1946. In this selection from Trial and Error, *Weizmann discusses Zionist progress in Palestine from 1907 to 1914. It was the concrete presence and achievement of Jews in Palestine that gave Weizmann and others increased diplomatic leverage during the wartime negotiations which followed.*

The condition of the Zionist movement, in 1906, the year I turned back from my imperfect and fitful seclusion to give it again its proper role in my life, may be summarized thus: the controversy between the Ugandists and the "classical" Zionists had transformed itself into the controversy between "political" and "practical" Zionism; and this in turn was yielding to a fusion of the two schools. The political Zionists argued: "Palestine belongs to Turkey. The purchase of land is forbidden by law. We can do nothing now but work for the charter, and use the Great Powers, like England and Germany, to help us obtain the charter." It was a view shared by the German and Austrian Zionist organizations, and by most of the Westerners. A small group in England, headed by Dr. Gaster and Herbert Bentwich, opposed them. Gaster's opposition, however was not very useful. I had the highest respect for his scholarship and his Jewish feeling, but I could not escape the impression that his Zionist point of view was tainted by an ingrained personal opposition to Herzl. My chief source of strength was Ahad Haam and the group that gathered about him.

The second, or practical school—ours—took what I have repeatedly called a more organic view of Zionism, and of historical process. In reality the "cultural" and "practical" Zionists were not

From *Trial and Error: The Autobiography of Chaim Weizmann* by Chaim Weizmann, pp. 121–132. Copyright 1949 by The Weizmann Foundation. Reprinted by permission of Harper & Row, Publishers, Inc. and The Weizmann Foundation.

opposed to Zionist political activity, as has often been represented; they only sought to impress upon the Zionist world the obvious truth that political activity alone is not enough; it must be accompanied by solid, constructive achievement, the actual physical occupation of land in Palestine, which in turn would be accompanied by the moral strengthening of the Jewish consciousness, the revival of the Hebrew language, the spread of the knowledge of Jewish history, and the strengthening of the attachment to the permanent values of Judaism.

I repeat that the process of fusion of the two schools was not a simple matter. Such was the fascination of phrases, such the force of prejudices once they were given sway over the mind, that the first resumption of real colonizing activity ran up repeatedly against obstinate opposition. It was as if people felt that bringing Jews into Palestine, founding colonies, beginning industries, in a modest way, was not the real business of Zionism. *That* was quite different; that consisted of the repetition of our intention to create a Jewish commonwealth in Palestine; and until such a commonwealth was created in a charter no progress of any importance would be achieved.

The deadlock was broken, I believe, at the eighth Zionist Congress, held in The Hague in the summer of 1907. I made there an ardent plea for the views which I had been propagating since my entry into the movement. I said, in effect: "Our diplomatic work is important, but it will gain in importance by actual performance in Palestine. If we achieve a synthesis of the two schools of Zionism, we may get past the dead point. Perhaps we have not done very much till now. But if you tell me that we have been prevented by local difficulties, by the Turkish authorities, I will not accept it. It is not wholly the fault of the Turks. Something can always be done." I pleaded that even if a charter, such as Herzl had dreamed of, were possible, it would be without value unless it rested, so to say, on the very soil of Palestine, on a Jewish population rooted in that soil, on institutions established by and for that population. A charter was merely a scrap of paper; unlike other nations and governments, we could not convert it into a reality by force; we had nothing to back it with except work on the spot. It was, of course, necessary for us to keep our case before the tribunals of the world, but the presentation of our case could only be effective if, along with it, there was immigration, colonization, education.

To carry my point, I coined the phrase "synthetic Zionism," which became a slogan among the practical Zionists. It was with this rallying cry that we managed to effect a change in the Executive, and in the program. David Wolffsohn was displaced from the presidency. A Presidium was formed, to which the younger men were admitted— Victor Jacobson and Shmarya Levin among others—together with some of the "practical" Zionists, like Ussishkin and Tchlenov. Professor Otto Warburg, the distinguished botanist, a definite exponent of "practical" Zionism, was elected chairman of the Presidium. Dr. Arthur Ruppin, who was to become our foremost colonizing expert, was invited to go out to Palestine and organize a Colonization Department, doing the best he could in the political circumstances then prevailing.

For those who are interested in the genesis of things, for whom an existing community is not something self-understood, but an organism which had a beginning, and a period of first growth, the early history of Jewish Palestine will have a special fascination. Today a strong, well-knit, and vigorous Jewish nation in the making, numbering over 600,000 souls, exists in Palestine, with its agriculture, its cities, industries, schools, hospitals, and university. Today the acquisition of a few thousand acres of land at a single purchase is a commonplace. We have seen—and I trust we shall again see— tens of thousands of Jewish immigrants drawn annually into Palestine and integrated with its economy and culture. But in the years of which I am speaking a few hundred acres of land was a vast territory; the arrival of a handful of immigrants was an event; a single little industry was a huge achievement. Capital was not yet tempted to seek out Palestine. A powerful workers' movement did not exist because there was no working class yet in Palestine. Seen in retrospect our outlook of those days was not merely modest; it was almost pitiful. Yet the prewar years 1906 to 1914 were decisive in a sense. The stamp of their work is still visible in Palestine. For we accumulated a body of experience which was to stand us in good stead in the years that followed the First World War. We anticipated many of the problems which were to confront us in the days of larger enterprise. We laid the foundations of institutions which are part of the re-created Jewish national home. Above all, we got the feel of things so that we did not approach our task after the Balfour Declaration like complete beginners.

It was not an accident that my own first contact with Palestine itself should have been made in the year 1907, the year in which the movement recovered the sober sense of reality. When the change was effected in the Zionist Executive, Johann Kremenetzky, of Vienna, one of the old Herzlian Zionists, not as deeply set in his ways as the Marmoreks and Fischers, was won to our view. Kremenetzky, like many others passed over hastily in these records, deserves, both as a person and a Zionist, much more generous treatment than can be given him here. He had migrated to Vienna from Odessa as a boy and had become a successful industrialist. He owned, at that time, a factory of electric bulbs, and had made it a model of its kind. The friendship we established lasted till long after the First World War, for he lived to a ripe old age—eighty-five, I think. He used to visit me in London, a gallant, beautifully groomed figure of a man, with undimmed vigor and undiminished faculties, devoted to Palestine to the end. Kremenetzky it was who made my first visit to Palestine possible. He challenged me, during the course of the Congress, to put into practice what I was preaching, to go out to the country, and to investigate, as an industrial chemist, the prospects of establishing an industry there. In particular, he suggested the possibility of the manufacture of essential oils. As it happened I was engaged in working out a process for the synthetic production of camphor which stands in near relation to that part of chemistry which deals with essential oils. I may as well say at once that nothing direct came of this particular project. But like many another experiment in those days it had great value in that it began the search for practicalities. Something was indeed to come, much later, of the application of my chemical training to the problem of the upbuilding of Palestine, and this first visit of mine to the country, in 1907, might have been made much later had it not been for the shift of emphasis which took place at the Hague Congress.

Thus it came about that, instead of returning to Manchester, where I had left my wife and our six-weeks-old baby, I set out at the end of the Congress for Palestine, traveling down first to Marseille, and taking a boat there. I had two companions on the journey, Manya Wilbushevitch Shochat, one of the great women pioneers, and a Dr. Klimker, a pioneer of the oil and soap industry of Palestine. All the way from Marseille to the eastern shores of the Mediterranean I kept preparing myself for the shock of the first contact. I damped

FIGURE 3. Chaim Weizmann, 1918. *(Ben-Dov Collection, The Central Zionist Archives. Copyright, Israel State Archives.)*

my hopes down, suppressed my excitement. I said to myself: "You must free yourself entirely from your romanticisms, from all the associations with which you have bound up the name of Palestine since your childhood. You will find a derelict country ravaged by centuries of Turkish misrule. You must look at things soberly and critically, with the eyes of the chemist rather than those of the Zionist." And thus the chemist and the Zionist were at constant war within me during the sea voyage. I was so anxious to be detached and objective that I denied myself the advantage of my emotions. Yet I knew then, and I have confirmed since, that while a cool, matter-of-fact estimate of the possibilities of Palestine is an absolute essential, the normal element of our historical and psychological attachment to the country is an invaluable ally in the struggle to overcome those material and moral difficulties which seem so formidable to the chemist and physicist. To ignore the force of sentiment in the name of practicality is to cease being practical.

However, if I was determined to find the minimum of encouragement, circumstances were not less determined to give my hopes no foothold. The journey took much longer than we anticipated. The last lap took us from Alexandria to Beirut, and there we were clapped into quarantine for ten days. The building in which we were interned was dignified by the name of "hospital." It was a dilapidated military barracks, with the most primitive sanitary arrangements, very poor food, and no attendance at all. If there had been any diseases about, this would have been the place to catch them. Fortunately there weren't any diseases about, either in Egypt, or on our boat, or in Syria; the quarantine had been instituted chiefly as a source of revenue for the local pasha and his henchmen. Cramped as I was for time, I would have been glad to give them their cut and get out; but that would have been a blow to the institution. So we sat it out. Manya Shochat and Klimker—both of whom had been in Palestine before—utilized the time to instruct me in the ways of the country, and to describe general conditions. Victor Jacobson, who was in Beirut as the director of the local branch of the Anglo-Palestine Bank, came to see us, and it was from him that I first heard something of the nascent Arab national movement.

Released at last from quarantine, I proceeded from Beirut to Jaffa by boat, and set foot on the land which had been such an integral part of my thoughts ever since my childhood. I was face to face at last with the reality, and as always happens in such cases, the encounter was neither as bad nor as good as I had anticipated.

A dolorous country it was on the whole, one of the most neglected corners of the miserably neglected Turkish Empire. Its total population was something above 600,000, of which about 80,000 were Jews. The latter lived mostly in the cities, Jerusalem (where they formed a majority of the population), Hebron, Tiberias, Safed, Jaffa, and Haifa. There were twenty-five colonies on the land. But neither the colonies nor the city settlements in any way resembled, as far as vigor, tone, and progressive spirit are concerned, the colonies and the settlements of our day. The dead hand of the *Halukkah* lay on more than half the Jewish population. That institution, historically significant in its time, calls for a word of description. For many generations pious European Jews had made it a practice to migrate to Palestine in their old age, so that they might die on holy soil. They were supported by a system of collections in the European communities. Their sole activity was the study of sacred books. They had never intended to take up gainful occupations, nor were they, as a rule, young enough to do so if they had had the intention. A few of them went into business in a small way. Historically speaking, they had been the expression of the undying Jewish attachment to Palestine; but in an age which was to witness the reconstruction of the Jewish Homeland, they were a useless and even retarding element.

The colonies were, with very few exceptions, in not much better case. When I was a boy in Motol and Pinsk the first wave of modern colonizers—the *Bilus,* as they were called—had set out for Palestine, under the impulse of the *Hibbat Zion* movement. They had been ardent, romantic, devoted, full of noble purposes and high dreams. But they had been inexperienced and impractical. They too had fallen into the grip of a kind of *Halukkah* institution, but the funds for them came, not from public collections, but from the never-ending generosity of Baron Edmond de Rothschild. They had not even started out with intelligent plans. They had not envisaged a process of national development, in which Jewish workers and Jewish landowners would form harmonious parts of a larger program. The colonies were more in the nature of businesses than agricultural enterprises. The settlers dealt in oranges as they had dealt in other commodities, back in Russia. Most of the labor was Arab, and the Jews were overseers. There was no pioneering spirit. Moreover, the few colonies were detached and scattered; they did not form blocks of territory. All this was particularly true about Petah Tikvah, Rishon le-Zion, and Ness Zionah in the south, of Rosh Pinah, Mishmar Ha-Yarden, and Metullah in the north. I found Ahad Haam's criticisms, his observations on the paralyzing effect of the baron's well-meant paternalism, thoroughly justified. Though there was an agricultural school at Mikveh Israel, there was no real scientific study of soil conditions, of crops, of the care of cattle. There existed no system of agrarian credits. There was no system for training newcomers.

The picture was not all dark. Our Zionist type of enterprise was to be found in a few places like Merhavyah, Ben Shemen, and Huldah. The young men and women who had come out of Russia in the last few years were establishing their first foothold in the Jewish colonies, competing, by superior intelligence and organization, with the cheaper Arab labor. There was a Jewish high school—the Gymnasium—in Jaffa; and the Bezalel Arts and Crafts School had been established in Jerusalem the year before I came out. Enough had been started to show that more could be done.

Joshuah Chankin, one of the famous original pioneers, was my guide on my first visit to Palestine. He accompanied me through the length and breadth of the country. We traveled mostly by carriage, for the only railroad then in existence ran—if that is the word—between Jaffa and Jerusalem, and took four or five hours to cover a distance which we now make in less than an hour by car.

I could not have had a better guide. He knew every nook and corner of the land; he knew the history and development of all the colonies, and spoke of them informatively as well as amusingly. We began our tour from Jaffa, and worked our way as far as Metullah, which is today on the Syrian border. I remember Nazareth vividly. We arrived there on a hot afternoon, riding southward, and from the hilltop we looked down on the wide stretch of the Valley of Jezreel, spreading at our feet like a vast carpet framed by the hills of Samaria and Ephraim, with Mount Tabor to the left. It was a superb sight, though the countryside was parched with the late-summer heat, and there was hardly a patch of green anywhere for the eye to rest on. How different that panorama looks today, with countless Jewish colonies covering the valley from end to end! Chankin told me how a part of the Emek—that is, the Jezreel Valley—had been bought, long before, by the *Hovevei Zion,* for a comparatively small sum and how, because of the lack of funds, the installments were discontinued, so that the first payments were lost and, with them, the opportunity. He said: "Of course we shall have to buy it again," and we did, later, paying ten to fifteen times the original price, because of the land values we ourselves had created. But I remember thinking how right I had been when I had told the Congress that, in spite of restrictions and difficulties, much more could be done in Palestine than had actually been done.

I spoke long and earnestly with Chankin about the disheartened and disheartening state of the colonies. New blood had to be brought into the country; a new spirit of enterprise had to be introduced. Once there had been a stream of immigration, the *Bilus* of the eighties, more than twenty years before; but there had been no follow-up. The pioneers that had once been so young, so full of energy and will power, had become old, tired, decrepit. The baron's regime had helped to undermine them. They had come to rely on his bounty; a bad harvest, a cattle plague, or any other calamity, sent them to him for help. Their initiative had been destroyed by the dictatorial bureaucracy of the baron's administration. They had lost hope; and they saw their children, born to them in Palestine, leaving the land and going to the cities, or, what was worse, returning to the exile from which they themselves had once fled in order to build a homeland for the coming generations.

The primary object of my visit, the establishment of a factory for essential oils, receded into the background of my thoughts. I was preoccupied with larger issues. Over and over again it was borne in on me that from a distance I had sensed the actual state of affairs; in spite of all political and administrative obstacles, there were great possibilities. Only the will was lacking. How was that to be awakened? How was a cumulative process to be set in motion? Our means were miserably small. The Jewish National Fund, created for the purchase of land as the inalienable property of the Jewish people, was little more than a charity-box collection. The Palestine office of the Zionist Organization, which Ruppin now headed, was no better off. When Ruppin demanded, in those days, that a land-development company be founded with the modest capital of 1 million marks—a quarter of a million dollars—the Organization placed at his disposal exactly one-tenth of that sum; and when we reflected that Baron Rothschild had sunk in the country something like 50 million marks, with the results I have described, we might well have been discouraged. If we were not, the fact must be ascribed to our feeling that a great source of energy was waiting to be tapped—the national impulse of a people held in temporary check by a misguided interpretation of historic method.

I made up my mind that I would go back to Europe to press with redoubled energy for immediate practical work in Palestine; and it was then, I think, that I laid out the program of my Zionist work for the next eight years. How, it will be asked, did we actually get past the dead point? The answer is: simply by getting past it! I have said that between 1906 and 1914 we accumulated a body of experience, anticipated our future problems, and laid the foundations of our institutions. But it must not be thought that these were merely token achievements. They had substance. By 1914 we had increased the Jewish population from 80,000 to 100,000, our agricultural workers from 500 to 2,000. The turnover of the Palestine office had grown thirtyfold. We had founded the Jewish National Library, and the *Technikum* of Haifa; our Gymnasium was attracting large numbers of Jewish students from abroad, who were bringing thousands of dollars annually into the country. These evidences of growth were, however, less important than the change of spirit which had come over the entire community. Apart from founding new colonies, like Kinneret and Deganyah, we had penetrated the old colonies, creating among them annexes of young people. The existence of 2,000 Jewish land workers acted as an attraction for young Jews from abroad. There was an instrument for them to turn to, an instrument which could absorb them into the new life. The transformation which was wrought in the old European-Palestine communities by the influx of young European Jews began to affect the old Sephardic, or Eastern, communities, and led to an influx of Yemenite Jews from Arabia. The *Halukkah* spirit of Palestine was at last being attacked—though it yielded very slowly. The Hebrew language had, thanks in part to the magnificent work of Eliezer Ben-Yehudah, been revived, and was the natural medium of converse for the majority of the Palestinian Jews, and wholly so for the young. The flow of migration back into the exile had fallen considerably.

Perhaps I can best sum up the progress of those years in a remark made to me by Baron Rothschild. Shortly before the First World War he paid a visit to Palestine, and saw for himself the change that had been wrought. I met him, soon after, in Paris, when I went to see him in connection with my work for the Hebrew University. I asked him for his impressions of Palestine, and he answered me simply and honestly: "Without me the Zionists could have done nothing, but without the Zionists my work would have been dead." The rapprochement between the baron and the Zionist movement dates from that period; he had become convinced at last that the Zionists were not simply idealistic agitators; they were capable of getting things done.

The man who during those years—and indeed throughout the quarter century following the First World War—played a decisive part in the colonization of Palestine was Arthur Ruppin. I suppose it was wholly fitting that I should have met this eminently practical Zionist during my first visit to Palestine, when I was establishing my own contact with realities. I had heard something of him, for it was the seventh Zionist Congress—that of The Hague—which decided to engage him as the director of the newly founded Palestine Department; and when I was introduced to him in Haifa I was somewhat taken aback. I saw before me a young German—I would almost have said Prussian—correct, reserved, very formal, seemingly quite remote from Jewish and Zionist problems. I was told that he was an assessor, or assistant judge, that he had had a successful business career, and that he had come out to Palestine in the spring of 1907, and spent several months there studying the land. All that one perceived on first meeting Ruppin was a German statistician and student of economics, but beneath that cool exterior there was a passionate attachment to his people, and to the upbuilding of Palestine. I learned this in the course of the years.

Ruppin was a man of brilliant mind, and of absolute integrity. His practical gifts were reinforced by equal gifts as a theoretician, and his books on Jewish sociology deservedly take a front rank in their field. His coolness misled people into thinking him an easygoing sort of person. Actually, whatever he said and wrote and did was the result of deep thought and a solid sense of responsibility. I remember few errors of judgment on his part, and when he differed with me—as for example in 1922, on the question of the minimum costs of colonization—he was usually right. In all disputes he used to disarm opposition by his imperturbability, and in a movement which had its very excited moments, he would never let himself be provoked into anger or abuse. He would answer quietly, with a kindness which killed opposition. I do not think I ever saw him angry, although, God knows, he had reason enough on occasion.

There was one case in which he was treated with the grossest unfairness. In 1919 he came to England from Palestine, and produced £200,000 out of moneys which he had handled for the Zionist Organization. This large sum, totally unexpected, was a godsend. It helped to fill up the deep cavity formed in the capital of the Jewish Colonial Trust by the losses sustained in Russia in consequence of the revolution, losses which made the position of the bank, at the beginning of our new period of work, rather precarious. But Ruppin was bitterly abused, and suspicion was cast on his integrity. This is how he had come by the money: during the war he had been receiving, from America, $25,000 a month, for work in Palestine. The money was sent to him via Constantinople, and he had paid out in Turkish pounds. As the war dragged on, the Turkish pound sank in relation to the American dollar, and Ruppin saved a considerable sum each month. He carried out his instructions to the letter, and the saving was not of his own making. This, on top of the dislike which he had occasioned by the socialist tendency of his colonization work, precipitated a bitter attack, and he was accused of being a speculator. I do not know of a more ridiculous and more unjustified accusation ever leveled at a man of absolute devotion and honesty. Curiously, the attack did not seem to touch him. His friends were furious, but he remained quite unmoved.

I have not had a better collaborator in my Zionist work than Arthur Ruppin. I received from him not only splendid service, but constant encouragement in enterprises which without his support would have lacked reality. He assured us all, in the old days, that Palestine was capable of absorbing large numbers of Jews in agriculture, and that we must not let ourselves be frightened off by the smallness of the country. One incident, which occurred during our first meeting in Palestine, illustrates the daring of his vision, concealed by his quiet, almost frigid, exterior. I was staying in Jaffa when Ruppin called on me, and took me out for a walk over the dunes to the north of the town. When we had got well out into the sands—I remember that it came over our ankles—he stopped, and said, very solemnly: "Here we shall create a Jewish city!" I looked at him with some dismay. Why should people come to live out in this wilderness where nothing would grow? I began to ply him with technical questions, and he answered me carefully and exactly. Technically, he said, everything was possible. Though in the first years communication with the new settlement would be difficult, the inhabitants would soon become self-supporting and self-sufficient. The Jews of Jaffa would move into the new, modern city, and the Jewish colonies of the neighborhood would have a concentrated market for their products. The Gymnasium would stand at the center, and would attract a great many students from other parts of Palestine and from Jews abroad, who would want their children to be educated in a Jewish high school in a Jewish city.

Thus it was Ruppin who had the first vision of Tel Aviv, which was destined to outstrip, in size and in economic importance, the ancient town of Jaffa, and to become one of the metropolitan centers of the eastern Mediterranean. Perhaps I should say that the most important consequence of the shift from purely political to "synthetic" Zionism was the introduction into Palestine, in those early years, of a number of first-class men who did excellent work then and in the postwar years. Ruppin was foremost among them. Not altogether in his class, but of high value nevertheless, was Samuel Pevsner, in whose house I met Ruppin. Pevsner had belonged to our Berlin Zionist group, and we had been friends nearly a decade before. He was a man of great ability, energetic, practical, resourceful, and, like his wife, highly educated. For such people, going to Palestine was in effect going into a social wilderness— which is something to be remembered by those who, turning to Palestine today, find in it intellectual, cultural, and social resources not inferior to those of the Western world. The Jewish community of Haifa was a tiny one, and nine-tenths of it was Sephardic. The bridge of Hebrew which was to unite Oriental and Occidental Jewry had not yet been created. So Pevsner and his wife lived almost in isolation. But Pevsner was a tremendous optimist, and though he died young, he lived long enough to see his optimism vindicated. He practically built up modern Jewish Haifa, that is to say, the splendid quarter of Hadar Ha-Carmel on the slopes above the old city.

During the first visit to Palestine I came across scattered reminders of my childhood days in Pinsk. The Eisenbergs were settled in Rehovoth. The Gluskins were in Rishon le-Zion. And others, whose names escape me, were taking root in the cities and colonies, tiny advance guards, the "Pilgrim Fathers" of the new Palestine to be.

My most unhappy experience during the three-weeks tour of the country—it would have been five weeks, but for the quarantine episode—was Jerusalem. I went up from Jaffa, not without misgivings. Jaffa already had the small beginnings of a new life, and the promise of a new society; Jerusalem was the city of the *Halukkah,* a city living on charity, on begging letters, on collections. Here the reality turned out to be as bad as the anticipation. From the Jewish point of view it was a miserable ghetto, derelict and without dignity. All the grand places belonged to others. There were innumerable churches, of every sect and nationality. We had not a decent building of our own. All the world had a foothold in Jerusalem—except the Jews. The hotel to which we were directed was a dilapidated and verminous ruin, with nondescript people pouring in and out all day long, and all of them engaged apparently in wasting their own and each other's time. It depressed me beyond words, and I left the city before nightfall. I remained prejudiced against the city for many years, and even now I still feel ill at ease in it, preferring Rehovoth to the capital.

But I was struck, as everyone must be, by the glorious surroundings of Jerusalem; and I thought then that there was only one place where, in time to come, we might erect some building worthy of the Jewish community; there was one hill still uncrowned by monastery or church—the Scopus, on which stood then only the small villa of Lady Grey Hill, and on which now stands the Hebrew University.

Those were unsensational years which preceded the First World War, a time of hard work and quiet growth. The modest progress which we were achieving in Palestine was mirrored in the steady evolution of the Zionist movement toward the serious appraisal of factual problems. When, in September 1913, Ruppin, addressing the eleventh Zionist Congress, in Vienna, said: "We have come to terms with the fact that we must achieve our object not via the charter, but via practical work in Palestine," he expressed the prevailing sentiment of the movement: we had not given up the hope of a charter, but we had come to terms with the conditions created by the lack of it. In short, the Zionist movement had become serious and realistic. We were not neglecting opportunities simply because they were for the time being limited ones.

Jewish Settlements in Palestine 1855 – 1914

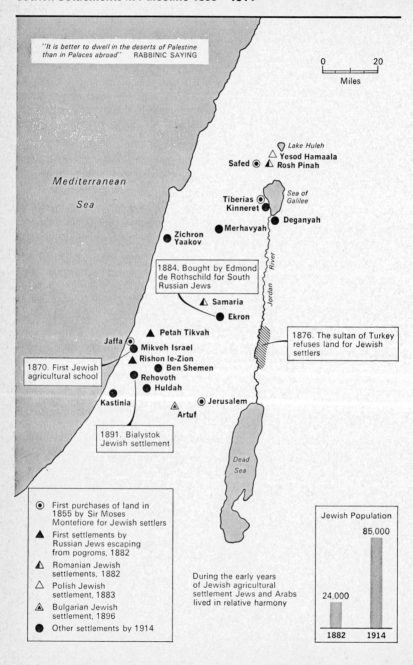

"It is better to dwell in the deserts of Palestine than in Palaces abroad"   RABBINIC SAYING

0   20
Miles

Mediterranean

Sea

Lake Huleh
△ Yesod Hamaala
Safed ◉   ▲ Rosh Pinah

Tiberias ◉   Sea of Galilee
Kinneret ●
●Deganyah

Zichron ●   ● Merhavyah
Yaakov

1884. Bought by Edmond de Rothschild for South Russian Jews

▲ Samaria
● Ekron

Jordan River

1876. The sultan of Turkey refuses land for Jewish settlers

▲ Petah Tikvah
Jaffa ◉
◉ Mikveh Israel
▲ Rishon le-Zion
● Ben Shemen
Rehovoth
● Huldah
Kastinia   ◉ Jerusalem
△ Artuf

1870. First Jewish agricultural school

1891. Bialystok Jewish settlement

Dead Sea

◉ First purchases of land in 1855 by Sir Moses Montefiore for Jewish settlers
▲ First settlements by Russian Jews escaping from pogroms, 1882
▲ Romanian Jewish settlements, 1882
△ Polish Jewish settlement, 1883
△ Bulgarian Jewish settlement, 1896
● Other settlements by 1914

During the early years of Jewish agricultural settlement Jews and Arabs lived in relative harmony

Jewish Population

85,000

24,000

1882   1914

Amos Elon

THE ISRAELIS: FOUNDERS

Amos Elon, an Israeli journalist living in Tel Aviv, has worked as a foreign correspondent for Ha'aretz, *one of Israel's leading papers. In 1967 he published* Journey through a Haunted Land *on present-day Germany. In this selection from his latest book,* The Israelis: Founders and Sons, *Elon captures the socialist and nationalist passion of the Russian Jewish pioneers in the second Aliyah (1904–1914). He also shows how the very programs which gave these pioneers strength aggravated the perhaps inevitable Arab-Zionist hostility.*

Although it hardly seemed so at the time, 1882 was an eventful year in the history of the Zionist settlement of Palestine. Levontin and his group were only the first. Throughout the summer and fall, prospective settlers continued to arrive. Petah Tikvah, abandoned three years earlier, was resettled by newcomers before the year was out. On the southern ridge of Mount Carmel a group of Romanian Lovers of Zion purchased and settled Samarin, the future Zichron Yaakov. Another group went further north to Upper Galilee, attractive to them because of its more European climate; after jogging through barren mountains on the backs of donkeys for almost a week, during which time one woman gave birth to a child, and much energy was wasted in quarrels with their Arab guides, the settlers reached a spot east of Safed and founded Rosh Pinah (literally, "Head Stone," the stone which "the builders refused is become the headstone of the corner," Psalms 118:22). Other colonies, in the north, south, and west on the coastal plain, soon followed.

Equally important, perhaps, was the fact that, in 1882, the British seized control over adjacent Egypt. This was a first step toward the extension of their rule to Palestine, which in turn led to the Balfour Declaration of 1917 and its recognition of a Jewish national home in Palestine.

Third, in that same year of 1882 there arrived in Palestine an obscure scholar from Lithuania named Eliezer Perlmann. Perlmann settled quickly in Jerusalem. He adopted a new name, Ben-Yehudah; returned his passport to the local Russian consul; and, unperturbed by the consul's retort that it was obviously not so, announced that Perlmann was dead.

This slightly-built, twenty-four-year-old philologist, whose constitution had been sapped by an early attack of tuberculosis, but whose nature was as hard as steel, lived under the ruthless tyranny of an idea—the revival of Hebrew as a spoken language. In his youth Ben-Yehudah had been an Orthodox rabbinical scholar. As a teen-ager he had renounced his studies to become a self-confessed "Russian nihilist." The Russian populist's classic tract, *What Is to Be Done,* became his Bible; Chernishevsky and Lavrov, his "rabbis." After his arrival in Jerusalem he did for Hebrew what Korais, the brilliant Corfu schoolteacher, did for modern Greek. Korais invented an intermediary language between that of ancient Greece and the current argot of his day. Ben-Yehudah searched classic Hebrew literature for words to be used in a modern context. The very first word he created was *millon* (dictionary), a derivative of *milla* (word). Another early coinage was *leumiut* (nationalism). In his memoirs he noted that there was one thing that he regretted all his life: "I was not born in Jerusalem, nor even in the land of Israel."

Looking back, Ben-Yehudah dramatically staged the decisive moment of his life at "midnight," shortly after the Russian-Turkish War of 1878. He had been at home, reading a Pan-Slavic tract by candlelight. Suddenly he realized the lesson implied for a small people like his own, and the imperative need to immediately "re-create Israel and its language upon the home soil. . . . " When he first broached this idea to an acquaintance, Ben-Yehudah (like Pinsker and Herzl after him) was warned that he was sick and must consult a doctor.

Ben-Yehudah's wife knew no Hebrew; while still on shipboard he told her that in Palestine they would speak nothing but Hebrew. He ruthlessly kept his vow. When his first son, Itamar, was born (by a curious coincidence on the same day the colony of Rishon le-Zion was founded) he became the first child in centuries to hear only Hebrew from both his parents and almost nothing from anyone else, for he was kept isolated from all human contact lest the purity of his Hebrew be spoiled by alien sounds. His mother, though weak and ailing, agreed to her husband's demand not to hire a servant in order that the child might hear nothing but the holy tongue. "We feared the walls of our home, the spaces of our room, lest they echo the sounds of a foreign language . . . and reach the child's ear. . . . We wished to keep all foreign sounds distant. . . ."

It was a risky undertaking. The language was still archaic. Many words indispensable in modern intercourse were missing. The child had no playmates; until his third year he remained almost mute and often refused to utter a word.

Ben-Yehudah's wife died in 1891 of tuberculosis that she had contracted from her husband. Ben-Yehudah, undeterred by the tremendous opposition from almost everyone he knew, remained firm, and by his fanaticism proved that Hebrew could become a language fit for ordinary daily usage. Sympathetic teachers in Jerusalem, Jaffa, and the new colonies joined his cause. Soon the children in all the new colonies spoke Hebrew fluently; while it was frequently a second language for them, after Yiddish, Russian, or French, it was "alive."

Many new settlers who followed in the steps of Levontin and Feinberg had been university students caught up by the double influence of Zionism and Russian populism; they interrupted their studies to go off to settle in Palestine as farmers. One pioneer, discussing works by two high priests of Russian populism, Alexander Herzen's *Who Is Guilty?* and Chernishevsky's *What Is to Be Done,* noted in his diary: "So agitated were young Russian revolutionaries by these books, that they decided to 'go to the people' and cause a revolution in their lives. The Russian people exist and live on native soil; [Jews] must re-create everything from scratch: the work, the land, the people and the society."

The ideas of Russian radicalism affected the new colonies from the beginning with varying results. An early manifesto by the Kiev Lovers of Zion denounced private ownership of land as the greatest evil of civilization; its authors warned the settlers against building Palestine on the "rotten basis" of the old world order. One charter forecast the extreme collectivism of the future *kibbutz*: ". . . one fortune for the entire society. No man has private property. Also his things, his clothes and whatever he may bring with him or receive from his home belong to the entire society."

Actually, none of these socialist and cooperativist ideas were put to practice at this early stage. With all their imported theories, the earliest settlers found Palestine a sobering experience. In reality most colonies quickly gravitated to private ownership of land, capitalist profit, and the exploitation of cheap (native Arab) labor. It was explained as the only realistic policy and was at least partly imposed from without. For within less than two years after settlement, in 1883, most of the newcomers were close to bankruptcy and some even to starvation. Baron Edmond de Rothschild of Paris came to their rescue.

Edmond de Rothschild (1849–1934) was one of the least known scions of a famous family of financiers, a dandy who through his Palestine venture inadvertently played a greater role in history than any of his more famous namesakes. He was inclined to leave the making of money to his brothers and cousins, and preferred rather to spend it as he saw fit. What seemed at the time an eccentric charity proved in the end a decisive political act. But for his lavish support of the early settlers, the Jewish colonization of Palestine would have started much later, perhaps even too late to succeed.

In October 1882 he willingly responded to the plea by Joseph Feinberg of Rishon le-Zion for a modest loan of 25,000 francs toward the digging of wells in the colony. He did so, as he later put it, as an "experiment" to see if it was possible to settle Jewish farmers in Palestine. The colonies soon became his main charity, surpassing even his generous support of French arts in general and the Louvre in particular. Between 1884 and 1900 he spent an estimated £1.6 million on purchase of land and the construction of houses for the colonists; he invested also in training and machinery, livestock, waterworks, and the like. His total expenditure has been estimated at £10 million. His entire property in Palestine was later turned over to the colonists or earmarked for a foundation which today supports various educational enterprises, including instructional television. Rothschild became a kind of benevolent feudal lord who owned villages and peasants in the Holy Land (the colonists were guaranteed a certain minimum income); he insisted upon tight controls through an extensive network of baronial overseers and administrators.

Rothschild's paternalism was of a type prevalent among many nineteenth-century philanthropists. In his vineyard he grew a Bordeaux-type wine. He resented his colonists' European clothes and wanted them to wear the local Arab dress; he insisted they observe meticulously the Jewish Sabbath, dietary, and other laws of Orthodox Jewish religion, which he himself—though not his pious wife—ignored. It is doubtful whether he ever hoped for a "Jewish state"; he was interested in "creating centers where Jewish intellectual and moral culture could develop." He met Herzl only once, for one brief and disastrous conversation. He considered Zionism dangerous both for the Jews of Europe and for those in his colonies, as it exposed them to accusation of not being "patriotic" Frenchmen, Russians, or Turks. His overseers were imported from France. They were professionals, thoroughly business-minded, deeply suspicious of the settlers whom they frequently accused of laziness and of harboring dangerous "Russian anarchist ideas." Bitter quarrels were common between the settlers and the baron or his overseers.

In later years Rothschild's opposition to political Zionism mellowed. Weizmann quoted him as saying: "Without me Zionism would not have succeeded. But without Zionism my work would have been struck to death."

Rothschild's administration kept a tight reign in the colonies, and, at least for a while, set the pattern of things. It was not socialist or cooperative, as some of the early Zionist Populists had hoped, but "colonial" in the accepted contemporary sense of that word. By 1902 there were already twenty-one colonies (eighteen others lay temporarily abandoned), with a total population of almost 5,000. All but a few were still subsidized by Rothschild. Some were beginning to show signs of prosperity, with fine, tree-shaded houses, schools and kindergartens, synagogues and parks, local periodicals, public libraries, amateur theatricals, etc.

A traveler in these colonies would probably not have found them much different from the English, French, or Dutch settlements in Kenya, Algeria, and the East Indies. Their economy was based largely on the supply of cheap native labor. It came from neighboring Arab villages as well as from farther-away places in Syria, Egypt, or the Horan in Transjordan. By 1889, barely seven years after its founding, the colony of Zichron Yaakov on Mount Carmel had 1,200 Arab workers serving a population of 200 Jewish settlers. In Rishon le-Zion —formerly an almost barren, waterless spot—an eyewitness reported that the first group of forty Jewish settler families attracted close to 300 Arab families of migrant laborers who squatted in courtyards or built shacks in the immediate neighborhood.

This imbalance precipitated an enormous *crise de conscience* abroad. Visiting Zionists noted with chagrin that some of the settlers were adopting the uglier aspects of colonialists elsewhere. They seemed no longer to conform to the original ideal of farmers who themselves tilled the soil, a work which, to the Zionists, was healthy and rejuvenating, both for the individual and the community; more and more were beginning to "resemble business entrepreneurs." According to one critic, some even "played cards at home while their Arab laborers did the work." Much of the criticism of the purists was doctrinaire or naive, full of the easy cleverness of those who observe a torturous experiment from a safe and comfortable distance. "How far they are from the life of the simple farmer," complained one visiting literateur from a Polish Hebrew periodical, who promptly returned to Warsaw. "How far they are from the life of the simple farmer who tills his land with his own hands without buying food [*sic*] and without worry that he may not find a buyer for his crop. When will this dire sight disappear? When shall the seed be sown from which will grow Israel's salvation?"

By 1902 the colonists, being human, were thinking above all of their own needs and not exclusively of a Jewish national revival in Palestine. They had become experienced in the hardships of life in Palestine; they had little patience for advice rendered gratuitously, they felt, from abroad by those who themselves were not willing to come.

In 1883, Zeev Vladimir Dubnow, a settler in Rishon le-Zion, described the early ardor of the settlers in a letter to his brother Simon, the well-known Jewish historian. He wrote that his aim was perhaps "magnificent and sublime" but "not unattainable. It is to inherit the land of Israel in time and to restore to the Jews the national independence they were robbed of two thousand years ago." Such passions did not last long. That two or three hundred settlers could imagine in 1883, as Vladimir Dubnow did, that they were about to "inherit" the land was a madly fantastic dream in the first place. Cortez took Mexico with a few hundred men only, but behind him lay the resources of an empire.

The Jewish settlers had little behind them beyond a loose network of peripatetic discussion groups. Moreover, Palestine and Syria by 1883 had already become a focus of imperialist Russian, French, German, and British designs, and a breeding ground for native nationalism as well. The first settlers were alone in a strange environment; if it was not yet as hostile as it would be a few decades later, it was nevertheless extremely difficult. They had no farm training. Rejecting Europe and settling in the ancient land of Canaan, tilling the barren fields, and singing hymns—all this had been a euphoric experience. Like most romance, it was of brief duration. Within a few years, even months, disenchantment set in. Even Levontin, the first of the new settlers and leader of Rishon le-Zion, returned to Russia after only eighteen months. A year later he sold his share of the land to Rothschild. His wife and mother had opposed his Palestine schemes from the beginning; the two women insisted upon accompanying him to Paris to complete the deed of sale, fearful that fantasy might again overtake him and he would change his mind in the last moment. Twenty years passed before Levontin returned once again to Palestine, as a functionary of the fledgling Zionist bank.

According to contemporary reports, a great number of settlers—or their sons—left the country. Some returned to Russia and Romania. Others wandered off as far as Kenya, America, South Africa, and Australia. Reemigration was hotly debated in the colonies. In the cemetery of Hadera, an early colony founded in the swampland of Sharon, where many first settlers died of malaria, the tombstone of a Peretz Herzenstein bears the inscription:

> He was his country's loyal son
> Until his final breath.
> His dying words to his children were
> Your country do not leave.

Those remaining relied more and more on cheap Arab labor and frequently turned away Jewish newcomers eager and willing to work. Some of the uglier aspects of colonialism everywhere became more and more common. "What the hell are *you* doing here!" a farmer in Rishon le-Zion hissed at a newly arrived young Zionist from Poland who was waiting with a group of Arab laborers in the main square of a colony for employment as a field hand. "Can't you find yourself a better place than among those blacks?" Moreover, by 1904, the majority of settlers had begun to doubt the Zionist dream could be fulfilled in Palestine. Newcomers would often be met in Jaffa by grumbling old settlers: "Madman! Irresponsible dreamer! Why have you come here? Go back to Russia, or move to America!"

Herzl died in 1904; in Europe his World Zionist movement was on the verge of disintegration. Even Eliezer Ben-Yehudah, the great fanatic of the Hebrew revival, became a so-called territorialist, a supporter of those seeking a territory in Uganda or Brazil as the site of the future Jewish national home. Ben-Gurion recalls that his greatest shock upon arriving in Palestine in 1906 was to hear of Ben-Yehudah's defection.

It was precisely at this low point in Zionist morale that the second wave of emigration from Russia was instigated by the pogroms of 1903 and the abortive revolution of 1905. This new influx was the "second *Aliyah*"; its men and ideas decisively changed the course of events.

The first wave of settlers, or those who remained of it, were slowly integrating into the economy of the country. Tiring of nationalist aspirations, they "lived with the Arabs" as colonial employers. The newcomers, for reasons of socialist doctrine, vehemently protested this "exploitation of Arab labor." They said that Jews must build their homeland with their own hands and not draw capitalistic profits from the employment of aliens. Their theorizing was a mixture of doctrine and self-interest, for they also desperately needed those jobs for themselves and were prepared to work for native wages.

In retrospect it seems that had the earlier settlers persevered in their course the Jewish population of Palestine, though growing, would have eventually become a wealthy colonial minority to be expropriated and expelled by the resurgent Arabs. The separate society and independent institutions created by the newcomers after 1905 in the end proved strong enough to avert such a possibility.

These newcomers were young and mostly unattached. Few married or bore children during their first fifteen years of settlement. Rabbis of a new secular faith, they were full of the fervor of Russian revolutionism which they transposed to Zionism with a tenacity and zeal such as had never fired the settlers of the first wave. Their missionary faith was stronger; above all they had been educated in a different political school. They produced leaders; they had "ideologists," whose dominant role was reminiscent of that of the clergy in Puritan New England. They were burning to work on the land, but an overriding preoccupation, at least among the leaders, was with abstract ideas and with the organization of political power to put their ideas into practice. Almost the moment they set foot on land they began to form overseas branches of their Eastern European–based political parties. Two main groups emerged, the Marxist *Poalei Zion* and the non-Marxist labor party, *Hapoel Hatzair.*

The two parties opposed one another with a religious ferocity. The total membership of both did not exceed a few hundred until after 1914 and their frequent "national conferences" were attended by almost the entire membership.

The Hebrew Social Democratic party, *Poalei Zion,* the party of Ben-Gurion and Ben-Zvi, considered itself as part and parcel of the international, revolutionary proletariat. "We are the party of the Palestinian working-class in creation, the only revolutionary party of the Jewish worker in Turkey," ran a party announcement published in Jaffa a short time after the first two dozen members disembarked at Jaffa. The men and women of *Poalei Zion* considered themselves engaged in a "class struggle" in Palestine, although the country had no industry, hardly any workers, and no capitalists to speak of. Ben-Zvi later rather pompously wrote: "Prognosis preceded reality and therein lay its glory." He took for granted the support of the "international proletariat"; in his eyes it followed logically from the precepts of Marxism. If it was not immediately forthcoming, that was certainly only a temporary aberration, a misunderstanding which would soon be cleared up in an atmosphere of international solidarity. One *Poalei Zion* leader delivered a series of lectures in Jaffa called "The Prophet Elijah and the Class Struggle in Ancient Israel."

Poalei Zion defined its Marxist doctrine in a curious document entitled "Platform of Ramleh, 1906"—so called after the little town on the Jaffa-Jerusalem highway where it was formulated, in the upstairs room of an Arab camel-driver's *khan,* or caravensery. A more improbable setting can hardly be imagined as the background for such a discussion. It was a clandestine meeting. In Ramleh, and under Turkish rule, there was no real need for such secrecy, but the participants—a dozen or so recent arrivals, including Ben-Gurion—kept up the Russian tradition of revolutionary conspiracy. They argued three days and two nights. The wording of the end product was in part a Zionist paraphrase of the *Communist Manifesto:*

> *The history of mankind is the history of national* [sic!] *and class struggle. . . . the natural and historical conditions of the process of production divide humanity into societies and classes. . . . in the revo-*

lutionary process [in Palestine] an important role is played by the pro-
ductive forces among the Jewish immigrants. . . .

Early in 1907 this "platform" was expanded to include (1) a demand for "public ownership of the means of production" (through the waging of a class struggle) and (2) ". . . with regard to the national problem, the party seeks political autonomy for the Jewish people in this country." This was later watered down to "create in Palestine a Jewish settlement, concentrated in its land and independent in the *economic* sense." For many newcomers the trappings of national sovereignty were less important than their ideal of a new, economically and socially just society.

Of all the amorphic groups who competed for membership among the newcomers, *Poalei Zion* was probably the furthest left. But it was only a matter of degree. The majority, whether they adhered to this group or to another, whether formally "Marxist" or not, were importers of social revolution. Revolution was a hope, a mood, a dream, a program; as the new settlers traveled steerage from Russia to Palestine, they carried it with them in their knapsacks, like Napoleonic soldiers their marshal's batons. Many were driven to these shores by the shattered hopes of 1905. What had so dismally failed in Russia, some now hoped would succeed in one of the more destitute corners of the Ottoman Empire—a safe haven for Jews, and a new paradise to boot. A kingdom of saints, a new world purged of suffering and sin. In this they would fail; but in the course of trying out their fantasy they forged reality as few men have in modern history. When, almost half a century later, the State of Israel was declared, at its helm stood the gray-haired survivors of that early group; a puritan oligarchy whose members had persevered, who had neither run away nor dropped from sight nor died. And because they had forced their will upon history they succeeded in making it.

Even a brief glance at their lives reveals an essential difference which separates many contemporary Israelis from the men and women of the second *Aliyah*. They were true believers. Contemporary Israelis lack the simplicity of their faith. They were moved by ideological convictions, by elaborate abstractions which were frequently divorced from any perceivable reality: modern Israelis are motivated by self-interest and the brutal realities of power. The early pioneers were dreamers; their innocence gave them great strength; courage came from inexperience. Modern Israelis are likely to be weakened by hindsight.

The early pioneers went to school with the idealists of the nineteenth century, for whom things were simpler than they are to us. Never were people more sure that they were on the right track. Some inevitably rationalized their action by reference to religious ties; but most were decidedly irreligious. One avowed atheist wrote shortly after his arrival in 1907: "What I do is not God's will—for I do not believe in God—but what simply is right morally and in practice absolutely necessary." The basic assumptions of their youth, derived almost exclusively from an Eastern European setting, remained with them throughout their lives.

When the first wave of settlers arrived in 1882 from Russia and Romania, the greatest difficulties were still relatively far off; even in 1906, few of the young enthusiasts of the second wave had an inkling of the bitter struggles and hopeless complications still before them. Unburdened by such knowledge, they proceeded upon their tasks with an energy that was made possible only by a sense of total self-righteousness and awareness of a higher purpose.

They were children of their time, as we are of ours. It has been said of the Russians of that period that they were the only people of Europe who lacked the "cement of hypocrisy." In this sense, too, the pioneers of the first and second waves were genuinely typical of their age, though it would be a mistake to think of them as a crowd of faceless conformists. Each had his own reasons, both personal and ideological, for coming, staying, or leaving. As a whole, those who arrived with the second *Aliyah* were not "tougher" than the earlier settlers. A very considerable number very soon left the country as had many pioneers of the first wave—tired, sick, unable to adapt in what often seemed a community of deranged fanatics; unable to stand the climate, the hard work, or the food; disappointed, or simply because of a change of mind.

Arrival in the country was often a depressing anticlimax. Herzl had envisaged the disembarkation as a dramatic event. His blueprint had sounded almost like a tourist brochure: "When the land comes into sight the flag is raised. . . . All must bare their heads [!] . . ." At disembarkation all must "wear the yellow tag." Elsewhere he wrote that the settlers' arrival would compare to the

Exodus of Moses as a "Wagnerian opera compares to a *Singspiel*
by Hans Sachs for Shrove Tuesday." The reality was neither Wagnerian nor a *Singspiel,* but rather often just a letdown. Embarrassing
scenes frequently occurred at the open roadstead in Jaffa. Groups
of arriving pioneers, enthusiastically coming ashore, at times even
kissing the dusty ground as they fell upon it, would mistake those
assembled on the quay for members of a welcoming party. In fact,
the latter were simply preparing to embark on the same ship to go
back to Europe. It was not the most encouraging first encounter.

Some contemporaries have put the number of those who left at
60 to 70 percent. David Ben-Gurion, who arrived in 1906, has even
spoken of 90 percent. We are concerned with those who remained,
and who eventually came into power; the hardened residue, the
toughest, who held out, surviving, one is tempted to say, in a Dar-
winian process of natural selection.

They were marked by a terrible sincerity and by an almost in-
human sense of rectitude. Inveterate diarists and eager composers
of polemic articles, they have left a vast body of written material.
S. N. Eisenstadt has noted that "never have so many volumes of
polemics been written about so many subjects by so few men in
such a short time." They were extremely self-conscious in their roles.
Some, like Ben-Gurion, recounted their own feats in the third person,
à la de Gaulle. With few exceptions not a glimmer of doubt flashes
through this voluminous output. On a summer night in 1910, J. C.
Brenner, the writer, who arrived with the pioneers of the second
wave, was walking with some friends at the farm at Ben Shemen
where they worked. Suddenly Brenner dropped to the ground. He
clutched in his fists a few clods of earth, kissed them, and with
tears in his eyes exclaimed: "Land of Israel, will you be ours? Will
you really be ours?" The cause was never questioned; only the power
of mean and petty humans to sustain it.

Brenner himself felt such inadequacy most acutely. His letters
reflect his own tortured hesitations before he finally went to Palestine. It took him nearly three years to decide. The irony in his letters
strikes a refeshingly candid tone among the letters—otherwise so
emphatic—of the time:

> *September 1, 1906: ". . . I am a typesetter . . . ready to go [to Pales-
> tine] at anytime. But who knows what will happen there? . . . What
> do I care for London, what do I care for Jerusalem?"*

September 4, 1906: ". . . As for Eretz Israel, it seems that my position is clear. I would go if I knew that I would be able to do something decent there. . . ."

October 10, 1906: "As for my journey to Eretz Israel, I have decided to come in any case. . . . But please explain: (1) Is there a decent Hebrew printing press in Jaffa? (2) Is the censorship difficult? (3) Does one suffer a lot from the Turkish officials and the Arab neighbors? (As for suffering at the hands of our Hebrew brethren—I know.)"

November 6, 1906: "When I consider the matter, [my] possibilities in Eretz Israel are terribly doubtful: censorship, and no money, and a new place and the present atmosphere of Eretz Israel, and its Jews, etc. etc."

November 15, 1906: "I have decided to postpone my decision to go to Eretz Israel for a full year at least."

March 25, 1907: "[I am a man] who sees no glimmer of hope. . . . I'll go to Palestine, but not as a believing and hopeful Zionist, but as a man who misses the sun. I want to work as a field laborer."

July 20, 1907: ". . . To Palestine I will not go. I hate the Chosen People, I hate the dead Country, the so-called Land of Israel, Fie! . . ."

December 26, 1907: "I want to move. In the past I thought about Palestine. Now I have decided to go to Galicia [Poland]."

March 16, 1908: ". . . I'll go to Palestine. . . . But I won't stay long."

September 18, 1908: "You are going to Palestine. . . . But what will you do there? I would go to New York. . . ."

January 27, 1909: "Today I leave Galicia [for Palestine]."

Some pioneers of the second wave have described their decision to emigrate to Palestine in almost mystic terms. "Everything was suddenly crystal clear; the fog parted, my entire body shook with excitement. . . . It was as if I had suddenly awakened from a bad dream. I knew what I had to do. Nothing else mattered."

Others claimed that at the very moment they set foot in Palestine they had been "reborn." Ben-Gurion started to count his years afresh from that date on, considering everything that preceded it a waste of time. "I wish that the remaining years shall not go up in smoke," Berl Katzenelson, the labor leader, wrote shortly after his arrival, "and that the *real* life will soon begin."

The poet Bialik wrote to the pioneers: "The very dust will come alive under your bare and sacred feet." This indeed was how they felt in the ecstasy of the first months or years, even before the barren fields they had sown turned green, or the virgin hills they had cleared of boulders were covered by forests. There is an ecstatic quality in the letters and notes written at the time by pioneers. There are the usual terms such as "homecoming" and "rebuilding," but other, stranger, descriptions occur: notions of return to the "womb" of history, and even to Zion the "betrothed." One spoke solemnly of his desire to achieve a "libidinous link with the soil." In Jewish liturgy there were always frequent references to a mystical "betrothal" between Israel and its promised land; this was now given a modern, personal, and political meaning.

Although most had hardly more than a rudimentary command of the language, the pioneers were fanatical Hebraists. Disembarking at Jaffa, Ben-Gurion and many others—like Ben-Yehudah in 1882— vowed never again to use a foreign language, but to speak only Hebrew. While such solemn vows were frequently impractical and often broken, they were sometimes kept with a stubborn will and an inhumanity that shocked only the noninitiated. When Ben-Yehudah's aged mother, who spoke no Hebrew, arrived in Palestine shortly before her death, Ben-Yehudah, who had not seen her in years, refused to talk with her in a language she could understand. (Nevertheless, he is said to have broken his vow—in speaking French with Baron Edmond de Rothschild on one of the latter's visits to the country.) In a makeshift clinic for malaria-struck pioneers, a girl patient who spoke Russian in a delirium was rudely chastised by the nurse for not using Hebrew.

Hebrew was more than a language. The insistence on its usage reflected a program, an attitude to life, to history, and to society. Joshua Altermann, a pioneer of the second *Aliyah,* was working in the Rothschild vineyards at Rishon le-Zion. The Baron's overseers ran the farm rather high-handedly and shared their employer's disdain of Hebrew and political Zionism. A few persisted in speaking Yiddish only. Altermann played deaf.

Until his orders are translated to Hebrew I just would not do what he wanted.

One day he again told me in his Rumanian-accented Yiddish to close a wine tap. I decided to keep it open even if he exploded with anger. He repeated his order. I went on asking him in Hebrew: "What are you say--ing?" By this time he was furiously screaming in Yiddish: "Vermach den

Kran!" Again I asked calmly "What is it that you want me to do?" And all this time the wine was pouring out before our eyes.

After much screaming back and forth between the two, the overseer finally shouted in Hebrew:

"Shut that tap you idiot! And get out of here immediately!" I closed the tap and said: "Now I know what you are." Neverthless he fired me. That day I knew that I had not been defeated but, to the contrary, had been gloriously victorious.

Technically speaking, they were colonists. Yet by temperament, motivation, circumstance, and choice they differed sharply from other emigrants of that period who colonized Australia, Africa, Canada, or the United States. They were not in search of fertile land, gold, unlimited opportunity, or steady employment in a fast-expanding economy. Nor were they sent by chartered companies or governments anxious to rid themselves of surplus populations, expand the territories under their control, or make the flag follow the trade.

This was colonizing without a motherland, an attempt to establish a state without the backing of state power; it was also a dramatic reversal of the then current village-to-city trend. Some of the early pioneers of 1882 had dreamed of industry and commercial enterprise; the newcomers after 1905 turned to agriculture. They became farmers less for practical than for ideological reasons. They thought little of profits, at least in the first period; they were trying to live a theory. It might have been easier and quicker to develop trade and industry; but for ideological reasons they did not. The pioneers believed that nations, like trees, must be "organically" rooted in the soil and that anti-Semitism was a result of the "unnatural" occupational structure of Jews in Eastern Europe.

Properly speaking, they were immigrants. But the messianic temper frequently breeds its own special language and the new arrivals rarely used that word. Instead, echoing the American "pilgrim," they referred to themselves as *olim,* a near-mystic term supercharged with emotion, primeval faith, and historic associations. It means, "those who ascend" who go on pilgrimage, rise above earthly desires. Immigration into Palestine was called *Aliyah* (literally "ascension"), hence "first *Aliyah*," "second *Aliyah*," etc.

Those *olim* who went into agricultural work were called *"halut-*

zim," literally, "vanguard," but in the current Hebrew usage charged
with ecstasy such as was never associated with the closest English
or American equivalent "pioneer." In America, the "pioneer" ethos
stressed individuality, daring, go-gettism. In modern Hebrew,
"halutz" connotes above all *service* to an abstract idea, to a political
movement, and to the community. A biblical term, it meant not only
"to pass over armed before the Lord into the land of Canaan" (Numbers 32:32) but also liberation, exaltation, expedition, rescue. The
ecstatic quality of being a *halutz* was well reflected in a popular
Yiddish song:

> *We are, we are, we are*
> *Pioneers, Pioneers! (Halutzim! Halutzim!)*
> *On burning fields*
> *On barren fields of waste.*
> *The first to arrive*
> *Like swallows in spring*
> *We believe . . .*
> *We'll cover the stony fields*
> *With golden bloom.*

The term *halutz* soon served as basis for derivatives such as do
not exist in other languages: halutzism, halutzistic approach, halutzistic culture, education, values, and even halutzistic morality. Cum-
bersome portmanteau words of considerable imprecision but of such
tremendous emotional force that they are still widely used in Israel
today. The pioneers of the second wave saw themselves less as
nation builders than as *halutzim* of a new social order.

Their orthodoxy was of that peculiar, innocent optimistic kind
which was a common trait of nineteenth-century reformers. The idea
of progress which had remained for such a long time a mere specu-
lative toy became in the nineteenth century an operative principle.
The pioneers of the second wave deeply believed in the possibility
of human progress, a faith which may seem naive today only because
we are governed by a different set of immediate historical memories.
It was before the Russian Revolution and before Marxist-Leninism
degenerated into the Stalinist and post-Stalinist police state, a
process which, borrowing the words of Shigalev in Dostoyevsky's
The Possessed, started from "unlimited liberty" and ended in "unlimited despotism." It was before two world wars were waged "to

end all wars"; before nationalism emerged not as Mazzini had hoped, as a vehicle of liberal humanism, but as a recrudescence of tribal savageries unprecedented in their ferocity; before the ennui engendered by the modern welfare state. It was the simpler, more hopeful world of yesterday. No problem seemed insoluble, if only properly analyzed and approached through the tenets of this or that philosophy.

Life for them was a perpetual striving, an incessant training course. Like so many Russian Populists they lived under an obsessive urge to conquer *themselves,* to fashion and forge their personalities after some great ideal, an ideal that was often taken from literature. Their letters and notes frequently express a powerful desire to discover the meaning of existence. This pursuit at times overshadowed their commitment to Zionism; but frequently the two achieved a near-mystic union. They were convinced that every man had a unique mission to fulfill in life and the first step was to define it. Zvi Schatz was a twenty-three-year-old worker at Migdal, on the Lake of Galilee, who, in his spare time wrote deeply melancholy Russian poetry. In 1913 he noted in his diary that "never in my whole life have I felt as far from human perfection as now, and never has there been in me as strong and deep a desire to begin deliberate work to perfect myself towards the great ideal of moral improvement."

For many young men and women who arrived with the second *Aliyah,* the magic key to a true perception of the self was physical labor. It was the beginning and end of morality. Like Levin in *Anna Karenina* they worked in the fields with scythe or shovel and decided they were finally beginning to understand life itself, communing with its deepest mysteries. In conquering work they were conquering themselves. There is a characteristic story of the young, frail, and pale girl who insists upon doing a man's heavy field work on a hot *Chamsin* day, digging trenches in difficult soil. She is taken on by a reluctant farmer on a trial basis; upon being told that she has passed the test and is accepted for work, she collapses, exhausted, in near-hysterical laughter of joy. This story later served as the backdrop for a successful Israeli play (*Kinneret, Kinneret* by Nathan Altermann) much as the fall of the Bastille served as the backdrop for many a nineteenth-century play on the French Revolution. Today the scene may seem unduly melodramatic, its heroes "too positive" for the modern taste; yet it clearly echoes the mood of the years 1905–1914.

The poetess Rachel Bluwstein (1890–1931)—a former art student who worked as a farmhand in Palestine in the years between 1908 and 1913—could easily have been the girl in Altermann's story. She wrote of "making music with the shovel and painting on the soil." Others wanted "to be slaves to the soil . . . kneel and bow down to it daily. Nurse its furrows until even the stony clods will yield a blessing."

"What is the point of your working as a laborer in Palestine?" the parents of Noah Naftulski complained in a letter written in 1907. "After all you are only twenty-two years old . . . you still have many possibilities to succeed in life; it is not yet too late. . . ." Naftulski was a gifted young man; barred as a Jew from the Russian gymnasium, he had taught himself mathematics, botany, and biology. He left for Palestine in 1906. His parents pleaded with him to try now to enter a Western European university. Young Naftulski wrote back: "There is a hidden delight in God's treasury . . . its name is labor; blessed is the man who has found it."

He adorned his letter with dried red poppies, from the fields of Petah Tikvah where he worked. "These days of April," he wrote, "when everything around you is covered by ice and the bitter cold is raging, here the soil of our land is covered with flowers, and by the curing, soothing sun of spring. . . ." Naftulski and his fellow pioneers sang together what was probably the leitmotiv of their generation,

> *Work is our life's elation*
> *From all troubles the salvation,*
> *Yah-hah-li-li labor mine!*

and would immediately pass on to melancholy Russian songs. But if they sang of the Volga, their thoughts were on the Jordan. Many shared a feeling of holy orders. Lebi Ben Amitai, after slaving all day in the heat of the Jordan Valley, visualized himself dressed in

> *a shirt of clean white cloth*
> *and in the company of priests I take my place*
> *and on the table find my bread and broth.*

In some of the pioneers of the second wave, physical labor assumed an almost transcendental meaning; it afforded most of the psychological satisfactions commonly supplied by religion. The word *avoda* in Hebrew means both labor and worship. Labor was worshipped. The harder it was, in terms of pure exertion—and at times it led to total exhaustion—the more it was held up as a means to realize one's true self. Not all, of course, worked with the same amount of sincerity. Every religion has its hangers-on, its phonies and hypocrites. S. Y. Agnon, the novelist who later became the first Israeli to win a Nobel Prize, lived in Palestine at that time, and cast a skeptical eye upon the scene. In his novel *Tmol Shilshom* set in Jaffa and Jerusalem of the time, he ironically distinguished between those who came to work and those "who came to write a great book on labor."

The great prophet of the religion of labor was Aharon David Gordon. His influence was considerable and lasted for decades, long after his death in 1922. Like Tolstoi in later life, Gordon abandoned his family in order to commune with nature and soul. At the age of forty-seven, a weak and ailing man with a flowing white beard, he became a manual laborer in the fields of Palestine. He quickly attracted a large following among the young pioneers, who called him *Hazaken,* the old man. His teaching was a curious amalgam of cabalistic mysticism, populist agrarianism, Zionism, and socialism, in that order of importance. He preached that only through hard physical labor could a man be redeemed. He called upon his fellow pioneers to become "zealots of labor." This was their only cure as men; as Jews they must not live by their wits but by their sweat. Gordon slaved by day in the fields. At night he would join the young workers in dancing the *hora,* and while intoning a monotonous Yiddish refrain, *"frailich! . . . frailich! . . . frailich! . . ."* (Joy! . . . Joy! . . . Joy! . . .), would whip himself and his fellow dancers into a state of near ecstasy. He wrote:

> *In my dream I come to the land. And it is barren and desolate and given over to aliens; destruction darkens its face and foreign rule corrupts it. And the land of my forefathers is distant and foreign to me, and I too am distant and foreign to it. And the only link that ties my soul to her, the only reminder that I am her son and she my mother, is that my soul is as desolate as hers. So I shake myself and with all my strength I throw*

. . . the [old] life off. And I start everything from the beginning. And the first thing that opens up my heart to a life I have not known before is labor. Not labor to make a living, not work as a deed of charity, but work for life itself . . . it is one of the limbs of life, one of its deepest roots. And I work. . . .

Gordon worshiped labor, the soil, and the nation as cosmic forces; he viewed "society" as a sheer mechanical, unstable entity. Man, instead of theorizing, must "enter the great university of labor, where heaven and earth and all of nature are creating a new human species." A modern reader is inevitably disconcerted by all this worship of irrational cosmic forces, of nature and sweat with undertones of "blood and soil" theories consciously or unconsciously derived from the romantic precepts of German nationalism. A parallel exists but it must not be carried too far. Gordon was a pacifist. He had a profound horror of all bloodshed, of force, and of all government. There were no racial or militaristic features whatsoever in his teachings. In the tradition of Tolstoi and of the Hebrew prophets he did not believe in state power or politics, but in ethical action by the individual. The Jews had been the first to say that the individual was created in God's image. "We must amplify this," Gordon wrote hopefully, "by saying that the nation must likewise be formed in God's image."

*   *   *

The second labor party, *Hapoel Hatzair,* was non-Marxist. Its members were equally certain that in the long run there was no conflict of interests between the two nations. Leading European Socialists of the time assumed that war was becoming improbable because workers of one nation would refuse to shoot at workers of another. There is little surprise that many of the young worker-pioneers in Palestine—less sophisticated, less experienced than the intellectuals of Paris, Brussels, Amsterdam, Vienna, and Berlin—refused to see any real conflict emerging between their own "proletarian enterprise" and the indigenous population, whose peasants and workers were being exploited by a corrupt upper class of feudal landowners, and who, they felt sure, must soon awaken to a sense of solidarity with them. For the pioneers, whether Marxist or not, there was no such thing as an irresolvable problem. If indeed there was an Arab problem, they felt sure that they had found a practical and just solution for it.

Their solution was, naturally, an economic one; it tied in with the mysticism of physical work so prevalent among the pioneers. It was called *Avoda Ivrit* (Hebrew Labor) or the "conquest of labor" by the Jews. After some hesitation, the men and women of *Poalei Zion* concurred. The plan in effect aimed at the establishment of a completely separate economic sector for the newcomers. Native labor must not be "exploited" in the reconstruction of the country by the Jews. Jews must do everything themselves. The natives would continue to benefit indirectly from the general improvement and economic upsurge, particularly in trade. But henceforth Jews must try to be self-sufficient and do all the physical work with their own hands, including the most difficult, the least paying, and the most menial. If there was no "exploitation" of Arab labor, Arab laborers could not "objectively" be opposed to the Zionists.

It was realized that such self-sufficiency must raise the human and economic cost of settlement; for this reason most of the earlier "bourgeois" settlers were violently opposed to *Avoda Ivrit*. Public and private funds were severely limited. Some feared that *Avoda Ivrit* might delay further expansion of the Zionist enterprise. But in the eyes of the newly arrived young radicals from Eastern Europe this was a small price to pay for the kind of moral renewal they were striving for. Also, the newcomers needed these jobs desperately for their own daily bread.

Different people agreed to the *Avoda Ivrit* scheme for different reasons. Marxists of *Poalei Zion* assumed that since all national enmity had its roots in economic factors, as long as there was no economic exploitation of Arabs by Jews there could not be any lasting nationalist antagonism between the two. It took decades and much bloodshed before some of the pioneers outgrew this faith. We must not judge them more harshly than we judge other Marxists of that time. Together they were looking forward assuredly to the coming abolishment of politics and to the withering away in socialism of all state coercion through the dismantlement of all those authoritarian structures that cause alienation between people.

The men of *Hapoel Hatzair,* non-Marxist but under the powerful spell of Tolstoianism, concurred in this view and fought even harder for *Avoda Ivrit*. In their eyes a "moral" right to any country could be acquired only through manual work of the kind most Jewish planters were only too eager to leave to illiterate Arab farmhands. They were convinced that if they were taking the unusual step of claiming a country occupied by others, history would exonerate them of all guilt, not only because they had no desire to displace anybody, but above all, because they were evidently *re-earning* their historic birthright through the bitter sweat of their brows.

Those who slave in the sun with their own hands to make a desert bloom could not be considered conquistadores. Only work "creates an inner right for the country," Eliezer Shochat wrote in 1910. Only work "breeds the deep relationship that exists between an artist and his painting; not the superficial legal one that prevails between a purchaser and the painting he has bought." A. D. Gordon held a similar view. What is so puzzling in all this theorizing is that apparently it never occurred to Shochat or to Gordon that by their own definition of "right through labor" the vast majority of Arabs in the country were daily proving their own claim to it.

The policy of *Avoda Ivrit* was never fully implemented until the Arabs themselves, through violence that led to mutual self-segregation, enforced its near-total application during the Arab rebellion of 1936–1939. In retrospect, even its partial application appears as the most critical of all Zionist measures in the pre-Independence period. *Avoda Ivrit* was predicated in part upon a doctrinaire illusion; it was rampant with intellectual inconsistencies. In effect, it created a subculture, free from the demands of the larger society, not parasitic upon it, and above all enjoying that kind of immunity from "reality" —whether Turkish, British, or Arab—that permitted its members to indulge in their dreams.

The policy and practice of *Avoda Ivrit* left an indelible mark upon Israel's national character. Few measures affected as deeply the Israelis' image of themselves in history. By avoiding the typical pattern of colonial settlers elsewhere, the policy of *Avoda Ivrit* bred in their hearts a deeply felt, and totally sincere, sense of moral superiority over other colonialists. If this be a fallacy, it gained ground, again, because there was some truth to it. There was never a sense of "colonial vocation" among the Zionist settlers. There was a cultural arrogance here as elsewhere; but individual motivation was sharply different. Elsewhere, a colonial career frequently meant social and professional advancement. In Palestine the opposite was true. Elsewhere, those who failed to attain bourgeois status at home often found it in the colonies; again, here the opposite happened. The settlers were not looking for individual material benefits but aimed at achieving a collective goal.

A sense of high adventure certainly played a role, more than was admitted at the time. But there was little, if any, of that general ennui as expressed, for example, by the frustrated European in Flaubert's *Sentimental Education* which has been seen as one key to the Frenchman's colonial vocation: "I feel like running off to live among the cannibals."

O. Mannoni, in *Prospero and Caliban,* one of the few detailed studies of colonial psychology, has suggested that colonial settlers from highly competitive societies tended to compensate their European-bred sense of social or personal inferiority by living as white masters among more primitive, native weak. To the spirit conceived in its own inferiority the services and homage of dependents is balm and honey. The humiliations of anti-Semitism were so obviously a prime factor in Zionism that one would have expected widespread and rather ugly compensatory reactions in the behavior of Jewish settlers toward the primitive Arab natives who worked for them. There were such "compensatory reactions," of course, especially during the earliest period, but neither widespread nor for very long. The first settlers in the Rothschild colonies occasionally behaved despotically toward their Arab employees, for which they were invariably berated by visiting Zionist intellectuals from abroad. The arrival of the young socialist radicals of the second *Aliyah* after 1905 precipitated a marked change of atmosphere.

The young pioneers who were now arriving in the country rarely looked down upon the natives. They were competing with Arab *felahin* for jobs on the Jewish plantations. As a rule they admired the Arab *felah* because he was so marvelously "rooted" in labor and agriculture, which the pioneers considered sacrosanct. The new pioneer emulated the *felah* by voluntarily renouncing the minimal living standards of a European. Shmuel Dayan, father of the future general, described his work with Arabs on a plantation: "I saw myself surrounded by strange foreign people; they were mocking me in a strange language. I took courage and worked with unestimable drive, without exactly knowing the job. I drank swamp water from a kerosene tin." At the end of the day he felt deliriously happy for having dug a trench as long and as well as most of his Arab co-workers.

Avoda Ivrit is a key, not only to the Israelis' historic self-image but also to much that happened later on. The separate economic sector implied in *Avoda Ivrit* was the beginning of the Zionist state within a state, which by 1933 had already become a major political factor. The inexorable logic of *Avoda Ivrit* led from a deliberate partition of the economy to the indeliberate partition of the country in bloodshed. There is a deep and tragic irony in the fact that the policy of *Avoda Ivrit* was in its time seen as a means to avoid or allay conflict between the two nations. In some ways it made the conflict worse. It might have given Jewish colonists a sense of moral superiority over colonial settlers elsewhere; at the same time it compounded the future tragedy by causing the deliberate exclusion of the natives from the New Society. It prevented the establishment of a joint basis upon which, *perhaps,* in the fullness of time, a binational polity, open to all, might have been tried; or perhaps the commonwealth of *Altneuland,* which Herzl had recommended, with the proviso: "If you will it, it is no fairy tale."

After settlement had begun and before World War I there were only a few isolated voices warning the settlers that they might be treading a path more dangerous than appeared through the tinted spectacles of ideology. Ahad Haam, the writer, in 1891 protested the view that the "Arabs are wild men of the desert, an ignorant people who did not see and do not understand what is going on around them. . . . in time, when our people in Palestine shall have developed to such an extent that they will begin more or less to push aside the natives, the latter will not easily give way." This was probably the darkest warning sounded at the time: but Ahad Haam did not follow it up with any practical conclusions.

The young pioneers after 1905, who adored Ahad Haam, took his words as another reason for fully implementing the policy of *Avoda Ivrit. . . .*

III TO THE BALFOUR DECLARATION: 1914–1918

Doreen Ingrams

PALESTINE PAPERS: 1917–1918

Doreen Ingrams is a British scholar working on the history of British policy in Palestine. She is well known as a writer and speaker on the Arab world. Consisting largely of British government documents, this selection clearly shows the Balfour Declaration as a contested decision, the immediate results of which in Palestine revealed the contours of the Arab-Jewish tensions in the Holy Land that would face the British for the next thirty years.

It was in November 1914, three months after the declaration of war with Germany, that Britain declared war on Turkey. At that time Palestine formed a part of the Turkish Empire. It was divided administratively into the vilayet of Beirut in the north and the independent sanjak of Jerusalem in the south. Its population consisted of some 500,000 Moslems, 60,000 Jews, and about the same number of Christians. Among the Jewish population about 12,000 were immigrants living in agricultural colonies.

Both the Arab Nationalist movement and the Zionist movement had by this time become more pressing in their demands: the former for freedom from foreign domination, the latter for the setting up of a Jewish state in Palestine. Arab nationalism was directed against the Turks. In Syria, Lebanon, and Iraq, groups of intellectuals and young army officers had ideas of democracy and freedom, while in the more remote Arab areas the movement was largely among tribes seeking independence. The only link between the two groups was Sherif Hussein of Mecca, respected by traditional tribal leaders for his position as custodian of the holy cities of Mecca and Medina, and recognized by the intellectuals as a man who had shown an independent spirit when under surveillance for sixteen years in Constantinople. His son, Amir Abdulla, had become involved in the nascent Arab movement in Constantinople and he had approached Lord Kitchener, then consul-general in Egypt, to ask whether the British government would help the Arabs if they rose against the Turks. Kitchener's answer was cautious as at that time Britain's policy was

From *Palestine Papers 1917–1922*, compiled by Doreen Ingrams, pp. 1–26. Copyright © 1973 by George Braziller, Inc. Reprinted with permission of George Braziller, Inc. and John Murray (Publishers) Ltd.

one of friendship with Turkey, but, six months later, when war broke out and Turkey became an enemy, the British government approached Sherif Hussein, as not only would an Arab revolt help the Allies in their war against Turkey, but the sultan of Turkey had proclaimed a *jihad* or holy war and was trying to induce the Sherif to support it. The Sherif agreed to side with the Allies providing that, when the Turks were defeated, the British would support Arab independence in the whole of the Arabian Peninsula (with the exception of Aden), Syria, Lebanon, Palestine, Transjordan, and Iraq.

A number of letters were exchanged between Sherif Hussein and the high commissioner in Egypt, Sir Henry McMahon, the most important of which was the letter of October 24, 1915, in which McMahon informed the Sherif:

> *The two districts of Mersina and Alexandretta and portions of Syria lying to the west of the districts of Damascus, Homs, Hama and Aleppo cannot be said to be purely Arab, and should be excluded from the limits demanded.*
>
> *With the above modification, and without prejudice to our existing treaties with Arab chiefs, we accept those limits.*
>
> *As for those regions lying within those frontiers wherein Great Britain is free to act without detriment to the interests of her ally, France, I am empowered in the name of the Government of Great Britain to give the following assurances and make the following reply to your letter:*
>
> *(I) Subject to the above modifications, Great Britain is prepared to recognize and support the independence of the Arabs in all the regions within the limits demanded by the Sharif of Mecca. . . .*[1]

Palestine was not mentioned by name in that letter, and in later years, when arguments arose over its interpretation, the Arabs maintained that it was not geographically possible for Palestine to be included in the "portions of Syria lying to the west of the districts of Damascus, Homs, Hama and Aleppo." The British government, however, maintained that it had always been intended to exclude Palestine from the area of independence. These opposing points of view became the cause of bitter controversy.

It has been suggested that the imprecision of the McMahon letter was intentional[2] because, whilst the British government was encouraging Arab hopes for independence, it was also having to con-

---

[1] For full text see Laqueur, *The Israel-Arab Reader*, pp. 33–35.
[2] Monroe, *Britain's Moment in the Middle East*, pp. 31–32.

sider its French ally. France had long had cultural links with Syria and Lebanon and considered she had claims to those countries after the Turks were defeated. Early in 1916 Sir Mark Sykes, who was attached to the Foreign Office as adviser on Near Eastern affairs, signed an agreement on behalf of the British government with François Georges-Picot, representing the French government, by which there was to be an independent Arab state—or confederation of states—in the area known today as Saudi Arabia and the Yemen Arab Republic: the French were to have control of Lebanon and Syria, the British that of Iraq and Transjordan. Palestine was to be under an international administration. This agreement was kept secret, because at the time of its signing it was thought that knowledge of it might prejudice the Allied cause. However czarist Russia had been kept informed and when the Bolsheviks came to power they published the document, with consequent dismay and consternation among the Arabs.

There were, thus, by 1917 two contradictory promises made by the British government regarding the disposal of Turkish-held territory after the war: first, the promise of independence to the Arabs given in the letter from Sir Henry McMahon to Sherif Hussein, and, second, the promise to the French given in the Sykes-Picot Agreement. In 1917 the British government made a third promise, this time to the Zionists.

The modern Zionist movement was founded by Theodor Herzl, who wrote in 1896: "The Idea which I have developed . . . is a very old one: it is the restoration of the Jewish State." At the first Zionist Congress held in Basel in 1897 it was stated that "the aim of Zionism is to create for the Jewish people a home in Palestine secured by public law." The Congress contemplated attaining this by "the promotion . . . of the colonization of Palestine by Jewish agricultural and industrial workers; the organization and binding together of the whole of Jewry: . . . the strengthening and fostering of Jewish national sentiment," and "preparatory steps towards obtaining government consent, where necessary, to the attainment of the aim of Zionism."[3]

The Zionist movement gained many supporters among prominent Jews and Christians in Europe and America, and when war with

[3] Laqueur, *The Israel-Arab Reader,* pp. 22–29.

Turkey was declared, Zionists saw an opportunity to realize their aspirations. Dr. Weizmann, president of the English Zionist Federation, recalls that in December 1914 when he was breakfasting with Lloyd George (then chancellor of the Exchequer), Herbert Samuel, M.P. (then president of the local government board), said that he was preparing a memorandum for the prime minister (Asquith) on the subject of a Jewish state in Palestine.[4] In fact Samuel wrote three memoranda on the subject. In January 1915 he submitted the first:

> *The course of events opens a prospect of change, at the end of the war, in the status of Palestine. Already there is a stirring among the twelve million Jews scattered throughout the countries of the world. A feeling is spreading with great rapidity that now, at last, some advance may be made, in some way, towards the fulfilment of the hope and desire, held with unshakable tenacity for eighteen hundred years, for the restoration of the Jews to the land to which they are attached by ties almost as ancient as history itself.*
>
> *Yet it is felt that the time is not ripe for the establishment there of an independent, autonomous Jewish State. Such increase of population as there has been in Palestine in recent years has been composed, indeed, mostly of Jewish immigrants . . . but in the country, as a whole, they still probably do not number more than about one-sixth of the population.*
>
> *If the attempt were made to place the 400,000 or 500,000 Mahommedans of Arab race under a Government which rested upon the support of 90,000 or 100,000 Jewish inhabitants, there can be no assurance that such a Government, even if established by the authority of the Powers, would be able to command obedience. The dream of a Jewish State, prosperous, progressive, and the home of a brilliant civilization, might vanish in a series of squalid conflicts with the Arab population. . . .*
>
> *I am assured that the solution of the problem of Palestine which would be much the most welcome to the leaders and supporters of the Zionist movement throughout the world would be the annexation of the country to the British Empire. . . . It is hoped that under British rule facilities would be given to Jewish organizations to purchase land, to found colonies, to establish educational and religious institutions, and to spend usefully the funds that would be freely contributed for promoting the economic development of the country. It is hoped also that Jewish immigration, carefully regulated, would be given preference so that in course of time the Jewish people, grown into a majority and settled on the land, may be conceded such degree of self-government as the conditions of that day may justify. . . .[5]*

Besides Herbert Samuel himself, there were a number of Zionist

[4] Weizmann, *Trial and Error*, p. 192.
[5] PRO. CAB. 37/123/43.

sympathizers among members of Parliament, and in the government, but, as Samuel wrote in his memoirs, the support of Lloyd
George, when he became prime minister in 1916, was essential.
Lord Reading, in a letter to Samuel, explained Lloyd George's
attitude: "Your proposal appeals to the poetic and imaginative as
well as to the romantic and religious qualities of his mind."[6] In 1917
the British government made a declaration to the Zionists that they
would look with favor on the establishment of a national home for
the Jews in Palestine.

It was at the Basel Conference in 1897 that the term "National
Home" was first used instead of Jewish state, as explained by Max
Nordau, an associate of Herzl: "I did my best to persuade the claim-
ants of the Jewish State in Palestine that we might find a circum-
locution that would express all we meant, but would say it in a way
so as to avoid provoking the Turkish rulers of the coveted land. I
suggested '*Heimstätte*' as a synonym for 'State'. . . . This is the
history of the much commented expression. It was equivocal, but we
all understood what it meant. To us it signified '*Judenstaat*' then and
it signifies the same now."[7]

The promise to the Zionists was given in the form of a letter from
the foreign secretary, Arthur Balfour, to Lord Rothschild, a leading
British Zionist. Probably no other scrap of paper in history has had
the effect of this brief letter, the cause of a conflict that has lasted
half a century and still shows no sign of settlement.

The Balfour Declaration

Many reasons have been put forward as to why the British government approved the Balfour Declaration. It was a matter of conjecture
in Whitehall five years later, in 1922, when the Hon. William Ormsby-
Gore, M.P., who was parliamentary under secretary of state for the
colonies, wrote a memorandum on the origins of the declaration
for Winston Churchill, then secretary of state for the colonies:

> . . . Such papers as it has been possible to obtain are very meagre and
> do not afford material for anything like a complete statement of the
> case . . . indeed, little is known of how the policy represented by the
> Declaration was first given form. Four, or perhaps five, men were chiefly

6 Quoted in Thomas Jones, *Lloyd George*, p. 126.
7 Quoted in Sykes, *Cross Roads to Israel*, p. 24.

concerned in the labour—the Earl of Balfour, the late Sir Mark Sykes, and Messrs. Weizmann and Sokolow [Chief London representative of the Zionist Organization], with perhaps Lord Rothschild as a figure in the background. Negotiations seem to have been mainly oral and by means of private notes and memoranda, of which only the scantiest records are available, even if more exist. . . . The earliest document is a letter dated 24th April 1917 in which a certain Mr. Hamilton suggested that a Zionist mission should be sent to Russia for propaganda purposes. It is clear that at that stage His Majesty's Government were mainly concerned with the question of how Russia (then in the first stages of revolution) was to be kept in the ranks of the Allies. At the end of April the Foreign Office were consulting the British Ambassador at Petrograd as to the possible effect in Russia of a declaration by the Entente of sympathy for Jewish national aspirations. The idea was that such a declaration might counteract Jewish pacifist propaganda in Russia.

In the same month (April 1917) Mr. Balfour, then Secretary of State for Foreign Affairs, went on his official mission to the United States ["to scheme out ways of co-operating with them in prosecuting the war."[8]] The Foreign Office note observes that "during this visit the policy of the declaration as a war measure seems to have taken more definite shape." It was supposed that American opinion might be favourably influenced if His Majesty's Government gave an assurance that the return of the Jews to Palestine had become a purpose of British policy.

The Foreign Office papers show that during the next few months various conversations took place with Dr. Weizmann and other Zionists, and that much telegraphic correspondence passed on the subject with Sir Mark Sykes, who was then at Cairo. . . .[9]

The year 1917 was a grave one for the Allies. The Russian revolution weakened the struggle against Germany in the East, and the Germans were about to transfer divisions from the Russian to the Western front before the American troops reached France.

On June 13 Ronald Graham, assistant under secretary of state for foreign affairs (later to become ambassador to Italy), described by Weizmann as "of considerable help in bringing about the Balfour Declaration,"[10] addressed a memorandum to Lord Hardinge, permanent under secretary of state for foreign affairs and previously viceroy of India:

It would appear that in view of the sympathy towards the Zionist movement which has already been expressed by the Prime Minister, Mr. Balfour,

---

[8] Thomas Jones, *Whitehall Diary, 1916–1925.*
[9] PRO. CAB. 24/158.
[10] Weizmann, *Trial and Error,* p. 231.

Lord Robert Cecil [parliamentary under-secretary for foreign affairs], and other statesmen, we are committed to support it, although until Zionist policy has been more clearly defined our support must be of a general character. We ought therefore to secure all the political advantage we can out of our connection with Zionism and there is no doubt that this advantage will be considerable, especially in Russia. . . . I submit for consideration that the moment has come when we might meet the wishes of the Zionists and give them an assurance that His Majesty's Government are in general sympathy with their aspirations. This might be done by a message from the Prime Minister or Mr. Balfour to be read out at a meeting which could be arranged for at any time. Such a step would be well justified by the international political results it would secure.

Balfour wrote a Minute:

I have asked Ld Rothschild and Professor Weizmann to submit a formula.

AJB[11]

Lord Rothschild replied on 18 July:

At last I am able to send you the formula you asked me for. If His Majesty's Government will send me a message on the lines of this formula, if they and you approve of it, I will hand it on to the Zionist Federation and also announce it at a meeting called for that purpose. . . .

1. *His Majesty's Government accepts the principle that Palestine should be reconstituted as the National Home for the Jewish people.*
2. *His Majesty's Government will use its best endeavours to secure the achievement of this object and will discuss the necessary methods and means with the Zionist Organization.*

Balfour drafted a reply accepting the formula as proposed by Rothschild, but Lord Milner, minister without portfolio and a member of the War Cabinet, considered the words "reconstituted" and "secure" much too strong. He therefore submitted an alternative:

His Majesty's Government accepts the principle that every opportunity should be afforded for the establishment of a home for the Jewish people in Palestine, and will use its best endeavours to facilitate the achievement of this object, and will be ready to consider any suggestions on the subject which the Zionist Organization may desire to lay before them.[12]

[11] PRO. FO. 371/3058.
[12] PRO. CAB. 21/58.

According to Weizmann, Milner "understood profoundly that the Jews alone were capable of rebuilding Palestine and of giving it a place in the modern family of nations," and had said publicly: " 'If the Arabs think that Palestine will become an Arab country, they are very much mistaken.' "[13]

The War Cabinet, according to the minutes, met on September 3 to consider the draft declaration. Lloyd George and Balfour, both Zionist sympathizers, were absent so that Edwin Montagu, secretary of state for India and an anti-Zionist, was able to have a decision deferred:

> . . . It was suggested that a question raising such important issues as to the future of Palestine ought, in the first instance, to be discussed with our Allies, and more particularly with the United States . . .
> The Acting Secretary of State for Foreign Affairs [Lord Robert Cecil] pointed out that this was a question on which the Foreign Office has been very strongly pressed for a long time past. There was a very strong and enthusiastic organisation, more particularly in the United States, who were zealous in this matter, and his belief was that it would be of most substantial assistance to the Allies to have the earnestness and enthusiasm of these people enlisted on our side. To do nothing was to risk a direct break with them, and it was necessary to face this situation.

The War Cabinet decided that:

> The views of President Wilson should be obtained before a declaration was made, and requested the Acting Secretary of State for Foreign Affairs to inform the Government of the United States that His Majesty's Government were being pressed to make a declaration in sympathy with the Zionist movement, and to ascertain their views as to the advisability of such a declaration being made.[14]

Balfour took up the case for the declaration when the War Cabinet met again on October 4, as recorded in the Minutes:

> The Secretary of State for Foreign Affairs stated that the German Government were making great efforts to capture the sympathy of the Zionist Movement. This Movement, though opposed by a number of wealthy Jews in this country, had behind it the support of a majority of Jews, at all events in Russia and America, and possibly in other countries. He saw

13 Weizmann, *Trial and Error*, p. 226.
14 PRO. CAB. 23/4.

nothing inconsistent between the establishment of a Jewish national focus in Palestine and the complete assimilation and absorption of Jews into the nationality of other countries. Just as English emigrants to the United States became, either in the first or subsequent generations, American nationals, so, in future, should a Jewish citizenship be established in Palestine, would Jews become either Englishmen, Americans, Germans, or Palestinians. What was at the back of the Zionist movement was the intense national consciousness held by certain members of the Jewish race. They regarded themselves as one of the great historic races of the world, whose original home was Palestine, and these Jews had a passionate longing to regain once more their ancient national home. Other Jews had become absorbed into the nations among whom they and their forefathers had dwelt for many generations. Mr. Balfour then read a very sympathetic declaration by the French Government which had been conveyed to the Zionists, and he stated that he knew that President Wilson was extremely favourable to the Movement.

Mr. Montagu urged strong objections to any declaration in which it was stated that Palestine was the "national home" of the Jewish people. He regarded the Jews as a religious community and himself as a Jewish Englishman. He based his argument on the prejudicial effect on the status of Jewish Britons of a statement that His Majesty's Government regarded Palestine as the national home of Jewish people. Whatever safeguarding words might be used in the formula, the civil rights of Jews as nationals in the country in which they were born might be endangered. How would he negotiate with the peoples of India on behalf of His Majesty's Government if the world had just been told that His Majesty's Government regarded his national home as being in Turkish territory? He specially urged that the only trial of strength between Zionists and anti-Zionists in England had resulted in a very narrow majority for the Zionists, namely, 56 to 51 of the representatives of Anglo-Jewry on the Conjoint Committee.

This Committee was composed of representatives of the Anglo-Jewish Association and the Board of Deputies, both bodies described by Weizmann as consisting of "old-fashioned, well-to-do assimilationist Jews."[15] The minutes continued:

He also pointed out that most English-born Jews were opposed to Zionism, while it was supported by foreign-born Jews, such as Dr. Gaster [Chief Rabbi of the Sephardic Communities of England] and Dr. Herz [Chief Rabbi of the United Hebrew Congregation of the British Empire], the two Grand Rabbis, who had been born in Roumania and Austria respectively, and Dr. Weizmann, President of the English Zionist Federation, who was born in Russia. He submitted that the Cabinet's first duty was

---

[15] Weizmann, *Trial and Error*, p. 200.

to English Jews, and that Colonel House had declared that President Wilson is opposed to a declaration now.

Lord Curzon [Lord President of the Council] urged strong objections upon practical grounds. He stated, from his recollection of Palestine, that the country was, for the most part, barren and desolate; there being but sparse cultivation on the terraced slopes, the valleys and streams being few, and large centres of population scarce, a less propitious seat for the future Jewish race could not be imagined. How was it proposed to get rid of the existing majority of Mussulman inhabitants and to introduce the Jews in their place? How many would be willing to return and on what pursuits would they engage?

To secure for the Jews already in Palestine equal civil and religious rights seemed to him a better policy than to aim at repatriation on a large scale. He regarded the latter as sentimental idealism, which would never be realised, and that His Majesty's Government should have nothing to do with it.

It was pointed out that during recent years before the war, Jewish immigration into Palestine had been considerably on the increase, and that several flourishing Zionist colonies were already in existence.

Lord Milner submitted an alternative draft declaration, as follows:

His Majesty's Government views with favour the establishment in Palestine of a National Home for the Jewish Race, and will use its best endeavours to facilitate the achievement of this object; it being clearly understood that nothing shall be done which may prejudice the civil and religious rights of the existing non-Jewish communities in Palestine, or the rights and political status enjoyed in any other country by such Jews who are fully contented with their existing nationality and citizenship.

The War Cabinet decided that:

Before coming to a decision they should hear the views of representative Zionists, as well as of those who held the opposite opinion, and that meanwhile the Declaration, as read by Lord Milner, should be submitted confidentially to (a) President Wilson, (b) Leaders of the Zionist Movement, (c) Representative persons in Anglo-Jewry opposed to Zionism.[16]

During October replies were received from the representative Jews:

The Chief Rabbi, Dr. J. H. Herz
It is with feelings of the profoundest gratification that I learn of the intention of His Majesty's Government to lend its powerful support to the re-

16 PRO. CAB. 23/4.

*establishment in Palestine of a national home for the Jewish people. . . .
I welcome the reference to the civil and religious rights of the existing
non-Jewish communities in Palestine. It is but a translation of the basic
principle of the Mosaic legislation: "And if a stranger sojourn with thee
in your land, ye shall not vex (oppress) him. But the stranger that dwelleth
with you shall be unto you as one born among you, and thou shalt love
him as thyself." (Lev. xix. 33, 34) . . .*

Lord Rothschild
*Personally, I think that the proviso is rather a slur on Zionism, as it pre-
supposes the possibility of a danger to non-Zionists, which I deny. . . .
One of the chief aims of the Zionist Federation, when the settlement in
Palestine takes place, is to see that while obtaining as large a measure
of autonomy as possible, no encroachment on the rights of the other inhabitants of the country should take place. . . .*

Sir Stuart Samuel, Bart., Chairman of the Jewish Board of Deputies
*I think that Jews resident in Great Britain are by a large majority favour-
able to the establishment of a national home for Jews in Palestine, under
proper safeguard. . . . Non-Jewish opinion would, I think, be conciliated
if a statement were made simultaneously that the Holy Places in Jerusalem and vicinity would be internationalized, or at any rate not be placed
under entirely Jewish control.*

Dr. Weizmann, President of the English Zionist Federation
*It is my deep conviction that the declaration framed by His Majesty's
Government will, when announced, be received with joy and gratitude
by the vast majority of the Jewish people all over the world. . . .*

*As to the wording of the declaration, may I be allowed respectfully
to suggest one or two alterations?*

*(a) Instead of "establishment," would it not be more desirable to use
the word "re-establishment"? By this small alteration the historical connection with the ancient tradition would be indicated and the whole matter
put in its true light. . . .*

*(b) The last lines of the declaration could easily be interpreted by
ill-wishers as implying the idea that, with the re-establishment of the
Jewish national home, only those Jews will have a right to claim full
citizenship in the country of their birth who in addition to being loyal and
law-abiding citizens would also totally dissociate themselves from the
Jewish national home, showing no interest in, or sympathy with, its successful development. This unnatural demand is surely not in the mind of
His Majesty's Government and in order to avoid any misunderstanding
I respectfully suggest that the part of the declaration in question be replaced by the following words: "the rights and political status enjoyed by
Jews in any other country of which they are loyal citizens."*

(c) May I also suggest "Jewish people" instead of "Jewish race"?

Mr. Nahum Sokolow, Chief London Representative of the Zionist Organisation
I received with profound pleasure and satisfaction your letter of the 6th instant, and I wish to express to His Majesty's Government the deep gratitude of the Zionist Organization for the spirit of sympathy and justice manifested in the proposed declaration. . . .

His Majesty's Government is aware that it is the Zionist movement which is responsible for such steps as have been taken towards the realization of Jewish national aims in Palestine, and that the future prosecution of these aims, with the invaluable aid which His Majesty's Government so generously offers, will be the particular charge of the representatives of the Zionist movement. The safeguards mentioned in the draft are not open to any objections, since they are and always have been regarded by Zionists as a matter of course.

Sir Philip Magnus, M.P.
In replying to your letter of the 6th October I do not gather that I am expected to distinguish my views as a Jew from those I hold as a British subject. Indeed, it is not necessary, even if it were possible. For I agree with the late Chief Rabbi, Dr. Hermann Adler, that "ever since the conquest of Palestine by the Romans we have ceased to be a body politic," that "the great bond that unites Israel is not one of race but the bond of a common religion," and that we have no national aspirations apart from those of the country of our birth. . . . I cannot agree that the Jews regard themselves as a nation, and the term "national" as applied to a community of Jews in Palestine or elsewhere seems to me to beg the question between Zionists and their opponents, and should, I suggest, be withdrawn from the proposed formula. Indeed, the inclusion in the terms of the declaration of the words "a national home for the Jewish race" seems to me both undesirable and inferentially inaccurate. . . . It is essential . . . that any privileges granted to the Jews should be shared by their fellow-citizens of other creeds. . . .

Mr. C. G. Montefiore, President of the Anglo-Jewish Association
For the true well-being of the Jewish race emancipation and liberty in the countries of the world are a thousand times more important than a "home." In any case only a small fraction of the Jews could be collected together in Palestine. . . .

I and my friends do not desire to impede colonization and immigration into Palestine, on the contrary we desire to obtain free facilities for them. We are in favour of local autonomy where ever the conditions allow it. Whoever the suzerain Power of Palestine may be, we are in favour of the Jews, when their numbers permit it, ultimately obtaining the power which any large majority may justly claim.

Mr. L. L. Cohen, Chairman Jewish Board of Guardians
The establishment of a "national home for the Jewish race" in Palestine, presupposes that the Jews are a nation, which I deny, and that they are homeless, which implies that, in the countries where they enjoy religious liberty and the full rights of citizenship, they are separate entities, un-identified with the interests of the nations of which they form parts, an implication which I repudiate.[17]

Meanwhile numbers of letters from Jews in Britain and abroad pressing for the declaration were received at the Foreign Office. Ronald Graham addressed a memorandum to Mr. Balfour regretting the Cabinet's delay in giving an assurance to the Zionists as this delay would throw them into the arms of the Germans. The moment, he said, this assurance is granted the Zionist Jews are prepared to start an active pro-Ally propaganda throughout the world.[18]

The War Cabinet met on 31 October and according to the Minutes:

The Secretary of State for Foreign Affairs [Balfour] stated that he gathered that every one was now agreed that, from a purely diplomatic and political point of view, it was desirable that some declaration favourable to the aspirations of the Jewish nationalists should now be made. The vast majority of Jews in Russia and America, as, indeed, all over the world, now appeared to be favourable to Zionism. If we could make a declaration favourable to such an ideal, we should be able to carry on extremely useful propaganda both in Russia and America. He gathered that the main arguments still put forward against Zionism were twofold:

(a) That Palestine was inadequate to form a home for either the Jewish or any other people.

(b) The difficulty felt with regard to the future position of Jews in Western countries.

With regard to the first, he understood that there were considerable differences of opinion among experts regarding the possibility of settling any large population in Palestine, but he was informed that, if Palestine were scientifically developed a very much larger population could be sustained than had existed during the period of Turkish misrule. As to the meaning of the words "national home" to which the Zionists attach so much importance, he understood it to mean some form of British, American, or other protectorate, under which full facilities would be given to the Jews to work out their own salvation and to build up, by means of education, agriculture, and industry, a real centre of national culture and

[17] PRO. CAB. 24/4.
[18] PRO. FO. 371/3054.

focus of national life. It did not necessarily involve the early establishment of an independent Jewish State, which was a matter for gradual development in accordance with the ordinary laws of political evolution.

With regard to the second point, he felt that so far from Zionism hindering the process of assimilation in Western countries, the truer parallel was to be found in the position of an Englishman who leaves his country to establish a permanent home in the United States. In the latter case there was no difficulty in the Englishman or his children becoming full nationals of the United States, whereas, in the present position of Jewry the assimilation was often felt to be incomplete, and any danger of a double allegiance or non-national outlook would be eliminated.

Lord Curzon stated that he admitted the force of the diplomatic arguments in favour of expressing sympathy and agreed that the bulk of the Jews held Zionist rather than anti-Zionist opinions. He added that he did not agree with the attitude taken up by Mr. Montagu. On the other hand he could not share the optimistic view held regarding the future of Palestine. These views were not merely the result of his own personal experiences of travel in that country, but of careful investigation from persons who had lived for many years in the country. He feared that by the suggested declaration we should be raising false expectations which could never be realized. He attached great importance to the necessity of retaining the Christian and Moslem Holy Places in Jerusalem and Bethlehem, and, if this were to be effectively done, he did not see how the Jewish people could have a political capital in Palestine. However, he recognized that some expression of sympathy with Jewish aspirations would be a valuable adjunct to our propaganda, though he thought that we should be guarded in the language used in giving expression to such sympathy.

The War Cabinet authorized:

The Secretary of State for Foreign Affairs to take a suitable opportunity for making the following declaration of sympathy with the Zionist aspirations:

His Majesty's Government view with favour the establishment in Palestine of a national home for the Jewish people, and will use their best endeavours to facilitate the achievement of this object, it being clearly understood that nothing shall be done which may prejudice the civil and religious rights of the existing non-Jewish communities in Palestine, or the rights and political status enjoyed by Jews in any other country.[19]

The letter embodying this declaration was sent by Balfour to Lord Rothschild on November 2, 1917.

[19] PRO. CAB. 23/4.

Palestine 1918

The Foreign Office set up a special branch for Jewish propaganda within the Department of Information under the control "of a very active Zionist propagandist named A. Hyamson, whose business it is to produce suitable literature and ultimately as soon as can be arranged, look after its distribution."[20] Propaganda material was distributed to virtually every known Jewish community in the world through local Zionist societies and other intermediaries.[21] Leaflets containing the text of the Balfour Declaration were dropped over German and Austrian territory: pamphlets in Yiddish were circulated to Jewish troops in Central European armies—after the capture of Jerusalem—which read: "Jerusalem has fallen! The hour of Jewish redemption has arrived. . . . Palestine must be the national home of the Jewish people once more. . . . The Allies are giving the Land of Israel to the people of Israel. Every loyal Jewish heart is now filled with joy for this great victory. Will you join them and help to build a Jewish homeland in Palestine? . . . Stop fighting the Allies, who are fighting for you, for all the Jews, for the freedom of all the small nations. Remember! An Allied victory means the Jewish people's return to Zion. . . ."[22]

Meanwhile the war against the Turks in Palestine was gradually proving successful. Sherif Hussein had raised the Arab revolt in June 1916. In December of that year the British occupied el Arish. In March 1917 their attack on Gaza failed and the British commander, Sir Archibald Murray, was replaced by General Allenby. The Arabs captured Aqaba in July 1917: Allenby's forces took Beersheba in October, then Jaffa, and, on December 9, 1917, captured Jerusalem. After the taking of Jerusalem Allenby issued a proclamation in which he stated that:

> . . . The object of war in the East on the part of Great Britain was the complete and final liberation of all peoples formerly oppressed by the Turks and the establishment of national governments and administrations in those countries deriving authority from the initiative and free will of those people themselves. . . .[23]

[20] PRO. FO. 395/202.
[21] Howard Sacher, *The Emergence of the Middle East,* p. 215.
[22] Aharon Cohen, *Israel and the Arab World,* p. 124.
[23] Quoted in Hansard, 21 June 1922.

FIGURE 5. General Allenby entering Jerusalem, 1917. (Courtesy, The Central Zionist Archives)

Allenby set up a military administration in the captured area of Palestine, known as Occupied Enemy Territory Administration or OETA, and General Gilbert Clayton, who had been involved in the negotiations with Sherif Hussein, was appointed chief political officer with his headquarters in Cairo. Publicity for the Balfour Declaration was not undertaken in Palestine, but the Arabs were aware of Zionist activity as Clayton reported to the Foreign Office on 20 December:

> *The Arabs are still nervous and feel that Zionist movement is progressing at a pace which threatens their interest. Discussions and intercourse with Jews will doubtless tend to calm their fears, provided latter act up to liberal principles laid down by Jewish leaders in London.*[24]

On January 14, 1918, Clayton reported:

> *In Palestine task of restoring normal conditions and general relief at expulsion of Turks still precludes any great preoccupation in political questions, but local Arabs still evince some uneasiness at Zionist activity and fear a Jewish government of Palestine as eventual result. . . .*[25]

Back in London the Middle East Committee, set up by the War Cabinet, which dealt with the affairs of Palestine, met on January 19. It consisted of Curzon—the chairman—Balfour, Hardinge, Sir Mark Sykes, negotiator of the Sykes-Picot Agreement, Major-General Sir G. M. W. Macdonogh—director of military intelligence—Lord Islington (formerly Sir John Dickson-Poynder who had been undersecretary of state for India), Mr. Shuckburgh (later Sir John Shuckburgh), who was a secretary in the Political Department of the India Office, and Captain the Hon. William Ormsby-Gore, M.P., the committee's secretary who was to become closely involved with the affairs of Palestine.

The committee discussed sending a Zionist Commission to Palestine, the need for which appeared to the members to be urgent for the following reasons:

> *. . . (1) The important political results that had accrued from the declaration of His Majesty's Government to the Zionists and the need for putting the assurance given in this declaration into practice.*

[24] PRO. FO. 371/3054.
[25] PRO. FO. 371/3391.

(2) The inadequacy of existing Zionist representation in Egypt and Palestine.

(3) The necessity of bringing the British authorities in Egypt and Palestine and the Arabs into contact with the responsible leaders of the organization in Entente countries.[26]

The despatch of the Zionist Commission was approved. Its leader was Dr. Weizmann, Levi Bianchini of Italy and Sylvain Lévi of France were members, and it was accompanied by Ormsby-Gore, with the rank of assistant political officer. Sir Reginald Wingate, high commissioner in Egypt, was informed of the decision by a telegram from the Foreign Office:

. . . Object of Commission is to carry out, subject to General Allenby's authority, any steps required to give effect to Government declaration in favour of the establishment in Palestine of a National Home for the Jewish people.

Should military exigencies permit, foundation of Jewish University, Medical School, to which Jewish world attaches importance and for which large sums are coming in, might be laid. Government favours this project.

Among the most important functions of the Commission will be the establishment of good relations with the Arabs and other non-Jewish communities in Palestine, and to establish the Commission as the link between the Military Authorities and the Jewish population and Jewish interests in Palestine.

It is most important that everything should be done to obtain authority for the Commission in the eyes of the Jewish world, and at the same time allay Arab suspicions regarding the true aims of Zionism. . . .[27]

In order to explain the commission to the Arabs and other communities Sir Mark Sykes wrote to the Syria Welfare Committee. This had been set up by General Clayton in Cairo and it included Arabs, Zionists, and Armenians.

Sykes at this time was a member of the team which served as a "brains trust" for the prime minister and had direct access to ministers. The team was nicknamed "the garden suburb" because it was housed in huts in the garden of No. 10 Downing Street.[28]

Weizmann later wrote of Sykes: "I cannot say enough regarding the services rendered us by Sykes. It was he who guided our work

---

[26] PRO. CAB. 27/23.
[27] PRO. CAB. 27/23.
[28] Monroe, *Britain's Moment in the Middle East*, p. 39.

into more official channels. He belonged to the secretariat of the War Cabinet, which contained, among others, Leopold Amery, Ormsby-Gore, and Ronald Storrs. If it had not been for the counsel of men like Sykes and Lord Robert Cecil we, with our inexperience in delicate diplomatic negotiations, would undoubtedly have committed many dangerous blunders."[29]

Sykes informed the Syria Welfare Committee that:

The Zionist Commission which is shortly proceeding to Egypt will be able to go into details in regard to co-operation and alliance which at this distance of time and space it is impossible to discuss.

Our mutual tasks are exceedingly difficult and require all the statesmanship and goodwill that it is possible to bring to bear.

But so much has been achieved so conciliatory a spirit has shown itself on all hands that I have confidence that the dearest wish of my life will be realized, and that is that peace and justice should at last reign from the Taurus to the Persian Gulf, and from the Mediterranean to the Persian Frontier, and all that vast area as interdependent, fiscally and politically. If one element is sacrificed or abandoned the whole fabric subsides. Short of a settlement which is satisfactory to the three peoples there are only two alternatives, Turkish tyranny or Anarchy, either the one or the other signifies that Jew, Armenian, Syrian, Mesopotamian, Palestinian and the people of the Arabian Peninsula must return to the hideous night of misery from which we strive that they shall emerge. . . .[30]

Sir Ronald Storrs, then Colonel Storrs and military governor of Jerusalem, received the commission when it reached Jerusalem on April 10. Ormsby-Gore telegraphed to Sykes:

Zionist Commission . . . officially received by Military Governor who introduced chief notables and dignitaries of the Holy City.

Commission much struck by cordiality of their reception by latter who included Grand Mufti, Father Diotallevi, the Custode representative of the Greek and Armenian convents, as well as prominent Moslem and Christian laity. The following morning a Zionist demonstration attended by between 4,000 and 5,000 people was held on summit of Mount of Scopus. . . . Dr. Weizmann replied to speeches of welcome in Hebrew and turning to me in English requested me to convey to Mr. Balfour the thanks of the meeting and of all Palestine Jewry for his historical declaration and to General Allenby an expression of assurance of loyalty and regard for his deliverance of Jerusalem thus enabling the establishment of a rule of freedom and justice for all creeds and peoples in Palestine.[31]

[29] Weizmann, *Trial and Error*, p. 230.
[30] PRO. FO. 371/3398.
[31] PRO. CAB. 27/25.

Six days after the arrival of the commission in Jerusalem, Weizmann wrote a note to Ormsby-Gore:

> *We were prepared to find a certain amount of hostility on the part of the Arabs and Syrians, based largely on misconception of our real aims, and we have always realized that one of our principal duties would be to dispel misconceptions and to endeavour to arrive at an amicable understanding with the non-Jewish elements of the population on the basis of the declared policy of His Majesty's Government. But we find among the Arabs and Syrians, or certain sections of them, a state of mind which seems to us to make useful negotiations impossible at the present moment, and so far as we are aware—though here our information may be incomplete—no official steps have been taken to bring home to the Arabs and Syrians the fact that His Majesty's Government has expressed a definite policy with regard to the future of the Jews in Palestine.*
>
> *A striking illustration of this condition of affairs occurred in Jerusalem only last week. On the 11th of April the Military Governor of Jerusalem was present at a performance in aid of a Moslem orphanage. We have seen extracts from two speeches delivered by Arabs on that occasion. . . . Both speakers used the kind of language which would be appropriate if an attempt were on foot to enslave and to ruin the Arabs of Palestine. They called on the Arab Nation to wake from its torpor, and to rise up in defence of its land, of its liberty, of its sacred places against those who were coming to rob it of everything. One speaker adjured his hearers not to sell a single inch of land. Nor is that all. Both speakers took it for granted that Palestine was and must remain a purely Arab country. In fact, a map of Palestine bearing the inscription "La Palestine Arabe" was prominently displayed. . . . While the speakers had no scruple about avowing their unmistakably anti-Jewish sentiments in the presence of the representative of the Government, the Military Governor, as far as our information goes, uttered no word to suggest that there was any discrepancy between those sentiments and the Government's policy. . . .*

Weizmann's note was forwarded to the Foreign Office on April 22 with comments by the military governor, Ronald Storrs, who wrote:

> *. . . the play was a somewhat crude allegory in which Palestine was represented as Andromeda whose chains of Turkish despotism were burst during two hours of characteristic absence of action and excess of verbosity by an Arab Perseus. . . . The play was written several years ago and could therefore hardly be said to be aimed at the Commission. In order to probe the matter yet further I sent for Mr. Hain Ben Attar, a Sephardim Jew of Moroccan origin . . . who had supplied the account of the proceedings. Mr. Ben Attar admitted that there had been no overt*

allusions to the Jews, but was still of opinion that isolated phrases could be construed into an anti-Zionist sense. . . . Mr. Ben Attar then proceeded slightly to shift his ground by telling me that none of the objectionable phrases had been pronounced until after my departure. . . . I find that here he was alluding to a poem which is stated to have been anonymously distributed in Jerusalem over a year ago . . . and which was considered by the Turks so undesirable in character that they deported Sheikh Al Tazi, the supposed author, to Konia. . . .

From the first announcement of the formation of the Zionist Commission, the Arab and Christian elements of Palestine have been labouring under grave disquietude which has not been allayed by the arrival of the gentlemen themselves. A variety of enthusiastic articles upon the future of Zionism published in many organs of the British Press have for obvious reasons wrought uneasiness and depression in the other elements of Palestine generally, and in particular, the Moslems. These feelings have been accentuated by numerous meetings of Jews. . . . On the 17th February Dr. Mekler speaking upon the geographical, agricultural, and health situation of Palestine closed his speech by attempting to show "how the Jewish people in their present state could take over the Holy Land." . . . At the beginning of March in the Hebrew Seminary Dr. Morchak delivered a speech on the return of Israel to Zion in which he elaborated a system of the future ruling of Palestine by the Jews. Such proceedings, reported perhaps as inaccurately to Moslems as their Arab play had been to the Zionists, caused no little despondency and searchings of heart and produced, as might have been expected, the usual ineffectual rejoinders in the shape of Moslem and Christian Land Unions for the protection of the soil, with a heroic programme and no subscriptions or results. . . .

I cannot agree that, as Dr. Weizmann would seem to suggest, it is the business of the Military Authorities "to bring home to the Arabs and Syrians the fact that H.M.G. has expressed a definite policy with regard to the future of the Jews in Palestine." This has already been done by Mr. Balfour in London, and by the Press throughout the world. What is wanted is that the Zionists themselves should bring home to the Arabs and Syrians an exposition at once as accurate and conciliatory as possible of their real aims and policy in the country. . . .

Speaking myself as a convinced Zionist, I cannot help thinking that the Commission are lacking in a sense of the dramatic actuality. Palestine, up to now a Moslem country, has fallen into the hands of a Christian Power which on the eve of its conquest announced that a considerable portion of its land is to be handed over for colonization purposes to a nowhere very popular people. The dispatch of a Commission of these people is subsequently announced. . . . From the announcement in the British Press until this moment there has been no sign of a hostile demonstration public or private against a project which if we may imagine England for Palestine can hardly open for the inhabitants the beatific vision of a new Heaven and a new Earth. The Commission was warned in Cairo of the numerous and grave misconceptions with which their enterprise was regarded and strongly advised to make a public pronouncement to put an end to those misconceptions. No such pronouncement has yet been made; and yet an inaccurate and unchecked account of an unimportant amateur performance in a small Boys School is considered a sufficient reason for asking the Commander-in-Chief to rub in to the people for whose moral and public security he is responsible full, and almost certainly unwelcome, details of His Majesty's Government's Zionist policy which have never yet been disclosed to the general public, nor, so far as I am aware, to any living soul. . . .[32]

Howard M. Sachar

AN INDUCEMENT FOR THE JEWS

In this selection from The Emergence of the Middle East: 1914–1924 *Sachar describes the complex diplomacy preceding the issuance of the Balfour Declaration. Sachar clearly demonstrates the importance of Anglo-French rivalries in the Middle East for the effective operation of Zionist diplomacy during World War I.*

Palestine and the Jews

Even as their troops were marching toward an "internationalized" Palestine, British Foreign Office and military officials shared growing misgivings about the prize their diplomacy had forfeited: the opportunity for total and unilateral control of the Holy Land. As early as March 22, 1915, months before the Sykes-Picot Agreement was even mooted, T. E. Lawrence had expressed Cairo's well-nourished hope "that we can rush up to Damascus, and biff the French out of all hope of Syria." He recalled later: "For my part, I did not tell Brémond (but he knew) that I meant to defeat his efforts and to take the Arabs soon into Damascus." The ambition to exert the dominating influence in the Levant became all but obsessive when, in the spring of 1917, the British were marshaling tens of thousands of their own

[32] PRO. FO. 371/3398.

From *The Emergence of the Middle East: 1914–1924* by Howard M. Sachar, pp. 187–189, 192–203, 208–222. Copyright © 1969 by Howard M. Sachar. Reprinted by permission of Alfred A. Knopf, Inc. and Penguin Books, Ltd.

men for the offensive against Palestine. For that reason the War Cabinet flatly vetoed repeated French demands to participate in the enterprise. Indeed, Britain's intention to reverse the Sykes-Picot Agreement hardened after her realization that the treaty permitted France to maintain its competitive prewar railroad concession in southern Palestine. On April 19 a special Committee on Territorial Terms of Peace under the chairmanship of Curzon reevaluated the strategic vulnerability of the Suez Canal, and all but unanimously emphasized the importance of unilateral British control in Palestine after the war. Two days later, Lloyd George informed Lord Bertie, his ambassador in Paris, that "the French will have to accept our Protectorate over Palestine." The prime minister noted later that an international regime in the Holy Land "would be quite intolerable to ourselves. . . . Palestine is really the strategic buffer of Egypt." A Foreign Office memorandum stated the issue succinctly: "The presence of a foreign Power in Palestine might seriously affect the position of Great Britain both in the Suez Canal and in adjacent Arab areas."

That was the essence of the issue. For several decades, in truth, London had been acutely sensitive to Palestine's strategic importance. Beginning in the 1890s, the British agent-general in Cairo had conducted a resolute, if oblique, political campaign to get a foothold in the Holy Land. His approach (not altogether successful) was to redefine Egypt's Sinai boundaries at the expense of Ottoman Palestine. Similarly, in the Anglo-French-German agreements of 1914 that allocated areas for railroad construction in the Ottoman Empire, the British had insisted on the privilege of a rail link between the Persian Gulf and Suez via Palestine's Negev. Most conclusively of all, Djemal's two Sinai expeditions appeared to confirm Palestine's importance as a staging base for offensives against the canal. In the hands of a major European power, such military value would unquestionably be compounded many times. Nevertheless, even with this consideration in mind, Whitehall had been prepared as late as 1916 to settle for a "condominium" in the Holy Land. Perhaps the compromise was inevitable at a time when the British had been thrust back onto the defensive in the Middle East, licking their wounds after Gallipoli and Kut. It was also the period when the French were carrying the heaviest burden of the struggle on the Western front. In any case, by the terms of the Sykes-Picot Agreement, the British had taken care to guard their crucial rail interests in southern Palestine and Haifa Bay, and thus to preclude the threat of direct French access to the Sinai Peninsula.

As the months passed, however, the prospect of a French military enclave in Palestine, even as an integral part of an Allied condominium, became increasingly unpalatable to London. The idea was to become altogether unacceptable when Allenby launched his full-scale invasion of the Holy Land and planted his troops on the country's soil. Unfortunately for Great Britain, the old equation of possession with nine points of the law was hardly an appropriate basis for dealings between wartime partners. A more impressively "idealistic" rationale would still have been preferred at a time when Sir Mark Sykes's signature was barely dry on the 1916 agreement with Georges-Picot. Initially Whitehall failed to appreciate that such a rationale already existed. It had been supplied by a rather unlikely source, the Jews, ostensibly the most internationalist of all Europe's peoples. Actually the Jews had provided an interesting opportunity for a foothold in Palestine as early as 1902. In October of that year, Theodor Herzl, founder of the modern Zionist movement, first approached British Colonial Secretary Chamberlain with a proposal for a charter of Jewish settlement in el Arish in the eastern Sinai Peninsula. An astute diplomat, Herzl suggested to Chamberlain that once the Jews were in el Arish under the Union Jack, Palestine, too, would be drawn into the British sphere of influence. Nothing came of the plan, since it was rejected by Lord Cromer, the British agent-general in Cairo. But the episode offered the British their first momentary glimpse of a volatile, highly charged nationalism which even then was sweeping with increasing passion and momentum through a large part of the Jewish world. This folk movement was particularly vigorous in the densely packed Jewish hinterland of Eastern Europe, where some 5 million Jews lived entirely to themselves, speaking their own language, nurturing their own religion and folk mores, and responding to Gentile contempt and persecution with a reciprocal ethnic clannishness of their own.

In its literary and polemical origins, Jewish nationalism bore a

FIGURE 6. From Walter Laqueur, *A History of Zionism*, p. 85. Copyright © 1972 by Walter Laqueur. Reproduced by permission of Holt, Rinehart and Winston, Inc. and George Weidenfeld and Nicolson Ltd.

Frontier Proposals for Palestine 1892 – 1919

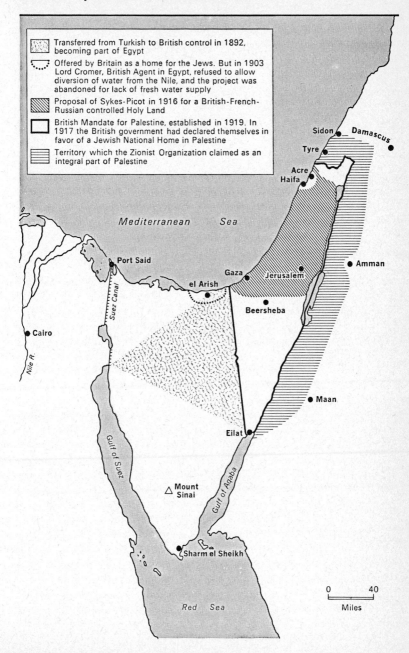

Transferred from Turkish to British control in 1892, becoming part of Egypt

Offered by Britain as a home for the Jews. But in 1903 Lord Cromer, British Agent in Egypt, refused to allow diversion of water from the Nile, and the project was abandoned for lack of fresh water supply

Proposal of Sykes-Picot in 1916 for a British-French-Russian controlled Holy Land

British Mandate for Palestine, established in 1919. In 1917 the British government had declared themselves in favor of a Jewish National Home in Palestine

Territory which the Zionist Organization claimed as an integral part of Palestine

Mediterranean Sea

Sidon
Damascus
Tyre
Acre
Haifa
Port Said
Gaza
Jerusalem
el Arish
Amman
Beersheba
Cairo
Suez Canal
Nile R.
Maan
Eilat
Gulf of Suez
Gulf of Aqaba
△ Mount Sinai
Sharm el Sheikh
Red Sea

0   40
Miles

close similarity to the romantic awakening of Balkan and other Ottoman millet peoples in the nineteenth century. Even in its physical urgency, the Jewish response to Alexander III's pogroms resembled the dynamic Bulgarian and Armenian reaction to Abdul Hamid's massacres. The uniqueness of Zionism was to be found, rather, in the homeland on which it focused.

*   *   *

By 1914, some 85,000 Jews lived in the Holy Land. Admittedly, they still lacked juridical status. In the 1908 and 1914 elections to the Ottoman Parliament, for example, not one Jew was returned as a delegate. Few Jews could so much as vote. But if the Zionists enjoyed little standing in Turkish eyes, in their own eyes they had taken great strides toward national regeneration. Their rural settlements numbered forty-three. On the coastal plain their citrus groves were earning profits for the first time. So were their shops, foundries, and printing presses in the cities. They spoke Hebrew as their daily vernacular by then, and guarded their own farms. Even the nucleus of self-government was dimly perceptible by 1914 in the grass-roots democracy of collective settlements, the federation of Judean colonies in the south, and the organization of lower Galilee in the north. The official Zionist Office in Palestine already was printing its own stamps and its own scrip. When, therefore, a Zionist leader like Chaim Weizmann . . . spoke to British statesmen of a Jewish national home, he was not speculating about the future alone. He also had in mind the tangible accomplishments of the present.

Yet the war, which opened new vistas for Zionist diplomacy on the world scene, very nearly throttled the Jewish settlement in Palestine itself. Most of the Jews settled there by 1914 were still not Ottoman subjects, and had come to depend upon the European consuls to ensure their elementary physical security. With the abolition of the Capitulations, that assurance was now gone. On December 17, 1914, Beha-a-Din, the Turkish governor of Jaffa, ordered the 6,000 Russian Jews who lived in his port city to be immediately expelled from the country. In terror of future deportations, Jewish communal leaders urged all Jews then domiciled in Palestine to apply immediately for Ottoman citizenship. Offices for that purpose were opened throughout the country, even at the home of the chief rabbi of Jerusalem. Within several weeks an effective naturalization campaign had avoided at least the physical danger of mass expulsion. A number of Jewish officials, including the Zionist Labor spokesman David Ben-Gurion and Yitzhak Ben-Zvi, sought to go further and petitioned the Ottoman authorities for the right to establish a Jewish militia to share in the defense of the country. The appeal was curtly rejected, an omen of things to come.

Early in 1915, Beha-a-Din was appointed to the staff of Djemal Pasha, as "secretary of Jewish affairs." A remorseless enemy of Zionism and Arab nationalism alike, the former governor of Jaffa launched a systematic attack on the entire Jewish redemptive effort in the Holy Land. Zionist newspapers, clubhouses, and schools were closed down. Hebrew posters and stamps were forbidden, Zionist flags confiscated. All Zionist public activities were banned. The Anglo-Palestine Bank was closed. Even more ominously, Jewish land titles were called into question, and Arabs were encouraged to pillage Jewish colonies. When Ben-Gurion and Ben-Zvi ventured to protest these measures, they and other Zionist leaders were summarily exiled.

It was not the hostility of the Ottoman authorities alone that threatened the security of Palestine Jewry. The "normal" hardships of war were bad enough. The British naval blockade choked off philanthropic remittances and food imports from abroad. The citrus crop withered and died on the trees, and with it the basis of the Jewish agricultural economy. Ruthless and arbitrary Turkish requisitions of animals and foodstuffs intensified the suffering, reducing many formerly prosperous Jewish and Arab families to maize grits as their basic staple and to flint and steel for fire. By the end of 1915, the Jews of Palestine, no less than the Arabs of the entire Levant area, were critically debilitated by hunger and disease. Still, remarkably, widespread starvation was avoided. The intervention of two influential Western Jews proved especially timely. One was Dr. Arthur Ruppin, director of the Zionist office in Jaffa, a German citizen who was permitted by the Ottoman authorities to distribute funds received from German Jewish sources. Far more important was the intercession of the American ambassador to Turkey, Henry Morgenthau. As a Jew, Morgenthau felt it necessary to lean far over backward in the studied impartiality and mildness of his protests. On the other hand, as the representative of a powerful neutral country, enjoying the full personal support of President Wilson, Morgenthau was bound to be taken seriously in his concern for the fate of the Jewish minority. It was principally at Morgenthau's request that Djemal gradually eased his repressive measures during the spring of 1915 and ended the wave of expulsions and arrests. The American ambassador even secured permission for American cruisers to bring occasional relief shipments of food and money to Palestine. This uncertain trickle of supplies and funds from abroad enabled the Palestine Jewish community to survive the war, however precariously.

Yet the fundamental brutality of Ottoman officials was neither forgotten nor forgiven by many hundreds of younger Jews who had been driven into exile during the early months of war. Interned in Alexandria, they petitioned the British authorities for the right to serve as a Jewish legion in an offensive against the Turks in Palestine. Sir Henry McMahon, the high commissioner in Cairo, approved the idea. The émigrés were promptly organized into a special transportation unit, the Zion Mule Corps. Their assignment was not Palestine, however, but the impending Dardanelles campaign. Although a British officer, Lieutenant Colonel John Patterson, was placed in charge of this unit, its animating spirit was Patterson's deputy, Captain Joseph Trumpeldor. A seasoned veteran of the Russian army, decorated for his heroism in the Russo-Japanese War, in which he lost an arm, Trumpeldor in recent years had been serving as a farmer-pioneer on a collective settlement in northern Palestine. When the world war began, he departed for Alexandria and volunteered his services to the British army. Patterson found him indispensable now in organizing the new Jewish force.

Its numbers were not large. By the end of August 1915, about 500 Palestinian and Egyptian Jews had joined the Zion Mule Corps. The recruits took the military oath in the presence of the chief rabbi of Alexandria, who enjoined them to be loyal and devoted soldiers of the "exalted British Government." The men were not informed until the last moment that they were going to Gallipoli. Upon being landed at Helles beach, the Corps performed creditably enough, the men leading their supply mules to the front trenches through heavy fire. Trumpeldor himself was wounded. Many other casualties were suffered, but were immediately replaced by new Jewish volunteers. The effort was apparently unavailing either for the Jews or the British. With the end of the Gallipoli campaign, the order came on December 28, 1915, for the Zion Mule Corps to be disbanded. Unrealized at the time, however, the first tentative step in Anglo-Zionist collaboration had already been taken.

The Origins of the Anglo-Zionist Alliance

Following the outbreak of the war, the leadership of the World Zionist Organization painstakingly avoided suspicion of collaboration with any of the belligerent nations. A special "Bureau for Zionist Affairs" was established in neutral Copenhagen to maintain contact with Jewish communities among both the Central Powers and the Entente. Within individual countries, too, local Zionist federations patriotically identified themselves with the respective national war efforts. Thus, the German Zionists courted officials in Berlin, urging the government to take the initiative in establishing a Jewish homeland in Palestine—which then would surely form a "bastion" of German influence in that part of the world. The Wilhelmstrasse rejected these overtures; it was not prepared to alienate its Turkish ally by making a public statement of support for Jewish nationalism. Elsewhere, the government of France was aware that Herzl, Wolffsohn, and other early Zionist leaders were Central European Jews by training and culture, if not by birth, and Paris therefore suspected Jewish nationalism as "the advance guard of German influence." In Russia, in whose Jewish community Zionism was a considerably more powerful movement than in any other, the czarist government was hardly likely to evince any sympathy for Jewish nationalism at a time when it was driving half a million Jews like cattle into the Russian interior. England appeared an even less likely source of help for the Zionist cause. Its Jewish community of a quarter million consisted largely of Russian immigrants. Although their sympathies were Zionist, most of the newcomers were far too poor and inchoate to exert any influence in public or communal affairs. Conversely, the older, acculturated, and well-established Jewish families were largely unsympathetic to Jewish nationalism. As a consequence, the British government was perhaps less aware of the Zionist renaissance in Palestine than that of any other major power.

Ironically enough, nevertheless, within two years after the outbreak of the war, the Zionist connection with official circles was stronger in England than in any other nation. One reason, although not the exclusive one, was the extraordinarily persuasive group of

Zionist leaders who happened to be living in England at the time. Their acknowledged spokesman was Chaim Weizmann, then in his early forties, a reader in chemistry at the University of Manchester. Russian-born, and university-trained in Switzerland, Weizmann was an extraordinarily lucid and convincing propagandist. He soon won a loyal following for the Zionist cause among a number of distinguished personalities in the Anglo-Jewish community. Perhaps the most influential of these after Weizmann himself was Herbert Samuel, a president of the local government board and later home secretary in the Asquith government. Samuel's concept was not simply of a Jewish homeland, but of a Jewish homeland under a British protectorate in Palestine, an arrangement that would conveniently forestall occupation of Palestine by any other power. He was the first to moot this idea to Asquith and Sir Edward Grey, both of whom viewed it with some reserve. "I confess," Asquith wrote later, "I am not attracted by the proposed addition to our responsibilities, but it is a curious illustration of Dizzy's [Disraeli's] favorite maxim that 'race is everything' to find this almost lyrical outburst proceeding from the well-ordered and methodical brain of H. S."

Samuel persisted, however, and, with others, introduced Weizmann to several luminaries of the Establishment. These included Charles P. Scott, editor of the Manchester *Guardian,* and Henry Wickham Steed, editor of the London *Times*, both of whom became devoted advocates of the Zionist cause. Through them, too, Weizmann met several of the key political figures of the day: Lloyd George, Winston Churchill, Lord Robert Cecil. Indeed, Weizmann's relationship with these men was strengthened by a vital service that he performed for the British Admiralty. In March 1916, he was summoned to London to help solve the shortage of acetone, the solvent used in making the naval explosive cordite. It required two years of experimentation, but Weizmann eventually accomplished the task by devising an ingenious process of fermentation. During those two years, moreover, the friendships Weizmann had made earlier were cemented on the highest level. As always, the force of the man's personality was almost irresistible. He was physically imposing, for one thing, the brow of his massive bald head finely etched with veins, his eyes shrewd and piercing, his mustache and goatee elegant, his clothing always superbly tailored. A slight Russian accent lent a touch of exoticism to Weizmann's perfect command of the English language. "As a speaker," wrote Sir Ronald Storrs later, "[he] was almost frighten-ingly convincing. . . ." Mark Sykes recalled: "I sometimes wonder whether his fellow Jews realize how deeply he impressed us Gentiles by his heroic, his Maccabean quality."

Weizmann's efforts were buttressed by other advantages. One was the almost mystical veneration with which many devout Anglo-Saxon (or Welsh or Scottish) Protestants regarded the Old Testament tradi-tions, the Children of Israel, and particularly the Holy Land itself. Lloyd George recalled that in his first meeting with Weizmann, in December 1914, place names of Palestine were mentioned that were "more familiar to me than those of the Western front." Balfour, too, had evinced a lifelong interest in the Holy Land and its history; like Lloyd George and Smuts, he felt deeply Christianity's debt to the Jews. That debt was compounded not merely by Weizmann's per-sonal services to the Allied war effort, but also by his uncompromis-ing devotion to Britain, his public and repeated insistence that the fate of Zionism was inexorably linked to that of the Allies. Thus, Weizmann's letter severing relations with the "neutralist" Zionist Bureau in Copenhagen was kept by Scotland Yard (unknown to Weiz-mann) and certainly influenced the authorities as much in his favor as did his scientific research for the admiralty.

Against this background of Anglo-Zionist cordiality, Weizmann's allusions to a "British protectorate over a Jewish homeland" struck an increasingly responsive chord among government officials. The basic moment of reappraisal in Middle Eastern policy came in De-cember 1916, when Lloyd George and Balfour succeeded Asquith and Grey as prime minister and foreign secretary. If, as the new government recognized, the Sykes-Picot Agreement was no longer a sufficiently watertight safeguard for British interests in Palestine, then perhaps the Jews as a client people might be as useful an opening wedge for England as the Lebanese Christians for France or the Armenians for Russia. The proposal was forthrightly advocated by Lord Milner, Lloyd George's closest friend and collaborator in the War Cabinet, by Lord Robert Cecil, undersecretary for foreign affairs, by Philip Kerr, the prime minister's personal adviser on foreign policy (later ambassador to the United States), and, perhaps most im-portantly, by the three young men who served as the Middle East specialists of the War Cabinet secretariat: Sir Mark Sykes, Leopold Amery, and David Ormsby-Gore (Lord Harlech). Sykes was the most influential of this group, the man who served as "marriage broker" in the progressively intimate relationship between the British government and the Zionist leadership.

This was a strange role for Sykes, who really never cared much for Jews at all. His Zionism stemmed in part from personal snobbery, a dislike of the "hyphenated" and "diluted" Jews who were beginning to make their way in English society. In truth, Sykes was unshakably convinced that the Jews were incapable of becoming a "normal" people until they produced "a virtuous and simple agrarian population" rather than, as he saw it, financiers, cosmopolitans, and radicals (in some degree, this was also a Zionist argument). During his travels in Palestine, Sykes had come to admire the Zionist colonies and to recognize their potential value as a rejuvenating force among the Jewish people. Plainly, however, more than concern for the future of the Jews animated Sykes's emerging Zionism. Although initially reluctant to upset the 1915 agreement with France, by autumn of the following year he had reluctantly come to share his colleagues' ambitions for a revisionist imperial policy in the Middle East. Thus, the chain of liberated national groups (Armenians, Arabs, Greeks) whom Sykes envisioned as Britain's logical Middle Eastern allies against the Turks would necessarily include the Zionist Jews. The idea did not spring full-blown from his own mind. Rather, it was suggested to him in October 1916 by one James Malcolm, a Persian-born Armenian who had been raised in England, and whose family maintained intimate connections with Jews. Malcolm attached himself to the Zionist cause early, partly out of genuine conviction, and partly in the hope, too, "that Jewish haute finance will help the Armenians. . . ." Through Malcolm, Sykes met Weizmann. After that, it became Sykes's mission in life to wed Zionist and British interests.

Time now became a crucial factor, for by the opening days of 1917 the British military offensive in Palestine was approaching its planned fulfillment. On February 7, Sykes met with the key Jewish leaders and hinted that the government was prepared to view favorably a Zionist solution to the Palestine question. Obviously, Sykes was not in a position to reveal the existence of the Sykes-Picot Agreement and the inhibition that this treaty placed on the cabinet's freedom of action. He observed simply that the Zionists themselves would have to take the initiative in persuading the Allied governments of the need for a Jewish homeland and in making evident to them the Zionist preference for a British protectorate. Weizmann and the others agreed. They set about immediately presenting their case in Paris and Rome. The effort was not unsuccessful. Both the French and the Italians expressed a friendly interest in the Jewish homeland, although they remained noncommittal on the question of British patronage. All the while Sykes, in the background, carefully stage-managed the negotiations. Nahum Sokolow, Weizmann's most intimate collaborator and the Zionist representative in these Allied discussions, wrote later:

> . . . As I was crossing the Quai d'Orsay on my return from the Foreign Ministry I came across Sykes. He had not had the patience to wait. We walked on together, and I gave him an outline of the proceedings. This did not satisfy him; he studied every detail; I had to give him full notes and he drew up a minute report. "That's a good day's work," he said with shining eyes. The second [meeting] was a day in April, 1917, in Rome. Sykes had been there before me and could not wait my arrival. He had gone to the East. I put up at the hotel; Sykes had ordered rooms for me. I went to the British Embassy; letters and instructions from Sykes were waiting for me there. I went to the Italian Government Offices; Sykes had been there, too; then to the Vatican, where Sykes again prepared my way.

The other Allies were hardly unaware of what Britain was up to. On April 6, 1918, Sykes actually informed Georges-Picot point-blank that Britain's military efforts in Palestine would have to be taken into account at the peace conference. "[Picot] is convinced," Poincaré wrote in his diary on April 17, "that in London our agreements are now considered null and void. British troops will enter Syria from the south and disperse our supporters." Neither were the Zionists ignorant of their function as an extension of British policy. Indeed, they welcomed the role, for the support and friendship of this mighty imperial power was now all but official. Precisely for that reason, Weizmann and the others, impatient for a public statement from the War Cabinet, were mystified that support continually fell just short of a public commitment. They knew nothing of the prior understanding with France, of course. "It was *not* from [Sykes] that we learned of the existence of the agreement," Weizmann recalled, "and months passed . . . before we understood what it was that blocked our progress." Charles P. Scott of the Manchester *Guardian* was the first to uncover the details of the Sykes-Picot understanding, and he immediately informed Weizmann. The Zionists were appalled. Evidently the disposition of Palestine was to have been a joint one between France and Britain all along. When Weizmann confronted Lord Robert Cecil with this information, the undersecretary neither confirmed nor denied it, although he warmly reiterated the government's sympathy for Zionism. And then, for the first time, Cecil suggested that perhaps more yet could be done in persuading the cabinet officially to declare the identity of British and Zionist goals, in this fashion undermining objections to a revision of the Sykes-Picot Agreement. It would be helpful, the undersecretary observed, if Zionists not simply in England but throughout the world should openly express themselves in favor of a British protectorate in the Holy Land. The implication was clear, too, that it would be no less useful if Jews throughout the world would use their influence generally on behalf of the Allied cause.

The *Quid Pro Quo* of Jewish Friendship

The hoary and tenacious myth of the power and wealth of world Jewry extended back to the Baroque Era, when Jewish court bankers functioned as dependable supporters of the absolutist dynasties. It was regarded with equal solemnity in the nineteenth century, when as astute a statesman as Palmerston could importune the Ottoman government to allow large-scale Jewish settlement in Palestine "because the wealth they would bring with them would increase the resources of the Sultan's dominions, and . . . would be a check upon any future evil designs of Mehemet Ali or his successor. . . ." It was taken no less seriously in the twentieth century. In February 1916, Sykes could write Georges-Picot: "If the great force of Judaism feels that its aspirations are not only considered but in a fair way to realisation, then there is hope of an ordered and developed Arabia and Middle East." Nearly all the major belligerent governments shared this awe for the—essentially legendary—power of world Jewry. It was significant that both Germany and France included Jewish "advisers" among their wartime missions to the United States, men ostensibly with special connections to help mobilize American Jewish support for their respective causes.

Lloyd George, too, expressed the prevailing conviction of Jewish "influence" in other lands, notably in the United States, where several powerful Jewish leaders were alleged to be inhibiting the American government from pulling its weight in the war. The notion was entirely spurious; but that was less important than what the prime minister believed. And Lloyd George's beliefs in 1917 were conditioned by the worst crisis of the war: Russia virtually out of action, France exhausted, Italy demoralized after Caporetto, German submarines taking a fearful toll of Allied shipping, not a single American division yet in the trenches. The need to exploit America's resources many times over, to keep Russia in the war, was all but overpowering. "In the solution of these two problems," Lloyd George wrote, "public opinion in Russia and America played a great part, and we had every reason . . . to believe that in both countries the friendliness or hostility of the Jewish race might make a considerable difference." Actually, the attitude of Jews was a negligible factor in both Russia and the United States. Weizmann must have suspected this; but he was willing at least to cultivate Jewish support in other lands for the much more limited cause of a British protectorate over a Zionist homeland. Even here his efforts were largely wasted. In the case of the United States, he was kicking at an open door. The country had already entered the war, the nationalist passions against the kaiser were by then well inflamed; Jewish influence, or lack of it, was no longer relevant. Until very shortly before, too, the Russian Zionist leadership's attitude toward the Entente had been poisoned by a grim and uncompromising hatred of the czarist regime and all that czarism meant in terms of Russian-Jewish suffering.

* * *

Faced with . . . equivocation at home and abroad, Weizmann and his colleagues might have proceeded far more cautiously in their effort to extract a pro-Zionist declaration from the British government. But changing circumstances were a relentless prod. Weizmann's knowledge of the Sykes-Picot Agreement convinced him that any danger had to be risked to avoid the dismemberment of Palestine and its Jewish settlement into disjointed and unwieldy zones of conflicting sovereignties. "This arrangement embodies all the faults of an Anglo-French and an international settlement," he protested angrily to Cecil on April 25, "and is aggravated by the fact that Palestine is cut up into two halves and the Jewish colonizing effort, which has been going on before the war for more than thirty years, is thus annihilated. . . ." Moreover, Allenby's Palestine offensive was imminent, and Weizmann sensed the urgent need for a government declaration strongly implying unilateral British control over the Holy Land. The Zionist leader's impatience was intensified by another factor. On May 24, 1917, several eminent Jewish communal leaders published a statement in the London *Times* violently attacking the Zionist position. These men were in turn repudiated by their own constituents, and by the *Times* itself, in subsequent published correspondence. But the exposure of an apparent schism within the Jewish community made it imperative for the Zionists and the government alike that the issue be resolved quickly.

The remote possibility existed, too, that the Turks still would prefer to extricate themselves from the war, and thus avoid the partition of their empire. Henry Morgenthau was convinced that such a possibility might usefully be explored with his own "reliable" Ottoman sources. When the former ambassador proposed to his government in May 1917 that he embark upon negotiations with certain "intermediaries" in Switzerland, Secretary of State Robert Lansing approved. Lansing suggested, however, that the mission ought to have a "cover." Eventually a ruse was devised by which Morgenthau would sail for Europe in June 1917 ostensibly to discuss the fate of Palestine Jewry with his "fellow Zionists." The British government, informed of the mission's real purpose, reacted coldly; the eve of Allenby's invasion was hardly the moment to give the Turks a way out of the war. The Zionists shared these misgivings. Thus, at the request of the Foreign Office, Weizmann agreed to intercept Morgenthau in Gibraltar. The extraordinary meeting took place. In a lengthy and occasionally heated interview, the Zionist leader bluntly warned Morgenthau that the chances of actual peace with the Turks were nil, and that indeed the British government wanted no part of the scheme and would do its best to scuttle it. Morgenthau was chagrined, but finally convinced. He passed another six weeks in aimless discussions with his "contacts" in Switzerland and then returned to the United States.

Weizmann, meanwhile, visiting Balfour on July 17, warned the foreign secretary that the risks of delay were mounting, and that an official declaration of governmental support for a Jewish homeland could no longer safely be delayed. Balfour did not have to be convinced. As early as 1906, during the closing months of his incumbency as Conservative prime minister, he had been perhaps the first of England's public figures to meet and respond to Weizmann. "It was from that talk with Weizmann that I saw that the Jewish form of patriotism was unique," he stated later. "Their love of country refused to be satisfied by the Uganda scheme [for an alternative Jewish homeland in Africa]. It was Weizmann's absolute refusal even to look at it that impressed me." With the memory of that original conversation still alive, Balfour received Weizmann in 1914, and the earlier cordiality between the two men was instantly revived. Weizmann's eloquence on behalf of a Jewish homeland literally stirred Balfour to tears. The Zionist leader wrote later: "In bidding me good-bye, he said with warmth: 'Mind you come again to see me. I am deeply moved and interested. It is not a dream. It is a great cause, and I understand it.' " Balfour's sympathy and encouragement did not flag after he became foreign secretary in Lloyd George's cabinet. There were those who considered him cold and emotionless, a rather forbidding man, reticent and impassive. But he was far from unfeeling, and particularly on the Jewish question. Like Smuts and Lloyd George, Balfour had been nurtured on the Old Testament, and his lifelong study of Jewish history had filled him with inner remorse about Christendom's treatment of the Jews. "The Jews are the most gifted race that mankind has seen since the Greeks of the Fifth Century," he told Harold Nicolson in 1917. "They have been exiled, scattered and oppressed. . . . If we can find them an asylum, a safe home, in their native land, then the full flowering of their genius will burst forth and propagate." Of course, imperial considerations were paramount in the government's calculations, together with the desire to mobilize "world Jewry" on behalf of the Allies. Yet, in Balfour's case, a genuine vein of Zionist mysticism unquestionably strengthened commitment to the Jewish national home. In response to Weizmann's pleas of June 17, the foreign secretary urged the Zionists themselves to draft an appropriate statement for presentation to the War Cabinet. He would stand behind it.

Weizmann and his closest associates labored intensively to prepare a suitable declaration, modifying and remodifying the text after numerous consultations with Balfour himself. The final statement was ready on July 18. It did not lack forthrightness. "His Majesty's Government," it declared, "accepts the principle that Palestine should be reconstituted as the National Home of the Jewish People. His Majesty's Government will use its best endeavours to secure achievement of this object and will discuss the necessary methods and means with the Zionist Organization." The letter, submitted to the ministers on September 3, elicited the warm approval of the cabinet majority. "It would affect Jewish national opinion," Smuts observed enthusiastically, "and nationally they are a great people." Ironically, the most forceful opposition came from the one Jew in the cabinet, Sir Edwin Montagu, secretary of state for India. Born and raised in London's East End, Montagu had fought an uphill battle to escape his ghetto origins and win acceptance in the privileged circles of government, as he himself once admitted to John Morley. In this case, a "national home" for the Jewish people seemed to raise for him embarrassing questions of Jewish dual loyalty. Now, on September 3, Montagu insisted that the proposed government statement would both alarm the Moslems of India and place the Jews of England in "an untenable position." Balfour's niece, Lady Dugdale, acidly noted later: "Mr. Montagu could not extend to his own people the sympathy he evinced later for nationalism in India." In any case, the vehemence with which Montagu opposed a pro-Zionist declaration persuaded the cabinet to drop the matter from the agenda.

Neither the Zionists nor their supporters in the government accepted this setback as more than temporary. Indeed, Lloyd George confidently put the question of the declaration on the agenda for the next cabinet meeting. And when the meeting took place, on October 4, Balfour himself emphatically presented the Zionist case, this time consulting a detailed personal memorandum from Weizmann which lay on the table before him. Once again, Montagu opposed the draft, with more intensity even than before. "I understand the man almost wept," Weizmann wrote. "When he had ended, Balfour and Lloyd George suggested that I be called in, and messengers were sent for me. They looked for me high and low—and I happened to be a few doors away in the office of Ormsby-Gore. I missed a great opportunity." Montagu's opposition had the effect not of changing the minds of Balfour, Smuts, Lloyd George, and other Zionist sympathizers, but of convincing them of the need for a compromise text simply to get the question resolved without endless delay. While Weizmann and his colleagues urgently maintained their pressure on the government, Amery and Milner labored over a compromise formula that became the essential draft of the Balfour

Declaration. The earlier phrase, "that Palestine should be reconstituted as the national home" of the Jews, was dropped in favor of
a somewhat more equivocal statement. . . . The Zionists were deeply
chagrined by the alteration. Nevertheless, they were fearful of tam-
pering with the modified resolution lest they jeopardize it altogether.

Lloyd George was prepared at last to force the issue through.
Before making his final move, however, the prime minister was determined to win a firm commitment of diplomatic support for Zionist
aspirations. It was by then open knowledge in Western government
circles that the very notion of a Jewish national home was wedded
to the corollary of British protectorate. Lloyd George therefore required assurance that a declaration implying such a protectorate
would not encounter serious opposition at the peace conference
later. At this point Sykes's tactics in dispatching Sokolow on the
round of Western capitals finally began to pay dividends. Received
at the Vatican in April 1917, Sokolow described the Zionist ideal to
Pius X and elicited from the pontiff a cordial statement of goodwill:
"I believe that we shall be good neighbors," Pius assured his Jewish
visitor. Equally friendly, if innocuous, statements were issued by the
Italian ambassadors in Paris and London, and by Paul Cambon, the
highly esteemed French ambassador in London. However much
Cambon may have resented a British-Zionist alliance, he, no more
than the English, dared ignore the alleged power of world Jewry.

Ultimately, the prestige and influence of the American government
proved decisive in resolving the issue for the British cabinet. Washington had never declared war on the Ottoman Empire. But the
United States, then mobilizing its immense strength for the Allied
military effort in Europe, would unquestionably exert a crucial impact on all phases of the future peace settlement. An emphatic pro-
Zionist statement from the American president would accordingly
insure Britain against diplomatic isolation on the Palestine issue. At
Weizmann's suggestion, the task of interceding with Woodrow Wilson
was undertaken by Louis Brandeis, a distinguished member of the
American Supreme Court and the most influential Zionist in the
United States. On September 23, Brandeis discussed the matter of
a Jewish national home with Colonel Edward House, the president's
intimate adviser. Exposed to the jurist's celebrated eloquence and
persuasive powers, House dropped his own earlier misgivings about
Zionism. When Brandeis was received by Wilson that same day,

therefore, he was able to confirm the president's support. "I find in my pocket the memorandum you gave me about the Zionist movement," Wilson wrote House a few days later. "I am afraid I did not say to you that I concurred in the formula suggested from the other side. I do, and would be obliged if you would let them know it." Actually, the formula Wilson thought he was endorsing was outdated. The text of the original Zionist draft had since been altered in favor of the more pallid Milner-Amery version. But the president probably did not know or care much what he was approving, for the question was of marginal interest to him. The fact of his endorsement, on the other hand, was all that mattered to the delighted pro-Zionist faction in the British government. The moment House's message arrived on October 16, they had what they needed.

The War Cabinet voted for the declaration on November 2—over Montagu's last dispirited objections. Significantly, the principal rationale by then was no longer the evident need to preclude French occupation of the Holy Land. Allenby's army was already on the verge of conquering Palestine, and the issue undoubtedly would be resolved by the substantial presence of the Egyptian Expeditionary Force. It was rather the vaunted power of world Jewry which influenced the War Cabinet's discussions of October 4 and 31, the obsessive desire to win the friendship of the Jewish community in both Russia and America. Lloyd George was counting on this support. "The Zionist leaders," he wrote later, "gave us a definite promise that, if the Allies committed themselves to . . . a National Home for the Jews in Palestine, they would do their best to rally to the Allied cause Jewish sentiment and support throughout the world. They kept their word in the letter and the spirit. . . ." Other factors determined the cabinet's vote, too. One was surely the genuine personal feeling of Balfour (and Smuts and Lloyd George) for the Holy Land and the Jewish people. "Near the end of his days," Balfour's niece wrote, "he said to me that on the whole he felt that what he had been able to do for the Jews had been the thing he looked back upon as the most worth doing." Others in the cabinet may have been animated by even more complex motives: Protestant millenarianism, an uneasy conscience about Christendom's treatment of the Jews, conceivably the need to endorse a humane and constructive act in the midst of the holocaust.

The declaration itself seemed curiously bland, however, and quite devoid of religious or mystical overtones of any kind. It took the form of a letter from Balfour to Lord Rothschild, president of the British Zionist Federation:

> *Dear Lord Rothschild, I have much pleasure in conveying to you, on be-half of His Majesty's Government, the following declaration of sympathy with Jewish Zionist aspirations which has been submitted to, and ap-proved by, the Cabinet: "His Majesty's Government view with favour the establishment in Palestine of a national home for the Jewish people, and will use their best endeavours to facilitate the achievement of this object, it being clearly understood that nothing shall be done which may prejudice the civil and religious rights of existing non-Jewish communities in Pales-tine, or the rights and political status enjoyed by Jews in any other coun-try." I should be grateful if you would bring this declaration to the knowledge of the Zionist Federation.*

The original Zionist draft of the declaration had called for "the reconstruction *of* Palestine [italics the author's] as the national home for the Jewish people." The phase "national home," employed in both versions, actually was unknown in international law and usage. The Zionists had coined the expression in 1897, at their first con-gress, to avoid the term "Jewish state," which the Ottoman govern-ment might have found provocative. Now, however, the Balfour version dispensed with the need of defining the boundaries of the Jewish settlement *in* Palestine. The "national home" might be no more than a small enclave within the country. Only five years later, the broad uplands of Transjordan were cut away, and fifteen years after that yet a further amputation would be proposed by the Peel Commission—all without violating the letter of this declaration. More-over, the need to protect "the civil and religious rights of existing non-Jewish communities in Palestine" could and would ultimately be interpreted as justification for limiting, even foreclosing, Jewish immigration in order to placate Arab nationalism.

Yet the eventual fate of the declaration was not necessarily con-sonant with the original intention of its authors. Colonel Meinertz-hagen, General Allenby's political officer, recorded a conversation in which Balfour stated: "My personal hope is that the Jews will make good in Palestine and eventually found a Jewish State." Lloyd George was quite explicit in his description of the cabinet's in-tentions:

It was not their idea that a Jewish State should be set up immediately by the Peace Treaty without reference to the wishes of the majority of the inhabitants. On the other hand, it was contemplated that when the time arrived for according representative institutions in Palestine, if the Jews had meanwhile responded to the opportunity afforded them by the idea of a National Home and had become a definite majority of the inhabitants, then Palestine would thus become a Jewish Commonwealth. The notion that Jewish immigration would have to be artificially restricted in order to ensure that the Jews should be a permanent minority never entered into the heads of anyone engaged in framing the policy. That would have been regarded as unjust and as a fraud on the people to whom we were appealing.

It is worth assessing the effectiveness of the appeal to "world Jewry." The Jews of England were thrilled and grateful, as their public meetings throughout the country and their innumerable resolutions of thanks made evident. Heartened by this response, in turn, and intent upon duplicating it in other countries, the government organized a special Jewish section within the Department of Information, staffing it primarily with Zionists. The task of these functionaries was to prepare literature for distribution through local Zionist societies and other intermediaries to virtually every known Jewish community in the world. Copies of the Balfour Declaration were circulated by the millions, including leaflets dropped from the air over German and Austrian towns. In Russia, news of the declaration evoked wild rejoicing. In the larger cities, huge, cheering crowds gathered outside the British consulates. In Odessa, a two-mile procession of Jews acclaimed the British consul on his balcony, their bands alternately playing *God Save the King* and *Hatikvah,* the Zionist anthem.

Meanwhile, embarking on a redoubled effort to mobilize Jewish support against the Central Powers, Weizmann and Brandeis cabled friends in Russia, entreating them to intercede with the new Communist government on behalf of the common Entente war effort. This, in the end, was wasted effort. The War Cabinet's notion that the Jews of Russia could somehow exert pressure on the Soviet regime was totally naive. The fifteen or twenty Jewish Bolshevists possessed of any real influence in the country were hostile to Jewish nationalism, and indeed were generally indifferent to the fate of their people altogether. On the other hand, the Jews of Germany and the Dual Monarchy remained steadfastly loyal to the cause of their governments. American Jewry, to be sure, was hardly less exhilarated by the news of the Balfour Declaration than were the Jews of Britain and Russia. Among them, too, public expressions and demonstrations of gratitude were evoked in the same full measure. But the United States was already at war. The hated Russian czar had already fallen. Nothing remained to inhibit the enthusiastic participation of American Jews in their national war effort, and nothing further was required to stimulate it. "The American Loan [to Britain] went much as had been anyhow expected," wrote Sir Ronald Storrs in 1937, "no sympathies for Britain accrued from the Soviet (which shortly denounced Zionism as a capitalistic contrivance); and the loyalty of German Jewry remained unshaken—with the subsequent reward that the world is now contemplating."

Perhaps the one tangible military result of the declaration was Jabotinsky's* belated success in organizing a Jewish legion. With the overthrow of the czar in March 1917, Jewish opposition to the plan largely evaporated. Moreover, by late spring, the imminence of a British offensive on Palestine all but dispelled fears of Turkish reprisals. For their part, Lloyd George and Balfour recognized that Zionist and British interests would equally be served by a Jewish legion entrenched in Palestine. Accordingly, after repeated appeals by Jabotinsky and Weizmann, the war ministry made the decision in August to establish a special Jewish infantry regiment. The unit would be awarded its own name and badge, the "Thirty-eighth Battalion of Royal Fusiliers," and its own privileged destination: i.e., Palestine. At this juncture, Colonel Patterson, former commander of the Zion Mule Corps, was summoned to London with orders to begin organizing the new group immediately. Not surprisingly, his first recruits were veterans of the original Zion Mule Corps. This time, too, their numbers were significantly augmented from the immigrant Jewry of London's East End. Nor was the recruitment effort limited to England. Patterson and Jabotinsky ordered the distribution of circulars to Jewish communities in America, Canada, and Argentina. The Balfour Declaration had been issued by then, and in the United States volunteers soon began registering at British consular offices. Among the first to enlist were Ben-Gurion and Ben-

---

* Vladimir Jabotinsky, in 1917 a young Russian-Jewish poet. During the British Mandate years, Jabotinsky came to head the militant revisionist wing of the Zionist movement.—Ed.

Zvi, whom Djemal Pasha had exiled from Palestine in 1915. They and other recruits were sent on to a military camp in Windsor, Nova Scotia, and by July of 1918 were on their way to England as members of the Thirty-ninth and Fortieth battalions of the Royal Fusiliers.

The initial vanguard of this legion disembarked at Alexandria as early as March 1918 and received advanced training outside Cairo. Whereupon Jabotinsky, serving as Patterson's aide, urgently set about recruiting among the Jews of southern Palestine and Jerusalem, the area already liberated by Allenby's army. "The anticipation [of Jabotinsky's arrival] was almost hysterical," wrote Eliahu Golomb, a founder of the original Palestine-Jewish self-defense force. "We had been waiting for the man with whose name was connected our greatest drama—the Jewish Army. We expected him to come and fulfill our vision." Thousands of Palestinian youth volunteered for service, although only several hundred of them could be accepted. Within a month the Thirty-ninth Battalion and units of the Fortieth arrived in Egypt. They were quickly sent to join the Thirty-eighth in patrolling the Jordan Valley against a threatened Turkish counterattack from across the river. For five weeks, the Jewish troops remained in the valley, the lowest spot on the earth's surface, suffering acutely from sunstroke and dysentery. When it became evident that the British staff officers, most of them anti-Zionist, intended to consign the Jews to this ordeal indefinitely, Patterson threatened to resign. The protest was effective, and the legion, now reduced by a third, was allowed to participate in Allenby's climactic autumn offensive. The Thirty-eighth Battalion was one of the first to enter Transjordan. By then the legion numbered 5,000 men, a sixth of the British army of occupation and half the size of Faisal's Arab force at its median strength in 1918. The legion did not remain in that sector long. Allenby soon transferred its men to the area west of the Jordan, while Arab troops to the south of the Dead Sea and east of the river continued to occupy the highlands. By then friction between the two peoples had to be avoided at all costs.

The Arabs and the Jews

The question of Arab-Jewish relations had not really been taken seriously earlier by either the Jews or the British. Before 1914, Zionist spokesmen had rarely considered the inchoate, largely illit-

erate Arab community in Palestine as a political factor. They were
largely indifferent to the heated press campaign that Arab nationalists, most of them Syrians, were mounting against Jewish settlement
and land purchases in the Holy Land during the immediate prewar
era. In 1913, Nahum Sokolow arranged several conciliatory parleys
with a group of Egyptian and Syrian notables. These conversations
did little to alleviate Arab misgivings, however, which most of the
Zionist leadership in any case still preferred to ignore. Neither,
during the war, did the British government sense any inconsistencies
between its patronage of an Arab revolt and its encouragement of
Zionist aspirations, or between the terms of its original promise to
Hussein and its subsequent declaration in favor of a Jewish national
home in Palestine. It will be recalled that in McMahon's crucial letter
to the sherif, on October 24, 1915, the British high commissioner
excluded from the area of Arab independence the land west of the
"districts" of Damascus, Homs, Hama, and Aleppo. A dispute erupted
at war's end and raged bitterly for years afterward on the question
of Britain's intention to exclude Palestine from the area of Arab independence. The wording in the correspondence was hardly precise,
for "district" was not a Turkish administrative term. Was McMahon
actually referring to "vilayets"? That was the Arab contention. Had
it been accepted, the strip of territory excluded from Arab rule
would have been far too narrow to embrace Palestine. The Jews
took the opposite position, arguing that exclusion of only a nominal
territorial enclave was something the French unquestionably would
not have accepted. If the high commissioner had intended to exclude all the land west of the vilayet of Aleppo, for example, no land
would then have been left to exclude; the vilayet extended to the sea.
For their part, the British always insisted that the term "district"
was being used simply in a loose sense, meaning vicinity; and thus
a line drawn west of the vicinities of Damascus, Homs, Hama, and
Aleppo, separating this territory from the coastal region, apparently
excluded Palestine.

McMahon did not content himself with excluding a specific area.
He informed the Arabs that British promises, even within the territory
conceded to Hussein and his followers, applied only to "those regions . . . wherein Great Britain is free to act without detriment to
the interests of her ally, France." . . . It was accepted both in Mecca
and in London that France was committed to the acquisition of a

major sphere of influence in western Syria and Palestine. Years later, in a letter to the London *Times* of July 23, 1937, McMahon restated the British case, emphasizing that "it was not intended by me in giving this pledge [to Hussein] to include Palestine in the area in which Arab independence was promised. . . ." Lloyd George took this qualification for granted in his discussion with Sykes on the eve of the latter's departure for the Middle East in April 1917. He cautioned Sykes to say and do nothing that might prejudice the Zionist cause, and, indeed, to refrain from making even the most general commitments to the Arabs on the subject of Palestine. The Arabs were aware that there was no likelihood of their being allowed even partial control over Palestine, the prime minister observed.

In January 1918, after the issuance of the Balfour Declaration, Commander Hogarth was dispatched from Cairo to Jedda to clarify for Hussein the implications of the Zionist program. After assuring the sherif that Arab freedom would be safeguarded in every way, Hogarth added, significantly: "In this connection, the friendship of world Jewry to the Arab cause is equivalent to support in all states where Jews have political influence. The leaders of the movement are determined to bring about the success of Zionism by friendship and cooperation with the Arabs, and such an offer is not one to be lightly thrown aside." The hint—perhaps it was too explicit an inducement to be called that—was received with alacrity by the Arab leader. Hogarth noted later: "[Hussein] probably knows little or nothing of the . . . economy of Palestine and his ready assent to Jewish settlement there is not worth very much. But I think he appreciates the financial advantage of Arab cooperation with the Jews." Initially, Hogarth's optimism did not seem misplaced, for the sherif issued several cordial invitations to the Jews to return to their "sacred and beloved homeland."

Immediately following Allenby's conquest of Palestine, however, the political future of the Holy Land was increasingly shaped by the British occupying authorities, many of whom shared the anti-Zionist sentiments of the Arab Bureau in Cairo. Clayton had opposed the Balfour Declaration. So had Wingate. Sykes himself apparently experienced misgivings about the direction Arab nationalism might take, for he cautioned a Jewish gathering on December 2, 1917, to deal generously with the Arabs and to recall that the Holy Land would have to be shared fully by both peoples. "You want to know the Arab is free," Sykes reminded his audience, "because he is, and always will be, your neighbor." The Zionist leadership was not oblivious by then to the need for manageable relations with the Arabs. In the summer of 1918, Weizmann met with a group of Syrian émigrés living in Cairo and used the full resources of his charm and persuasiveness to reassure them of Zionist intentions. Arab rights and sensibilities would be fully respected, he promised. The Arab representatives were neither charmed nor persuaded. They countered, rather, with a suggestion for the proportional representation of the Arab majority in any future Palestine government. This reaction so unsettled Weizmann that he decided that there was no further time to be lost before meeting personally with Faisal. To that end he and Ormsby-Gore departed on a ten-day journey to Amman, in Transjordan. The two men were greeted cordially, even lavishly, in the traditional Arab manner; a sumptuous banquet was prepared in their honor. Weizmann was eager to settle matters. He wrote later:

> *I explained to [Faisal] . . . our desire to do everything in our power to allay Arab fears and susceptibilities, and our hope that he would lend us his powerful moral support. He asked me a great many questions about the Zionist program and I found him by no means uninformed. . . . I stressed the fact that there was a great deal of room in the country if intensive development were applied, and that the lot of the Arabs would be greatly improved through our work there. With all this I found the Emir in full agreement, as Lawrence confirmed to me by letter.*

Faisal promised to convey the gist of the talk to his father. "The first meeting in the desert," Weizmann recalled, "laid the foundations of a lifelong friendship."

However warm the understanding between the two leaders, co-operation between their peoples was not destined to come that easily. Moslem-Christian societies were even then springing up throughout Palestine, not infrequently with the private encouragement of British military officials. . . . The Arab slogan *Falastin biladna* —"Palestine is our country"—was first uttered in the summer of 1918, at the very moment when Allenby's army was thrusting deep into Galilee. Even as the War Cabinet and the Zionist leadership in London exulted in the evident fulfillment of their joint ambitions for the Holy Land, the sound of the Arab challenge gained in intensity. It had its Hebrew counterpart, too—*Eretz Yisrael Shelanu*—as Jewish legionaries and veteran Zionist farmers greeted each other ecstatically in growing numbers of liberated Palestinian villages. In the not distant future both credos would sear themselves indelibly into the British conscience.

Chaim Weizmann

THE BALFOUR DECLARATION

In this second selection from Trial and Error, *Weizmann describes the skillful Zionist propaganda and diplomacy which preceded and made possible, despite the opposition of anti-Zionist Anglo-Jewry, the achievement of the Balfour Declaration. Revealed here is Weizmann's attitude toward Palestinian Arab opposition to Zionism in the immediate aftermath of the declaration. Omens of future British-Zionist conflicts are also evident as Weizmann describes his experiences in Palestine early in 1918.*

The reader will remember that from the beginning I had looked upon Zionism as a force for life and creativity residing in the Jewish masses. It was not simply the blind need of an exiled people for a home of its own. I could not agree with Herzl that the *Judennot,* the tragedy of Jewish homelessness, persecution, and poverty, was sufficient to account for the Zionist movement, and was capable of supplying the necessary motive power for the creation of a Jewish homeland. Need alone is negative, and the greatest productions of man spring from an affirmation. Jewish homelessness was not just a physical discomfort; it was also, and perhaps in larger measure, the malaise of frustrated capacities. If the Jewish people had survived so many centuries of exile, it was not by a biological accident, but because it would not relinquish the creative capacities with which it had been entrusted.

For assimilated Jews all this was a sealed book; in their complete alienation from the masses, the source of inspiration, they had not

Excerpts from pp. 176–180, 188–189, 193–194, 200–208, 211–214, 216–224 in *Trial and Error: The Autobiography of Chaim Weizmann* by Chaim Weizmann. Copyright 1949 by The Weizmann Foundation. Reprinted by permission of Harper & Row, Publishers, Inc. and The Weizmann Foundation.

the slightest concept of the inner significance, the constructive moral-ethical-social character, of Zionism. They looked upon it— Lucien Wolf, for instance—as a primitive tribalism. They felt themselves, when they were men of an ethical turn of mind like Claude Montefiore, called upon to "rescue" Judaism from Zionism, or to rescue it just so. It is worth noting, in this connection, that in the Second World War the only part of the entire Mediterranean basin on which the United Nations could count without reservation for full cooperation in the war against nazism and fascism, was Jewish Palestine. It would be wrong to ascribe this to the peculiar position of the Jews, who could never hope to come to terms with Hitlerism. The reverse is equally true; it was Hitlerism which could not come to terms with fundamental Jewish democracy. The character assumed by Jewish Palestine was a projection of the Jewish national, ethical, and social content. In a war for the assertion of world democratic principles, a Jewish Palestine could not have played any other role, whatever the attitude of antidemocratic forces toward the Jewish people.

The deeper meaning of Zionism must not be lost sight of in the record of practical steps, of day-to-day strategic adjustments, which led up to the granting of the Balfour Declaration, and which accompanied future developments. I am reverting now to the common accusation that Zionism was nothing but a British imperialistic scheme, the Balfour Declaration a quid pro quo, or rather payment in advance, for Jewish service to the empire. The truth is that British statesmen were by no means anxious for such a bargain. I wrote to Mr. C. P. Scott, in March 1915:

> *The British cabinet is not only sympathetic toward the Palestinian aspirations of the Jews, but would like to see these aspirations realized. I understand Great Britain would be willing even to be the initiator of a proposal to that effect at the peace conference. But at the same time Great Britain would not like to be involved in any responsibilities. In other words, they would leave the organization of the Jewish commonwealth as an independent political unit entirely to the care of the Jews. At the same time there is a view prevalent that it is not desirable that Palestine should belong to any great power.*
>
> *These two views are in contradiction. If Great Britain does not wish anyone else to have Palestine, this means that it will have to watch it and stop any penetration of another power. Surely, a course like that involves as much responsibility as would be involved by a British protectorate over*

Palestine, with the sole difference that watching is a much less effective preventative than an actual protectorate. I therefore thought that the middle course could be adopted . . . viz; the Jews take over the country; the whole burden of organization falls on them, but for the next ten or fifteen years they work under a temporary British protectorate.

In effect, this is an anticipation of the mandate system. Indeed, had the original idea, or the mandate system, been fully implemented, the service which Jewish Palestine, alone among the Mediterranean peoples, rendered to the cause of democracy in the Second World War would have been proportionately greater. I wrote, in the same letter, of the bond which such a Palestine would create between England and the Jewish people, and added: "A strong Jewish community on the Egyptian flank is an efficient barrier for any danger likely to come from the north." There was a time, in the Second World War, when this danger was very real. If it did not materialize, it does not cancel the value of the 30,000 Jewish soldiers who volunteered from Palestine for service with the United Nations armies of the Near East and Europe, or of the considerable role which Palestine played in the war as a minor arsenal of democracy.

I wrote further: "England . . . would have in the Jews the best possible friends, who would be the best national interpreters of ideas in the Eastern countries and would serve as a bridge between the two civilizations. That again is not a material argument, but certainly it ought to carry great weight with any politician who likes to look fifty years ahead." . . .

From part of the foregoing it is clear that England's connection with Palestine rested on the idea of a Jewish Homeland in Palestine; but for the idea of a Jewish Homeland, England would not have entertained the thought of a protectorate—or later of a mandate— over Palestine. In short, England felt she had no business in Palestine except as part of the plan for the creation of the Jewish homeland. Always (as we have already seen in the case of Asquith) there was a shying away from the assumption of "responsibility" bound up with Palestine as such. I wrote to Mr. Scott at about that time:

Sir E. Grey is in full sympathy with the Jewish national ideals, as connected with the Palestinian scheme, but would not like to commit himself as to the advisability of establishing a British protectorate over

Palestine. He thinks that such a step may lead to difficulties with France and, secondly, may go against the opinion of a certain school of liberals in this country. He would, therefore, be inclined to look for a scheme by which the Jews would not lay any additional burden on England.

These hesitancies, as we know, were later to introduce a note of uncertainty into the British attitude toward the Jewish homeland. How was it that the decision was actually made, and why was the pledge actually given? One factor, perhaps the decisive one, was the genuine appeal which the idea itself made to many of the leaders of Britain. One of the differences between that time and ours is in the approach to state problems. The so-called realism of modern politics is not realism at all, but pure opportunism, lack of moral stamina, lack of vision, and the principle of living from hand to mouth. Those British statesmen of the old school, I have said, were genuinely religious. They understood as a reality the concept of the Return. It appealed to their tradition and their faith. Some of them were completely baffled by the opposition to our plan on the part of assimilated Jews; others were actually rubbed the wrong way by it. Lord Milner was a great friend of Claude Montefiore, the spiritual leader of the anti-Zionists; but on this point he would not be influenced. Milner understood profoundly that the Jews alone were capable of rebuilding Palestine, and of giving it a place in the modern family of nations. He said, publicly: "If the Arabs think that Palestine will become an Arab country, they are very much mistaken." Wickham Steed, the editor of the *Times,* expressed intense annoyance to me at the action of the anti-Zionists—we shall come to the incident later—in publishing a series of letters against the plan in his paper. Philip Kerr, afterward Lord Lothian, an enlightened imperialist, saw in a Jewish Palestine a bridge between Africa, Asia, and Europe on the road to India. He, like many others, was taken aback by the anti-Zionism of the "leading" British Jews; but the measure of understanding which I expected from him—he was then secretary to Lloyd George—and from others may be gauged by the frankness of the following letter, which I wrote to him at the height of the Jewish anti-Zionist opposition, in 1917:

There is another aspect of the question which troubles me. It seems as if the cabinet and even yourself attach undue importance to the opinions held by so-called "British Jewry." If it is a question of the Jews who have settled in Great Britain, well, the majority of these Jews are in favor of Zionism. If on the other hand by British Jews one understands the minority of wealthy, half-assimilated Jews who have been living in this country for the last three or four generations, then, of course, it is true that these people are dead against Zionism. But here is the tragic misunderstanding. Zionism is not meant for those people who have cut themselves adrift from Jewry, it is meant for those masses who have a will to live a life of their own and those masses have a right to claim the recognition of Palestine as a Jewish National Home. The second category of British Jews will fall into line quickly enough when this declaration is given to us. I still expect a time, and I do so not without apprehension, when they will even claim to be Zionists themselves. Some Jews and non-Jews do not seem to realize one fundamental fact, that whatever happens we will get to Palestine. . . . No amount of talk by Mr. Montagu or people like him will stem the tide.

There were, at that time, alike in the highest government posts, and in those of secondary importance, men with a real understanding both of the moral implication of the Zionist movement, and of the potentialities of Palestine. To some extent before my moving to London, but much more afterward, I set myself to discovering these men, guided almost always by the indefatigable Mr. Scott. Some of them I met in the course of my work at the Admiralty and with the Ministry of Munitions. In the one department of the war where they really dealt with political problems—the War Office—there were men of first-rate political capacity and of deep appreciation of the Zionist movement, even if they did not always agree with all of its phases. There was a general atmosphere of sympathy, all the way from General Wilson, the chief of staff, who was a great friend of Lloyd George, to the lower ranks of the department, which were responsible for the detailed work. In the Foreign Office, too, there was a predisposition to look favorably on the Zionist problem. The tone of public opinion at large, as far as we could ascertain it, was one of interest, and not unfriendly. The Manchester *Guardian* was with us; the London *Times* was favorably inclined. There was an eager desire to win over the Jewish public opinion of the world. In this respect, too, there is a fundamental difference between then and now: Hitler taught the world not to attach too much importance to public opinion in general and to Jewish public opinion in particular.

In another sense, too, it was easier to work then than now because most of the discussions were in the realm of the abstract. The great difficulties, like the Arab problem, had not yet come to the fore. There were only doubts of the usual kind, such as one hears even now: "Are the Jews capable of building up a country? Isn't Palestine too small?"—although at that time the eastern boundary of Palestine went as far as the Hedjaz Railway and included Transjordan—"Will the Jews go to Palestine? Is not Zionism the dream of a few intellectuals and of a handful of poor Jews living in the ghettos of Poland and Russia?" But these doubts were without great weight. What mattered was the readiness of people to listen and be convinced; and I pleaded the cause of Palestine wherever I could obtain a hearing.

*　　*　　*

Of course, we had never been so naive as to imagine that nothing more was needed than England's consent. As far back as 1915 I had discussed the question with Mr. C. P. Scott, and a letter of mine to him, written on February 11 of that year, reads in part: "Firstly as for France, I don't think that she should claim more than Syria, as far as Beirut. The so-called French influence, which is merely spiritual and religious, is predominant in Syria. In Palestine there is very little of it—a few monastic establishments. The only work which may be termed civilizing pioneer work has been carried out by the Jews. From the point of view of justice, therefore, France cannot lay claim to a country with which it has no connection whatsoever."

It will be remembered that the sharp intramural Jewish struggle round the Haifa Technical College had, in fact, been the reflex of contending claims or ambitions on the part of various powers with regard to Palestine. This was familiar ground to us. What we did not know in the early stages of our practical negotiations was that a secret tentative agreement, which was later revealed as the "Sykes-Picot Treaty," already existed between France and England! And the most curious part of the history is this: Although Sir Mark Sykes, of the British Foreign Office, had himself negotiated this treaty with M. Georges Picot of the French Foreign Office, Sir Mark entered into negotiations with us, and gave us his fullest support, without even telling us of the existence of the tentative agreement! He was, in effect, modifying his stand in our favor, seeking to revise the agreement so that our claims in Palestine might be given room. But it was *not* from him that we learned of the existence of the agreement, and months passed—months during which we carried on our negotiations with the British and other authorities—before we understood what it was that blocked our progress.

The first full-dress conference leading to the Balfour Declaration took place at the home of Dr. Gaster on the morning of February 17, 1917, Dr. Gaster presiding. There were present, besides Dr. Gaster, Lord Rothschild, Herbert Samuel, Sir Mark Sykes, James de Rothschild, Sokolow, Joseph Cowen, Herbert Bentwich, Harry Sacher, and myself. Sir Mark attended, as he told us, in his private capacity.

The discussions touched on several points which were to constitute the heart of the problem in the ensuing months. First, we were determined that there was to be no condominium or internationalization in Palestine, with all the complications, rivalries, inefficiencies, compromises, and intrigues which that would entail, to the detriment or perhaps complete paralysis of our work. What the Zionists wanted was a British protectorate with full rights according to the terms of the memorandum. These arguments did not, however, apply to the Holy Places, which we wanted internationalized. Second, the term "nation," as applied to the emergent Jewish homeland in Palestine, referred to the Jewish homeland *alone,* and in no wise to the relationship of Jews with the lands in which they lived. So much was made clear by Herbert Samuel. To this I added that the Jews who *went* to Palestine would go to constitute a Jewish nation, not to become Arabs or Druzes or Englishmen.

We reviewed the international situation. It was the consensus that the Jews everywhere, in so far as they were interested in a Jewish homeland in Palestine, held the views we were putting forward. Of one country we could speak with official authority. Mr. Brandeis, the head of the Zionist movement in America, and adviser to President Wilson on the Jewish question, was in favor of a British protectorate, and utterly opposed to a condominium. This was true, also, of the Russian Zionists. We anticipated no objection on this score from any Zionist group, not even the German. Not so simple, however, was the external international situation, that is to say, the attitude of the other powers. On this subject Sir Mark Sykes talked at some length. He spoke with the utmost freedom of the difficulties which confronted us. I may say, in fact, that he placed all his diplomatic skill at our disposal, and that without it we should have had much heavier going than we did. There is, of course, no doubt in my mind that, on the

Sykes-Picot agreement, he was, like Georges-Picot, bound to secrecy by his government.

Sir Mark began by revealing that he had long considered the question of Palestine and the Jews, and that the idea of a Jewish Palestine had his full sympathy; moreover, he understood entirely what was meant by "nationality," and there was no confusion in his mind on that point. His chief concern, at the moment, was the attitude of the powers. Sir Mark had been in Russia, had talked with the foreign minister, Sazonov, and anticipated little difficulty from that quarter. Italy, he said, went on the principle of asking for whatever the French demanded. And France was the real difficulty. He could not understand French policy. The French wanted all Syria and a great say in Palestine. We (the Zionists) would have to discuss the question very frankly with the French—and at this point we interrupted to say that "we" did not at all relish having to conduct such negotiations: that was the business of the British government. Mr. James de Rothschild pointed out very correctly that if British Jews approached the French government, the latter would get French rabbis to press for a French Palestine.

Sir Mark then went on to speak of the Arab problem, and of the rising Arab nationalist movement. Within a generation, he said, the movement would come into its own, for the Arabs had intelligence, vitality, and linguistic unity. But he believed that the Arabs would come to terms with us—*particularly if they received Jewish support in other matters.* Sir Mark anticipated the attitude of the greatest of the Arabs, the Emir Faisal.

This, in brief, was the substance of our first "official" conference.

* * *

In the mobilization of Jewish public opinion, undertaken . . . at the instance of the British government, we had in mind England, South Africa, Russia, France, Italy, Canada, and America—but by far the greatest emphasis was placed on America. Of America's role in the movement I shall have much to say. At this point, one aspect of her immense services is relevant. Mr. Louis D. Brandeis was at the head of the movement then, and I was in constant touch with him. On April 8, 1917, I sent him a report on the general position, which I could say was developing very satisfactorily. "The main difficulty," I wrote, "seems to be the claims of the French. . . . We look forward here to a strengthening of our position, both by the American Government and American Jews, and on that point I had a conversation with Mr. Norman Hapgood in the presence of Mr. Herbert Samuel, Mr. Neil Primrose, Mr. James de Rothschild and Commander Wedgwood, M.P. An expression of opinion coming from yourself and perhaps from other gentlemen connected with the Government in favor of a Jewish Palestine under a British protectorate would greatly strengthen our hands."

Before long, Mr. Brandeis was able to throw the full weight of his remarkable personality onto the scales. America had entered the war in March of that year. On April 20, Mr. Balfour arrived in America on a special mission, and almost immediately met the justice at a party at the White House. Mrs. Dugdale, Balfour's biographer, reports that Balfour's opening remark to Brandeis was: "You are one of the Americans I had wanted to meet," and continues, "Balfour remarked to Lord Eustace Percy, a member of his Mission, that Brandeis was in some ways the most remarkable man he had met in the United States. It seems from such notes of these conversations as survive, that Balfour pledged his own personal support to Zionism. He had done it before to Dr. Weizmann, but now he was British Foreign Secretary. Mr. Justice Brandeis seems to have become increasingly emphatic, during the course of the British Mission's visit, about the desire of American Zionists to see a British Administration in Palestine."

My letter of April 8 must have reached Mr. Brandeis about the time of Balfour's arrival on the twentieth. I wrote again, on April 23:

> *Both Russia and America are at present proclaiming antiannexationist principles. . . . I need not dwell on the fact that Jewish National Democracy and the Zionist Organization which essentially represents this Democracy trust implicitly to British rule, and they see in a British protectorate the only possibility for a normal development of a Jewish commonwealth in Palestine. Whereas, in my opinion, Great Britain would not agree to a simple annexation of Palestine, and it does not desire any territorial expansion, it would certainly support and protect a Jewish Palestine. This is why American support for this scheme is so valuable at the present stage.*

Mr. Brandeis did more than press the idea of a Jewish Palestine under a British protectorate. He carried on a general work of clarification. In America as in England, then as later, Jewish opposition to

Zionism was confined to minority groups. Mrs. Dugdale records further: "As late as January, 1918, our Ambassador in Washington reported, on the authority of Mr. Justice Brandeis himself, that the Zionists were violently opposed by the great capitalists, for different reasons," and she adds, in passing, "This in itself shows how baseless was the idea, once very prevalent, that the Balfour Declaration was in part a bargain with American financiers."

But the most important feature of American help at that time issued from the policy proclaimed by President Wilson in repudiation of secret treaties. The Sykes-Picot arrangement was not a full treaty; but it was sufficiently official to create the greatest single obstacle to our progress. The proclamation of the Wilsonian principle of open covenants openly arrived at compelled the powers to put their cards on the table. The Sykes-Picot arrangement, or semiofficial treaty, faded into the background.

From all the foregoing it will be seen that our work was carried on harmoniously and systematically. As Mrs. Dugdale puts it, succinctly: "A Jewish national diplomacy was in being." She adds: "By the end of April [1917] the Foreign Office recognized, with some slight dismay, that the British Government was virtually committed."

The final struggle round the issuance of the Balfour Declaration was, however, still before us. . . .

* * *

It was an extraordinary struggle that developed within English Jewry in the half-year which preceded the issuance of the Balfour Declaration—a struggle which probably had no historic parallel anywhere. Here was a people which had been divorced from its original homeland for some eighteen centuries, putting in a claim for restitution. The world was willing to listen, the case was being sympathetically received, and one of the great powers was prepared to lead in the act of restitution, while the others had indicated their benevolent interest. And a well-to-do, contented, and self-satisfied minority, a tiny minority, of the people in question rose in rebellion against the proposal, and exerted itself with the utmost fury to prevent the act of restitution from being consummated. Itself in no need—or believing itself to be in no need—of the righting of the ancient historic wrong, this small minority struggled bitterly to deprive the vast majority of the benefits of a unique act of the world conscience; and it succeeded, if not in balking the act of justice, at least in vitiating some of its application.

The assimilationist handful of upper-class British Jews were aware that the Zionist cause was making great headway in government circles and in general public opinion. But it was only in the spring of 1917 that they felt the critical moment to be approaching, and I knew that action could be expected. On May 20, a special conference of delegates from all the constituent Zionist societies of Great Britain was held in London. I had been the president of the Zionist Federation for about a year, and in my official address to the assembly I issued a note of warning against the impending attack. We were already so far advanced on our path to recognition that I could speak of the dangers which attended success.

I said: "One reads constantly in the press, and one hears from friends, both Jewish and non-Jewish, that it is the endeavor of the Zionist movement immediately to create a Jewish State in Palestine. Our American friends have gone further, and they have even determined the form of this State, by advocating a Jewish Republic. While heartily welcoming all these demonstrations as a genuine manifestation of the Jewish national will, we cannot consider them as safe statesmanship. . . . States must be built up slowly, gradually, systematically and patiently." At that time the whole world—and the Jews more than anyone else—had been thrilled by the overthrow of the czarist regime in Russia, and the establishment of the liberal Kerensky regime. This, too, was a danger of a sort. "Some of us— some of our friends even, and especially some of our opponents," I told the conference, "are very quick in drawing conclusions as to what will happen to the Zionist movement after the Russian Revolution. Now, they say, the great stimulus of the Zionist movement has been removed. The Russian Jews are free; they do not need any places of refuge outside of Russia—somewhere in Palestine. Nothing can be more superficial, and nothing can be more wrong than that. The sufferings of Russian Jewry never were the cause of Zionism. The fundamental cause of Zionism was, and is, the ineradicable national striving of Jewry to have a home of its own—a national center, a national home with a national Jewish life. And this remains now stronger than ever. A strong and free Russian Jewry will appreciate more than ever the strivings of the Zionist Organization."

I was speaking the simple truth. The great outburst of enthusiasm with which the Balfour Declaration was received in Russia, the great revival of the Zionist movement, before its final extinction by the Bolshevik regime, was a stirring demonstration of the Jewish national will to live. But I reserved for the end of my address to the conference what weighed most heavily on my mind. I said:

> It is a matter of deep humiliation that we cannot stand united in this great hour. But it is not the fault of the Zionist Organization. It is, perhaps, not the fault of our opponents. It must be attributed to the conditions of our life in the Dispersion, which have caused in Jewry a cleavage difficult to bridge even at a time like this. It is unfortunate that there still exists a small minority which disputes the very existence of the Jews as a nation. But there need be no misgivings on that account; for I have no hesitation in saying that if it comes to a plebiscite and a test, there can be no doubt on which side the majority of the Jews will be found. And I warn you that this test is bound to come—and come sooner, perhaps, than we think. . . . We do not want to offer to the world a spectacle of a war of brothers. We are surrounded by too many enemies to be able to afford this luxury. But we warn those who will force an open breach that they will find us prepared to stand up united in defense of the cause which is sacred to us. We shall not allow anybody to interfere with the hard work which we are doing, and we say to all our opponents: "Hands off the Zionist movement!"

As I suspected, the attack had been prepared. Four days later, on May 24, the Conjoint Committee—or at least the two principal officers of the Conjoint Committee, Mr. David L. Alexander, president of the Board of Deputies of British Jews, and Mr. Claude G. Montefiore, president of the Anglo-Jewish Association—published a long statement in the London *Times,* violently repudiating the Zionist position, and urging the government against favorable action on our demands. All the old arguments that I had learned to expect since the time of my encounter with Western assimilation in the person of Dr. Barness of Pfungstadt were there. The Jews were a religious community, and nothing more. The Jews could not claim a national home. The utmost that could be demanded for the Jews of Palestine was enjoyment of religious and civil liberty, "reasonable" facilities for immigration and colonization, and "such municipal privileges in towns and colonies as may be shown to be necessary," and so on, and so on.

There were some interesting anomalies in the situation which

would have amused us if the matter had been less serious. Messrs.
Alexander and Montefiore repudiated the Zionist philosophy on the
ground that Judaism was nothing more than religion. The chief
rabbi of the British empire, Dr. Hertz, and the *Haham* of the Por-
tuguese and Spanish communities, Dr. Gaster, rebutted the attack!
Messrs. Alexander and Montefiore—and with them, of course, the
group to which I have alluded, Mr. Lucien Wolf, Mr. Edwin Montagu (by then secretary of state for India) and others—were afraid
of having their patriotism challenged. The London *Times,* in a
rather remarkable leading article, answered: "Only an imaginative
nervousness suggests that the realization of territorial Zionism, in
some form, would cause Christendom to turn round on the Jews and
say, 'Now you have a land of your own, go to it.' "

This leading article was written by Wickham Steed, after various
letters by Dr. Hertz, Dr. Gaster, Lord Rothschild, and myself had
appeared in the *Times.* I went to see Steed in order to hand him my
own letter. He received me with the utmost cordiality. I found him
not only interested in our movement, but quite well informed on it.
He had known Herzl in Vienna; he had known Leopoldstadt and the
Viennese Jews. He was not only glad to publish the Zionist statements but expressed downright annoyance with the heads of the
Conjoint Committee. For a good hour or so we discussed the kind
of leader which was likely to make the best appeal to the British
public, and when it appeared, on the twenty-ninth, it caused something like consternation among the assimilationists. It was a magnificent presentation of the Zionist case. I cannot refrain from quoting
two more sentences, aimed directly at the arguments of the Conjoint
Committee heads. "We believe it [Zionism] in fact to embody the
feelings of the great bulk of Jewry everywhere. . . . The importance
of the Zionist movement is that it has fired with a new ideal millions
of poverty-stricken Jews cooped up in the ghettos of the Old World
and the New."

The bringing of the fight into the open had made it imperative
that the government take action, and thus settle the issue. On
June 13, before I left on my Gibraltar "mission," I wrote Sir Ronald
Graham: "It appears desirable from every point of view that the
British Government should give expression to its sympathy and support of the Zionist claims on Palestine. In fact it need only confirm
the view which eminent and representative members of the Govern-

ment have many times expressed to us, and which have formed the basis of our negotiations throughout the long period of almost three years." And a few days later I went, together with Sir Ronald and Lord Rothschild, to see Mr. Balfour (this visit had nothing to do with the Gibraltar mission) and put it to the foreign secretary that the time had come for the British government to give us a definite declaration of support and encouragement. Mr. Balfour promised to do so, and asked me to submit to him a declaration which would be satisfactory to us, and which he would try and put before the War Cabinet.

While I was absent in Gibraltar, the Political Committee, under the chairmanship of Sokolow, busied itself with the preparation of the draft. A number of formulas were devised; in all of them we were careful to stay within the limits of the general attitude on the subject which prevailed among the leading members of the government. This is something to be borne in mind for the reconstruction of the complete picture. The final formula on which we agreed, and which Lord Rothschild handed to Mr. Balfour on our behalf on July 18, 1917, ran as follows:

> *His Majesty's Government, after considering the aims of the Zionist Organization, accept the principle of recognizing Palestine as the National Home of the Jewish people and the right of the Jewish people to build up its national life in Palestine under a protection to be established at the conclusion of peace, following upon the successful issue of the war.*
>
> *His Majesty's Government regard as essential for the realization of this principle the grant of internal autonomy to the Jewish nationality in Palestine, freedom of immigration for Jews, and the establishment of a Jewish National Colonizing Corporation for the re-establishment and economic development of the country.*
>
> *The conditions and forms of the internal autonomy and a Charter for the Jewish National Colonizing Corporation should, in the view of His Majesty's Government, be elaborated in detail and determined with the representatives of the Zionist Organization.*

It is only fair to note that the Jewish opposition to Zionism was mitigated by opposition within the ranks of the non-Zionists themselves. It transpired that the heads of the Conjoint Committee had acted without the knowledge and consent of the constituent bodies, the Board of Deputies of British Jews and the Anglo-Jewish Association, in issuing the anti-Zionist statement to the London *Times.* A vote of censure of those bodies actually forced the resignation of Mr. Alexander and a number of his colleagues. Small as the non-Zionist body of sentiment was, the active opposition was even smaller. And yet it was capable of working great harm, and we waited with much concern for the response of the government.

On August 17, I was able to write to Felix Frankfurter, in the United States: "The draft has been submitted to the Foreign Office and is approved by them, and I heard yesterday, it also meets the approval of the Prime Minister [Lloyd George]."

It remained, of course, to be approved by the War Cabinet—but from the individual expressions of opinion which had come from its members, there cannot be the slightest doubt that without outside interference—*entirely from Jews!*—the draft would have been accepted early in August, substantially as we submitted it.

Around September 18, I learned that our declaration had been discussed at a cabinet meeting from which both Mr. Lloyd George and Mr. Balfour were absent, and that the sharp intervention of Edwin Montagu had caused the withdrawal of the item from the agenda. The same day I received a letter from Lord Rothschild, in which he said: "I have written to Mr. Balfour asking him for an interview Thursday or Friday. . . . Do you remember I said to you in London, as soon as I saw the announcement in the paper of Montagu's appointment, that I was afraid we were done."

I did not feel as desperately as Lord Rothschild, but the situation was unpleasant. We saw Balfour separately, I on the nineteenth, Lord Rothschild on the twenty-first. I received the utmost encouragement from Balfour. He told me that his sympathies had not been changed by the attitude of Montagu. I was able to send the following cable to Brandeis on the same day:

> *Following text declaration has been approved Foreign Office and Prime Minister and submitted War Cabinet: 1. His Majesty's Government accepts the principle that Palestine should be reconstituted as the National Home of the Jewish people. 2. His Majesty's Government will use its best endeavors to secure the achievement of this object and will discuss the necessary methods with the Zionist Organization.*

I added that the opposition of the assimilationists was to be expected and that it would be of great assistance if the text of this declaration received the support of President Wilson and of Brandeis.

To Lord Rothschild, Balfour expressed the same unwavering firmness on the issue as to me. Lord Rothschild wrote to me, after his interview with Balfour on September 21: "I said I had evidence that a member of the cabinet was working against us. He [Balfour] hastily said: 'He is *not* a member of the cabinet, only of the *Government,* and I think his views are quite mistaken.' "

On the twenty-first I had another talk with Smuts—a member of the War Cabinet, and obtained from him the expected reiteration of his loyalty. At the same time we were doing our best to counteract the activities of the assimilationists, who were attacking us in a series of pamphlets, in the press, and in person-to-person propaganda, as well as in the cabinet. On the twenty-eighth I talked again with Lloyd George, who put our memorandum on the agenda of the War Cabinet for October 4. And on the third I wrote to the Foreign Office, for transmission to the War Cabinet:

> *We cannot ignore rumors which seem to foreshadow that the anti-Zionist view will be urged at the meeting of the War Cabinet by a prominent Englishman of the Jewish faith who does not belong to the War Cabinet. We are not in a position to verify these rumors, still less to criticize the fact should these rumors prove to be true; but we must respectfully point out that in submitting our resolution we entrusted our national and Zionist destiny to the Foreign Office and the imperial War Cabinet in the hope that the problem would be considered in the light of imperial interests and the principles for which the Entente stands. We are reluctant to believe that the War Cabinet would allow the divergence of views on Zionism existing in Jewry to be presented to them in a strikingly one-sided manner. . . . Where there is a human mass claiming recognition as a nation there the case for such recognition is complete. We have submitted the text of the declaration on behalf of an organization which claims to represent the national will of a great and ancient though scattered people. We have submitted it after three years of negotiations and conversations with prominent representatives of the British nation.*

Whether these sharp expostulations reached the members of the War Cabinet the next day I do not know. But the meeting of the War Cabinet to deal with the declaration was to be held, according to advice given me, on the fourth. That day I came to the office of Mr. Kerr, Lloyd George's secretary, and I had the temerity to say: "Mr. Kerr, suppose the cabinet decided to ask me some questions before they decide the matter. Would it not be well for me to stay here and be in readiness?" To this he replied, kindly, even compassionately: "Since the British Government has been a Government no private person has been admitted to one of its sessions. So you go back to your laboratory, Dr. Weizmann, and everything will be all right."

I did not go back to my laboratory. I could not have done any work. I went, instead, into the office of Ormsby-Gore, close by, and waited. There was nothing I could do, of course, but I should have had to be more—or less—than human, to have occupied myself during those hours with the routine of my laboratory. I learned too late that I might have done something.

When the Palestine item was laid before the War Cabinet, Edwin Montagu made a passionate speech against the proposed move. The tenor of his arguments will be gathered from the general propaganda of the anti-Zionists, given on the foregoing pages. There was nothing new in what he had to say, but the vehemence with which he urged his views, the implacability of his opposition, astounded the cabinet. I understand the man almost wept. When he had ended, Balfour and Lloyd George suggested that I be called in, and messengers were sent for me. They looked for me high and low—and I happened to be a few doors away in the office of Ormsby-Gore. I missed a great opportunity—and this was entirely due to Philip Kerr. Perhaps, however, it was better so. I might, in that setting, with Montagu in front of me, have said something harsh or inappropriate. I might have made matters worse instead of better. Certain it was that Montagu's opposition, coupled with the sustained attacks which the tiny anti-Zionist group had been conducting for months—their letters to the press, the pamphlets, some of them written pseudonymously by Lucien Wolf, their feverish interviews with government officials—was responsible for the compromise formula which the War Cabinet submitted to us a few days later.

It was on the seventh of October that I wrote to Kerr the letter quoted [earlier], expressing my chagrin and bewilderment at the attention paid by the British government to a handful of assimilated Jews, in their opposition to what was the deepest hope of millions of Jews whom we, the Zionists, represented. On October 9, I could cable as follows to Justice Brandeis:

The cabinet after preliminary discussion suggested following amended formula:

"His Majesty's Government view with favor the establishment in Palestine of a National Home for the Jewish race and will use its best endeavors to facilitate the achievement of this object; it being clearly understood that nothing shall be done which may prejudice the civil and religious rights of the existing non-Jewish communities in Palestine, or the rights and political status enjoyed in any other country by such Jews who are fully contented with their existing nationality and citizenship."

Most likely shall be asked to appear before the cabinet when final discussion takes place in about a week. It is essential to have not only President's approval of text, but his recommendation to grant this declaration without delay. Further your support and enthusiastic message to us from American Zionists and also prominent non-Zionists most desirable to us. Your support urgently needed.

A comparison of the two texts—the one approved by the Foreign Office and the prime minister, and the one adopted on October 4, after Montagu's attack—shows a painful recession from what the government itself was prepared to offer. The first declares that "Palestine should be reconstituted as the National Home of the Jewish people." The second speaks of "the establishment in Palestine of a National Home for the Jewish Race." The first adds only that the "Government will use its best endeavors to secure the achievement of this object and will discuss the necessary methods with the Zionist Organization"; the second introduced the subject of the "civic and religious rights of the existing non-Jewish communities" in such a fashion as to impute possible oppressive intentions to the Jews, and can be interpreted to mean such limitations on our work as completely to cripple it.

I was not given a chance to present our views to the War Cabinet, and the anti-Zionists alone had their say at the October 4 session. The cabinet actually did not know what to do with the obstructionist Jews. Sykes, Amery, Ormsby-Gore were nonplussed. In the end it was decided to send out the text to eight Jews, four anti-Zionists and four Zionists, for comments and suggestions, with a covering letter in which it was stated that "in view of the divergence of opinion expressed on the subject by the Jews themselves, they [the Government] would like to receive in writing the views of representative Jewish leaders, both Zionist and non-Zionist."

We, on our part, examined and reexamined the formula, comparing the old text with the new. We saw the differences only too clearly, but we did not dare to occasion further delay by pressing for the original formula, which represented not only our wishes, but the attitude of the members of the government. In replying to the letter of the government I said: "Instead of the establishment of a Jewish National Home, would it not be more desirable to use the word 're-establishment'? By this small alteration the historical connection with the ancient tradition would be indicated and the whole matter put in its true light. May I also suggest 'Jewish people' instead of 'Jewish Race.'" (This last suggestion actually came from Mr. Brandeis.)

It goes without saying that this second formula, emasculated as it was, represented a tremendous event in exilic Jewish history—and that it was as bitter a pill to swallow for the Jewish assimilationists as the recession from the original, more forthright, formula was for us. It is one of the ifs of history whether we should have been intransigent, and stood by our guns. Should we then have obtained a better statement? Or would the government have become wearied of these internal Jewish divisions, and dropped the whole matter? Again, the result might have been such a long delay that the war would have ended before an agreement was reached, and then all the advantage of a timely decision would have been lost. Our judgment was, to accept, to press for ratification. For we knew that the assimilationists would use every delay for their own purposes; and we also knew that in America the same internal Jewish struggle was going on—complicated by the fact that President Wilson, who was wholeheartedly with us, considered the publication of a declaration premature, in view of the fact that no state of war existed between America and Turkey. Brandeis's intention was to obtain from President Wilson a public expression of sympathy. In this he was not successful. But on October 16, Colonel House, acting for President Wilson, cabled the British government America's support of the substance of the declaration. This was one of the most important individual factors in breaking the deadlock created by the British Jewish anti-Zionists, and in deciding the British government to issue its declaration.

On November 2, after a final discussion in the War Cabinet, Balfour issued the famous letter known as the Balfour Declaration. It was addressed to Lord Rothschild. In an earlier talk with Balfour, when he had asked me to whom the forthcoming declaration should be addressed, I suggested Lord Rothschild rather than myself, though I was president of the English Zionist Federation. The text read:

> *His Majesty's Government view with favor the establishment in Pales-tine of a National Home for the Jewish people, and will use their best endeavors to facilitate the achievement of this object, it being clearly understood that nothing shall be done which may prejudice the civil and religious rights of the existing non-Jewish communities in Palestine or the rights and political status enjoyed by Jews in any other country.*

While the cabinet was in session, approving the final text, I was waiting outside, this time within call. Sykes brought the document out to me, with the exclamation: "Dr. Weizmann, it's a boy!"

Well—I did not like the boy at first. He was not the one I had expected. But I knew that this was a great departure. I telephoned my wife, and went to see Ahad Haam.

A new chapter had opened for us, full of new difficulties, but not without its great moments. . . .

A generation has passed since the Balfour Declaration became history. It is not easy to recapture, at this distance, the spirit of elation which attended its issuance—a spirit shared by non-Jews and Jews alike: on the Jewish side the expectation of imminent redemption, on the non-Jewish side the profound satisfaction awakened by a great act of restitution. Certainly there were dissident voices on both sides, but they were overborne by numbers and by moral authority. The foremost statesmen of the time had collaborated in the declaration. Balfour was to say later that he looked upon it as the great achievement of his life; Viscount Robert Cecil, one of the founders of the League of Nations, considered the Jewish homeland to be of equal importance with the League itself. And in spite of the phrasing the intent was clear. President Wilson declared: "I am persuaded that the Allied nations, with the full concurrence of our Government and our people, are agreed that in Palestine shall be laid the foundations of a Jewish Commonweath." Speaking for Balfour and himself, Lloyd George tells us in his memoirs:

> *As to the meaning of the words "National Home" to which the Zionists attach so much importance, he [Balfour] understood it to mean some*

form of British, American or other protectorate, under which full facilities would be given to the Jews to work out their own salvation and to build up, by means of education, agriculture and industry, a real center of national culture and focus of national life. . . . There can be no doubt as to what the [imperial War] Cabinet then had in their minds. It was not their idea that a Jewish State should be set up immediately by the Peace Treaty without reference to the wishes of the majority of the inhabitants. On the other hand, it was contemplated that when the time arrived for according representative institutions to Palestine, if the Jews had meanwhile responded to the opportunity afforded them and had become a definite majority of the inhabitants, then Palestine would thus become a Jewish Commonwealth. The notion that Jewish immigration would have to be artificially restricted in order that the Jews should be a permanent minority never entered the head of anyone engaged in framing the policy. That would have been regarded as unjust and as a fraud on the people to whom we were appealing.

It will be, among other things, my painful duty to retrace to their beginnings the steps which have placed such a gap between the promise of the declaration and the performance; and those beginnings, I regret to say, coincided with the first efforts to translate policy into actuality.

Early in 1918, His Majesty's Government decided to send a Zionist commission to Palestine to survey the situation and to prepare plans in the spirit of the Balfour Declaration. The commission was to be representative of the Jews of all the principal Allied countries; but as America was not at war with Turkey, she did not feel able to appoint representatives, and the Russian members, though duly appointed, were unable for "political reasons" to leave in time to join us. There came to join us, then, the Italians and the French.

The Italian government sent us Commendatore Levi Bianchini, who proved to be a most devoted worker, collaborating closely with every aspect of our work in Palestine; but one soon got the impression that his devotion had an Italian rather than a Palestinian bias. In the light of subsequent developments it is easy to understand the deep interest evinced by the Italians in Zionist activities in Palestine even in those early days. Already the Jewish national home was viewed with a certain jealousy and suspicion as tending to strengthen British influence in "Mare Nostrum"; and every effort was made to offset this by encouraging Italian participation in Palestine's economic development. It was repeatedly suggested to us that we might make use of Italian firms, Italian workers, Italian supplies for the execution of our preliminary work.

The French sent us Professor Sylvain Lévi, an avowed anti-Zionist! He was forced upon us by the French government—which had made strong representations to the British—and by Baron Edmond de Rothschild, who felt that the presence of Sylvain Lévi on the commission, in spite (or even because) of his known views, would help us to combat certain opposition currents in French Jewish opinion; this with especial reference to the anti-Zionist *Alliance Israélite,* of which Sylvain Lévi was the distinguished president. Like Commendatore Bianchini, Lévi was a devoted worker in the field—and in the same spirit. He seemed to feel that it was his business to keep the French end up. He showed great interest, of course, in the settlements of the PICA (Palestine Jewish Colonization Association) founded by Baron Edmond de Rothschild long before the Zionist Organization was in a position to take up practical work in the country. Sometimes one could not help feeling that M. Lévi looked a little askance at the growth of Zionist influence as an infringement on the virtual monopoly enjoyed till then by the PICA.

Mr. James de Rothschild, Baron Edmond's son, acted as a kind of liaison officer between ourselves and the PICA interests in Palestine, and was naturally somewhat biased in favor of the settlements created by his father. Mr. de Rothschild was and was not a member of the Zionist Commission. He attended all our meetings, but did not wish to be officially identified with us. Occasionally this state of things would create an awkward situation, which would usually be relieved by the diplomatic talents of Major Ormsby-Gore (now Lord Harlech), our liaison officer with the British military authorities.

The representatives of English Jewry on the commission were, besides myself, Mr. Joseph Cowen, Dr. David Eder, Mr. Leon Simon, and Mr. I. M. Sieff (secretary).

Our departure was set for Monday, March 8, 1918. A few days before that date Sir Mark Sykes, who was responsible for collecting and organizing us, and making our traveling arrangements—no easy task in wartime—suddenly had the idea that it would be useful for the prestige of the commission if I, as its chairman, were to be received by His Majesty the King before we left. I was deeply appreciative—as we all were—of the honor, but I had some misgivings as to the wisdom of the step. I knew that we were setting out on a long and difficult road, and I felt that it would be better to defer the audience until we had something substantial to our credit in Palestine, and could report progress. But the authorities whom we consulted thought otherwise, and naturally I fell in with their views.

Here the first of those incidents occurred which were to make the Zionist Commission a sort of prelude or thematic overture to the future. Arrangements were made for me to be taken to the palace on the Saturday morning preceding the departure. I bought, and put on, my first and last top hat, and came to the Foreign Office at the appointed hour, to find a very confused and apologetic Sir Mark Sykes, who informed me that he had just received some "very disquieting" telegrams from Cairo, to the effect that the Arabs were beginning to ask uncomfortable questions. . . . He was inclined to think that it might be better to cancel the audience.

In a sense this did no more than vindicate my first instinctive reaction to the suggested audience; but at this point I simply could not agree to the cancellation, and certainly not on the ground specified. The audience had, of course, not been given any publicity; but it was known in the narrow circle of my colleagues, and they would be deeply distressed by what they would regard both as a serious setback and a bad augury for the future. I told Sir Mark what I felt on this point and urged him to arrange another audience in spite of the shortness of time available. Sir Mark, while underlining his personal sympathy for our position, felt unable to do this, and so we stood in a corridor of the Foreign Office engaged in heated and at times painful discussion. We were joined by Major Ormsby-Gore, who was inclined to take my view of the subject. I remember maintaining with much emphasis and warmth that if we were going to be deflected from a considered line of action by such things as telegrams vaguely indicating some stirrings of the Arab world, our work in Palestine would be utterly impossible, and we had better not go out at all.

The argument went on for what seemed a long time; and eventually we decided that the best thing to do would be to put the position to Mr. Balfour, who happened at this moment to come into view mounting the Foreign Office stairs. Sir Mark suggested that I should see him; I preferred to have Sir Mark put the case, knowing he would present it in the fairest possible light. Major Ormsby-Gore and I waited outside the room for half an hour or so, and then Sir Mark emerged to say that Mr. Balfour thought that the audience should take place, and was at that moment telephoning to the palace to explain that the whole misunderstanding had arisen through his own late arrival at the office! A second audience was fixed there and then for the following Monday morning—the very day of our departure for Palestine.

And so I was presented to His Majesty King George. V. The first thing he said on greeting me was: "You know, Mr. Balfour always *does* come late to the office. I quite understand." He then turned the subject to Palestine, and showed great interest in our plans. Knowing me to be of Russian birth he also spoke at some length on the Russian Revolution—then front-page news—saying at one point: "I always warned Nicky about the risks he ran in maintaining that regime; but he would not listen." He then returned to the purpose of the audience and wished us success in our endeavors.

*   *   *

Within a week we found ourselves assembled in Palestine, settled in Tel Aviv in the house of David Levontin, who was then absent from the country. Tel Aviv at this time was a little seaside town consisting of perhaps a hundred houses and a few hundred inhabitants. It was quiet, almost desolate, among its sand dunes, but not unattractive, though it had been cut off from the outside world for nearly four years, and had suffered under both the German and Turkish occupations.

GHQ was in Ramleh—or rather in Bir Salem—in a building formerly a small German hospice, standing on a hill surrounded by orange groves, and visible from our present home in Rehovoth. It was a modest house but, for the prevailing conditions, quite comfortable. On my arrival I found myself at once in the war atmosphere, an abrupt and startling change from Cairo. At breakfast the first morning I was wedged in between General Allenby and General Bols, who talked war across me—casualties, attacks, retreats—and I could not but sense a certain strain in the atmosphere. In fact, I felt we could hardly have descended on GHQ at a more inopportune moment. The news from the Western front was bad; most of the European troops in Palestine were being withdrawn to reinforce the armies in France. The train which had brought me from Cairo had been promptly loaded with officers and men being rushed to the West. Allenby's own advance was completely checked; he was left with a small Indian Moslem force, and the Arabs, quick to sense the weakening in the British position, were showing signs of restiveness. Our arrival was definitely no accession of strength or comfort, especially as Arab agitators lost no time in proclaiming that "the British had sent for the Jews to take over the country."

This was only the beginning of our difficulties. I soon discovered that the Balfour Declaration, which had made such a stir in the outside world, had never reached many of Allenby's officers, even those of high rank. They knew nothing about it, and nothing about the sympathy shown at that time to our aims and aspirations by prominent Englishmen in every walk of life. They were cut off from Europe; their minds were naturally concentrated on the job in hand, which meant winning the war or—more precisely at the moment— holding their own on their particular front, and not being rolled back by the Turks under Liman von Sanders. Unfortunately this was not all; there were deeper and so to speak more organic obstacles in the mental attitude of many of Allenby's officers. The scanty Jewish population, worn out by years of privation and isolation, speaking little English, seemed to them to be the sweepings of Russian and Polish ghettos. And Russia at this time was hardly in the good books of the Allies, for it was soon after the Bolshevik revolution, which on the whole they identified with Russian Jewry; Russians, Jews, Bolsheviks were different words for the same thing in the minds of most of the British officers in Palestine in those days, and even when they were not entirely ignorant of developments, they saw little reason to put themselves out for the Jews—declaration or no declaration.

This peculiar situation had not, however, developed of itself. In an early conversation with General (now Sir Wyndham) Deedes (he was one of the few who *did* understand our position), I learned of at least one of the sources of our tribulations. Suddenly, and without introduction, he handed me a few sheets of typewritten script, and asked me to read them carefully. I read the first sheet and looked up in some perplexity, asking what could be the meaning of all this rubbish. General Deedes replied quietly, and rather sternly: "You had better read all of it with care; it is going to cause you a great deal of trouble in the future." This was my first meeting with extracts from the Protocols of the Elders of Zion.*

Completely baffled, I asked Deedes how the thing had reached him, and what it meant. He answered, slowly and sadly: "You will find it in the haversack of a great many British officers here—and they believe it! It was brought over by the British Military Mission which has been serving in the Caucasus on the staff of the Grand Duke Nicholas."

It would be a mistake to imagine that the views of the whole British army were tainted by the ideas expressed in the Protocols of the Elders of Zion; but at a time when the horrors of the Bolshevik revolution were fresh in everyone's mind the most fantastic rumors and slanders—operating frequently on existing backgrounds of prejudice—gained credence, and the extracts from the Protocols which I then saw had been obviously selected to cater to the taste of a certain type of British reader.

But even without this unpredictable blow at us our position was difficult enough. On meeting Allenby I had of course handed over my credentials and letters of introduction from Mr. Lloyd George, Mr. Balfour, and others; but warm though their terms were, I saw that they made little impression. Almost his first remark was: "Yes, but of course nothing can be done at present. We have to be extremely careful not to hurt the susceptibilities of the population." He was polite, even kind, in manner, but not at all forthcoming when we got down to the purposes of the commission. One felt that this was a military world, and in it only soldiers had a right to exist. Civilians were a nuisance. But here we were—a very motley group of civilians —injected into the military organism like a foreign body. . . . The messianic hopes which we had read into the Balfour Declaration suffered a perceptible diminution when we came into contact with the hard realities of GHQ.

I stayed three days at Bir Salem. Rightly or wrongly, I felt that those days were in the nature of a period of probation. Authority wanted to see a little more of me, and find out what kind of fellow had been inflicted on them by the politicians in London before they let me loose in Palestine. I had no chance of communicating with various

---

* Anti-Semitic forgery alleging a subversive Jewish world conspiracy.—Ed.

friends of mine in Rishon or Rehovoth, who had been eagerly await-
ing my arrival. I was little more than a mile away from them, but there
was no bridge leading from GHQ to the surrounding villages. I spent
an anxious three days. I had to mind every word I said, and suppress
a great many ideas I had brought out with me, putting them into cold
storage for the time being. Major James de Rothschild was of course
on much more intimate terms with the staff than I was; many of them
were old friends of his. But his contribution toward raising my morale
was confined to repeated warnings not to say anything and not to do
anything: "Remember, walls have ears!"

It was always a relief to go into Deedes's tent; with him I could
speak freely, dream freely. He it was who initiated me into the habits
of military camps, and eventually put me in touch with General Clayton, the political officer of the army in Palestine, in whose charge the
commission had been officially placed. The second night of my stay
in Bir Salem I spent entirely in Deedes's tent. We talked of the present and of the future, and I told him of my hopes and plans. He
listened patiently and benignly to it all; both critical and sympathetic,
he warned me of the many obstacles I should have to overcome, but
ended by reminding me that faith could move mountains. We talked
until we were exhausted, and eventually he had a camp bed put up
for me and I passed the remainder of the night—a short two hours!—
under canvas with him. We awoke to find that the "latter rains" had
come upon us while we slept, and the whole floor of the tent was
covered with spring flowers. We took them as a happy omen.

That morning, as I stood in front of my tent, which was near the
main road, I saw Allenby driving past. He stopped, and after a friendly
greeting motioned me to get into the car with him, saying that he was
going up to Jerusalem and thought I might like to go up with him.
He was right: I was devoured by the desire to "go up to Jerusalem."
But something within held me back. I remembered the rather curious
reticence of the last couple of days, and after a minute I said: "I
would like to come; but in the circumstances don't you think it would
be better for me to go a little later, and in my own time? It might be
embarrassing for you to be seen entering the capital with me." Allenby got out of the car and stood by me for a minute or two, apparently
deep in thought; then he smiled and held out his hand to me: "You
are quite right—and I think we are going to be great friends." From
that time I felt that, with the commander in chief anyhow, the ice

was broken. Eventually we did go up to Jerusalem together, but that was in July—just before the laying of the foundation stones of the Hebrew University.

After those three days I was, so to say, released from GHQ; my colleagues and I were given free passes, a car, petrol, and—greatest favor of all—our own telephone. We were, I believe, the only civilians in Palestine to be so privileged. I was determined that no action of mine should destroy the tender plant of confidence which had begun to grow up between GHQ and ourselves. And this—though mercifully I did not know it at the time—was the beginning of the hard road which I have had to tread for practically the rest of my life. I was placed between the hammer and the anvil—between the slow-moving, unimaginative, conservative, and often unfriendly British administration, military or civil, and the impatient, dynamic Jewish people, which saw in the Balfour Declaration the great promise of the return to them of their own country, and contrasted it resentfully with the administrative realities in Palestine.

There were, of course, notable and noble exceptions in those early days, like Wyndham Deedes and Gilbert Clayton and the commander in chief himself. But they were not the men in daily contact with the population; they were immersed in the conduct of the war, and had to leave the details of administration to men of lower rank in the military hierarchy; and these were, almost without exception, devoid of understanding, or vision, or even of kindness.

The governor of Jaffa—and thus of Tel Aviv—was at this time a Colonel Hubbard. Under him he had, if not the largest, then certainly the most active Jewish community in Palestine. But in all his actions and utterances, trivial as most of them were, he went out of his way to discourage the Jews and encourage the Arabs, in so far as it was possible for him to do so. A typical instance, taken from a note made at the time was his reception of a small committee of Jewish agricultural engineers, surveyors, and so on, who had occasion to visit Nablus (under official government auspices) to inspect some *Jiftlik* (state) land in the neighborhood. Colonel Hubbard told them—jokingly, perhaps, but if so it was a bad joke—that if they did not leave immediately they ran the risk of being half-killed by the excited populace. He added a contemptuous reference to President Wilson, "who meddles too much with Palestine," and concluded by saying that if the committee wished to travel through the *Jiftlik* it would have to take a regiment of soldiers along. In conversation with friends he was wont to say that if "trouble" should occur in Jaffa, he would take no responsibility for it, and would not interfere, or allow troops under his command to interfere.

Then there was Colonel Ronald Storrs, in Jerusalem. He was much more subtle in his approach. He was everyone's friend; but, try as he might, he failed to gain the confidence of his Jewish community. The chief administrator, General Money, had on his staff several advisers and officials who, from the first moment, felt it to be their duty to impress upon the Jewish communities under their charge that, whatever the politicians in London might have been fools enough to say or do, *here* we were in a quite different world: *"Nous allons changer tout cela."*

With the best will in the world those early days in Palestine would have been difficult enough. The Jewish community was depleted, derelict, and disorganized. Most of its leading figures had been banished by the Turkish authorities, either to Damascus or to Constantinople. Ruppin, our able colonization expert, was in Constantinople. We missed equally Meir Dizengoff, the distinguished mayor of Tel Aviv. This was a moderate, practical, level-headed man who served the city for nearly three decades after the period of which I am writing. He attended conscientiously to his duties and to the needs of the *Yishuv,* unbiased by party feeling. His opinions were respected by everyone, and almost universally accepted. Deprived of him and a few others like him, the Jews of wartime Palestine hardly knew which way to turn. The German and Turkish occupations had exhausted and disrupted the Jewish settlements, and numbers of Jews had fled to Egypt as refugees. After the occupation by the British army they began to drift back. There was, of course, a great scarcity of commodities, and as soon as the road to Egypt was opened people began to press for permits to go and replenish their stocks. This became a source of much trouble for the commission, for we were the official intermediaries between the Jewish population and the military authorities. Only one railway line connected Palestine with Egypt, and there was only one train daily in each direction. The limited accommodations were badly needed for military purposes, and it was not possible to obtain permits for civilians except for the most urgent reasons. With great reluctance I found myself obliged to forward applications to the transport officer from time to time, though I kept them down as far as possible. Even with a friendly attitude on the part of British officers such necessary restrictions were bound to become a source of grievance both against the commission and the British authorities.

But the attitude of far too many of the British officers toward the Jews could by no stretch of the imagination be called friendly, and this was particularly the case in the district of Jaffa. And in that atmosphere of tension and expectation the reasonable and the unreasonable restrictions were often lumped together; trivial things assumed the importance of affairs of state; and there were instances of discrimination which I did not consider trivial at all. I did my best to smooth over the rough places, but my assurances to the Jews that these frictions and inconveniences were inevitable in a period of transition went unheeded in the face of the realities of daily life. It was no use telling them that it was farfetched to draw ultimate conclusions from the attitude of this or that officer, and that the men who really counted understood our troubles and were with us, not against us. The fact was, after all, that though General Deedes and Clayton gave much of their time and diplomatic skill to easing the situation, the general relations between the British authorities on the spot and the Jewish population grew more and more strained, and there were only a few points where normal friendly relations existed and where the indispensable good will was actively being fostered.

And then an incident occurred which made it necessary for me to bring the whole matter to the attention of the commander in chief.

Some time in May 1918, we heard that the colony of Petah Tikvah (one of the premier settlements established by Baron Edmond de Rothschild in the early 1880s) would have to be evacuated for military reasons. Regrettable as this was from the point of view of the settlers, no reasonable person could raise any objection to it if military exigencies required it. The military authorities on the spot promised me that, should the suggested evacuation be definitely decided on, due notice would be given and the Zionist Commission would be allowed to help in the arrangements; that is to say, we would provide housing for the evacuees, in Tel Aviv and elsewhere, we would see to it that their plantations were looked after, and we would let them have reports from time to time. I had already informed the colonists of this understanding between us and the military, and they had naturally accepted it. Suddenly, on the eve of the Feast of Pentecost, a messenger came to us posthaste from Petah Tikvah, saying that orders had been given to evacuate the colony the next morning, and that all our careful preparations had apparently gone for nothing. What made matters worse was that there were two Arab villages nearer to the front than Petah Tikvah, and they had received no evacuation orders. For this, of course, there may have been military reasons, but it was very hard to understand just the same. Deductions—not pleasant ones—were naturally made from these developments: Jews were not trusted, and had to be turned out; Arabs, who were known to cross the enemy lines repeatedly, were left unmolested. It was difficult for me, inexperienced as I was, to appreciate the true position, and after a great deal of heartsearching I decided to go to the fountainhead, and asked for an interview with the commander in chief.

I was invited to dinner with General Allenby the same evening. I had not seen him since my first days in Palestine. After dinner, the general suggested that we find a quiet place to talk, as he had all the night before him: there would probably be some sort of skirmish before dawn, and he could not in any case expect any sleep. I began by explaining to him the Petah Tikvah tangle, about which he naturally knew little, since the orders had been given by the divisional officer and GHQ was not yet informed of them. He agreed, however, that the matter ought to be looked into, and asked his ADC to make inquiries there and then and report back to him immediately. The result was that the evacuation was postponed for a few days, and the arrangements previously made for it were upheld.

There was, however, more to our talk. The general asked me for a more detailed report on the relations between the Jewish population and his administration. This gave me my opening, and I proceeded to explain that, while we understood that matters of high policy could not at the moment be implemented, and that the Balfour Declaration could not find practical application till after the war, the continuance of strained relations between the Jewish population and the British military authorities was doing no good to anyone at present, and might seriously prejudice the future. It was not simply a matter of relations between the Jews and the British, nor was it the immediate question of the particular rebuffs or setbacks. It was rather the effect on the Arab mind. The Jews were anxious to help the British; they had received the troops with open arms; they were on the best of terms with the Anzacs. But it seemed as though the local administration was bent on ignoring the home government's attitude toward our aspirations in Palestine, or, what was worse, was going out of its way to show definite hostility to the policy initiated in London. The outlook for later relations between Jews and Arabs was, in these circumstances, not a promising one.

This was my first opportunity of discussing at length with General Allenby questions of policy and our future. Like most of the Englishmen at that time in Palestine the commander in chief, though not hostile, was inclined to be skeptical, though not because he feared trouble from the Arabs; it was rather that, in his view, Palestine *had* no future for the Jews. Indeed, the Arab question at that time seemed to give no grounds for anxiety. Such prominent Arab spokesmen as there were had more or less acquiesced in the policy; at any rate, they made no protest. With some of them—like the old mufti of Jerusalem, and Musa Kazim Husseini—we had established very friendly relations; and . . . the titular and actual leader of the Arab world, the Emir Faisal, was even enthusiastically with us. What I had to overcome in the commander in chief, then, was a genuine skepticism as to the intrinsic practicality of the plan for the Jewish homeland.

I pointed out to him that there were untapped resources of energy and initiative lying dormant in the Jewish people, which would be released by the impact of this new opportunity. These energies, I believed, would be capable of transforming even a derelict country like Palestine. I reminded him of the villages founded by Baron Edmond de Rothschild, which even in those days were oases of fertility in the surrounding wastes of sand—in startling contrast to the Arab villages, with their mud hovels and dunghills. I tried with all my might to impart to the commander in chief some of the confidence which I myself felt—in part because I had come to have a great personal regard for him, and also because I felt that his attitude might be crucial when the time came to get down to practical problems. I remember that toward the end of the long talk, when I felt his resistance yielding a little, I said something like this:

> You have conquered a great part of Palestine, and you can measure your conquest by one of two yardsticks: either in square kilometers— and in that sense your victory, though great, is not unique: the Germans have overrun vaster areas—or else by the yardstick of history. If this conquest of yours be measured by the centuries of hallowed tradi-

tion which attach to every square kilometer of its ground, then yours is one of the greatest victories in history. And the traditions which make it so are largely bound up with the history of my people. The day may come when we shall make good your victory, so that it may remain graven in something more enduring than rock—in the lives of men and nations. It would be a great pity if anything were done now—for instance by a few officials or administrators—to mar this victory.

He seemed at first a little taken back by this tirade; but when I had finished he said: "Well, let's hope it will be made good."

After this interview relations between ourselves and the administration underwent a certain improvement; but on the whole the spirit governing officialdom was not conducive to cooperation between ourselves and the British or between ourselves and the Arabs. There were constant changes of governors under the military occupation, with constant setbacks. Whether the Arabs got positive encouragement to oppose the Allied policy from one or two of the British officials, or whether they just drew their own conclusions from the day-to-day conduct of these gentlemen, it is impossible to say, much less to prove. Nor does it much matter. The fact was that Arab hostility gained in momentum as the days passed; and by the time a civil administration under Sir Herbert Samuel took over, the gulf between the two peoples was already difficult to bridge.

George Antonius

PLEDGES AND COUNTER-PLEDGES

George Antonius (1892–1942) was an Arab scholar of Lebanese origin and a senior civil servant in Palestine during the early days of the British Mandate. This section from his classic history, The Arab Awakening, *presents an Arab nationalist perspective on the events surrounding the issuing of the Balfour Declaration.*

The first step was for the British government to satisfy themselves that, in the event of their making a declaration in favor of Zionist aspirations, the Zionists would welcome and work for the establishment of British rule in Palestine. When Mr. Lloyd George came to power in December 1916, there was in existence a plan drawn up by the leaders of the Zionist movement, in which a program was outlined for the administration of Palestine in the event of an Entente victory. The plan was based on the assumption that, after the war, the administration of Palestine would be taken over either by France or by Great Britain or by both acting jointly in a condominium. The Zionist leaders were then unaware of the existence of the Sykes-Picot Agreement, and had naturally assumed that France might be successful in pressing her claim to Palestine as being part of Syria. As it stood, the Zionist program, with its equal regard for French and British designs on Palestine, did not altogether suit Mr. Lloyd George's book. But when the issue was discussed in exploratory conversations between British statesmen and Zionist leaders, the latter, taking the hint, decided with alacrity to eliminate France altogether from their scheme and to plump for an exclusively British Palestine. It was then that Mr. Lloyd George authorized Sir Mark Sykes to enter into negotiations with the Zionists; and accordingly, the first conference was held on the seventh of February 1917, in London. At that conference, the Zionist leaders gave Sykes a formal assurance that they were irrevocably opposed to any internationalization of the Holy Land, even under an Anglo-French condominium; and that, provided Great Britain would support them in their national aspirations, they would henceforth work for the establishment of a British protectorate in Palestine. That was the basis of the bargain which led to the issue of the Balfour Declaration nine months later when the cry went forth that Mr. Lloyd George and his colleagues, by their bold espousal of the cause of persecuted Jewry, had furnished the world with another proof of the humanitarian idealism with which they were inspired.

In recent years, statements have been made by both Mr. Lloyd George and Dr. Weizmann, purporting to give a different account of the motives which had prompted the issue of the Balfour Declaration. In an address he gave at the Royal Institute of International Affairs in London on June 9, 1936, Dr. Weizmann said:

> *The suggestion that is often heard that the Balfour Declaration was made . . . for Imperialist or any other similar vulgar reason is entirely false. I think one fact may disprove this legend. When the British Government agreed to issue the famous Balfour Declaration, it agreed on one condition: that Palestine should not be the charge of Great Britain.*

This statement is not in accordance with the facts or even with the very condensed version given in the report published in 1921 by the Executive of the Zionist Organization, in which it is stated that considerations of the strategic value of Palestine to the British Empire had weighed with the promoters of the Balfour Declaration, and that, at their very first formal conference with Sir Mark Sykes, the Zionist leaders had made it clear to him that their objectives envisaged the establishment of a British protectorate in Palestine. Dr. Weizmann was present at that conference. Nor does his statement tally with the account published by Asquith of the representations that were made to him as prime minister, as far back as the beginning of 1915. Among those representations was, as we have seen, a memorandum by Mr. Herbert Samuel advocating the annexation of Palestine by Great Britain with a view to settling some 3 or 4 million Jews in it—a proposal which had already found favor with Mr. Lloyd George, but which had been rejected by Mr. Asquith. This is what Asquith wrote, under an entry dated March 13, 1915:

> *. . . . I have already referred to Herbert Samuel's dithyrambic memorandum, urging that in the carving up of the Turks' Asiatic dominion we should take Palestine, into which the scattered Jews would in time swarm back from all quarters of the globe, and in due course obtain Home Rule. Curiously enough, the only other partisan of this proposal is*

Lloyd George who, I need not say, does not care a damn for the Jews or their past or their future, but thinks it will be an outrage to let the Holy Places pass into the possession or under the protectorate of "agnostic, atheistic France."

The declaration might have appeared sooner had it not been for certain political difficulties. One was the opposition of the non-Zionist Jews who were seriously alarmed at the nationalistic implications of political Zionism, and who gave publicity to their opposition in a remarkable statement, remarkable alike for its sincerity and, as has been amply shown in the event, for its foresight. The statement appeared in *The Times* of May 24, 1917, over the signatures of David L. Alexander, president of the Board of Deputies of British Jews, and Claude G. Montefiore, president of the Anglo-Jewish Association. In it, the signatories stressed their fidelity to *cultural* Zionism of which the aim was to make Palestine a Jewish spiritual center in which the Jewish genius might find an opportunity of developing on lines of its own. They entered a strong and earnest protest against the idea of *political* Zionism which claimed that the Jewish settlements in Palestine should be recognized as possessing a national character in a political sense, and that the settlers should be invested with certain special rights on a basis of political privileges and economic preferences. They prophesied that the establishment of a Jewish nationality in Palestine was bound to "have the effect throughout the world of stamping the Jews as strangers in their native lands, and of undermining their hard-won position as citizens and nationals of those lands." Events have proved that those fears were only too well grounded, for it cannot be denied that the development of Zionism in the postwar period has been one of the main psychological factors in the deplorable growth of anti-Semitism.

Another difficulty lay in the reluctance of the French government to give up their pretensions with regard to Palestine. There were powerful groups in French political life, in business and banking circles, and in the ecclesiastical world, to whom the proposal of excluding Palestine from the sphere of French influence would have been abhorrent; and the French cabinet, at whose head was the cautious Ribot, could scarcely be expected to countenance any such proposal. It was clear to the British government and to the Zionist leaders that they would have to act with infinite circumspection. The tactics they employed aimed at obtaining the assent of the French government to the principle of a Zionist establishment in the Holy Land, without specific reference to the question of future sovereignty in Palestine. At the first approach, the attitude of the French government was far from encouraging. Then it was that the Zionist leaders heard for the first time, through an accidental leakage, of the existence of the Sykes-Picot Agreement and of its provisions regarding the internationalization of Palestine; and, feeling that they were being duped, they protested angrily to the British government who, however, appear to have succeeded in reassuring them, for the negotiations proceeded as though the Sykes-Picot Agreement had not existed.

At last, after protracted negotiations, the assent of the French government was secured to the principle of a declaration in favor of Zionism. In the United States, Mr. Justice Brandeis, making a very able use of his influence at the White House, obtained President Wilson's approval of the terms of the proposed declaration. For a time, the progress of the negotiations was impeded by a division of opinion among the members of the British cabinet and by the vigorous opposition of Edwin Montagu, the only Jew in the cabinet. There was also a fundamental divergence as to the character of the future Jewish establishment in Palestine. The Zionists were pressing for a statement of policy accepting the principle "of recognising Palestine as *the* national home of the Jewish people." The British government, unwilling to commit themselves to so far-reaching a policy, refused to promise anything more than that they would view with favor "the establishment in Palestine of *a* national home for the Jewish people." The difference was one between a limited Jewish national home in Palestine and an unlimited one. In the end, the Zionists gave way and agreed to the text which was finally drawn up in the following terms:

> *His Majesty's Government view with favour the establishment in Palestine of a national home for the Jewish people and will use their best endeavours to facilitate the achievement of this object, it being clearly understood that nothing shall be done which may prejudice the civil and religious rights of existing non-Jewish communities in Palestine, or the rights and political status enjoyed by Jews in any other country.*

The Balfour Declaration, as it came to be universally known, was issued from the Foreign Office on the second of November 1917, and made public a few days later, that is to say, two years after the issue of Sir Henry McMahon's note of the twenty-fourth of October 1915, and eighteen months after the outbreak of the Arab Revolt, when the Sherif Hussein, relying on England's pledges of Arab independence, which he had every reason to believe applied to Palestine, had thrown in his lot openly with the Allies.

In those parts of the Arab world which were in direct touch with the Allies, the Balfour Declaration created bewilderment and dismay, even among those who were not aware of the exact nature of the British pledges to the Arabs. It was taken to imply a denial of Arab political freedom in Palestine. The news reached Egypt first, where it soon provoked a wave of protest on the part of the Arab leaders congregated in Cairo; and, for a time, the British authorities there, aided by a strict censorship and an active propaganda service, had much to do to allay Arab apprehensions and prevent a collapse of the revolt. In the occupied part of Palestine, the British command did their best to conceal the news, as though they had a bad conscience about it.

When the news reached King Hussein, he was greatly disturbed by it and asked for a definition of the meaning and scope of the declaration. This request was met by the despatch of Commander Hogarth, one of the heads of the Arab Bureau in Cairo, who arrived in Jedda in the first week of January 1918, and had two interviews with the king.

The message which Hogarth had been instructed to deliver had the effect of setting Hussein's mind completely at rest, and this was important from the standpoint of the morale of the revolt. But what is equally important from the point of view of the historian is that the message he gave the king, on behalf of the British government, was an explicit assurance that "Jewish settlement in Palestine would only be allowed in so far as would be consistent with *the political and economic freedom of the Arab population.*" The message was delivered orally, but Hussein took it down, and the quotation I have just given is my own rendering of the note made by him in Arabic at the time. The phrase I have italicized represents a fundamental departure from the text of the Balfour Declaration which purports to guarantee only *the civil and religious rights* of the Arab population. In that difference lay the difference between a peaceful and willing Arab-Jew cooperation in Palestine and the abominable duel of the last twenty years. For it is beyond all reasonable doubt certain that, had the Balfour Declaration in fact safeguarded the political and economic freedom of the Arabs, as Hogarth solemnly assured King Hussein it would, there would have been no Arab opposition, but indeed Arab welcome, to a humanitarian and judicious settlement of Jews in Palestine.

In his reply, Hussein was quite explicit. He said to Hogarth that in so far as the aim of the Balfour Declaration was to provide a refuge to Jews from persecution, he would use all his influence to further that aim. He would also assent to any arrangement that might be found suitable for the safeguard and control of the Holy Places by the adherents of each of the creeds who had sanctuaries in Palestine. But he made it plain that there could be no question of surrendering the Arab claim to sovereignty, although he would willingly consider when the time came, whatever measures might seem advisable to supply the future Arab government in Syria (including Palestine) with expert administrative and technical guidance.

In the months that followed, Hussein gave ample proof of the sincerity of his attitude. He sent out messages to his principal followers in Egypt and in the forces of the revolt to inform them that he had had assurances from the British government that the settlement of Jews in Palestine would not conflict with Arab independence in that territory; and to urge them to continue to have faith in Great Britain's pledge and their own efforts to achieve their freedom. He ordered his sons to do what they could to allay the apprehensions caused by the Balfour Declaration among their followers. He despatched an emissary to Faisal at Aqaba with similar instructions. He caused an article to be published in his official mouthpiece, calling upon the Arab population in Palestine to bear in mind that their sacred books and their traditions enjoined upon them the duties of hospitality and tolerance, and exhorting them to welcome the Jews as brethren and cooperate with them for the common welfare. The article appears to have been written by Hussein himself and is historically valuable not only as an instance of his freedom from religious prejudice or fanaticism, but also as reflecting the general Arab attitude towards Jewry prior to the appearance of political Zionism on the scene.

In Egypt, the efforts of the British authorities to explain away the political implications of the Balfour Declaration had met with some success. In March, a Zionist commission headed by Dr. Weizmann arrived in Cairo on their way to Palestine; and they, too, went to no little trouble to allay Arab apprehensions. Dr. Weizmann, with his great gift of persuasion, scored a temporary success in interviews he had with several Arab personalities, and in this he was ably and zealously seconded by Major the Hon. W. Ormsby-Gore, who was accompanying the commission as political officer delegated by the Foreign Office. They gave their hearers such a comforting account of Zionist aims and dispositions as dispelled their fears and brought them to a state of acquiescence in the idea of Zionist-Arab cooperation. Meetings were arranged and held between Zionist and Arab leaders. The proprietor of an influential newspaper in Cairo was so far impressed with Dr. Weizmann's and Major Ormsby-Gore's assurances that he made use of the weighty columns of his journal to dispel Arab fears about their political future and advocate an understanding between the two races.

IV EARLY ZIONISM AND THE PALESTINIAN ARABS

Walter Laqueur

THE UNSEEN QUESTION

Walter Laqueur is presently director of the Institute of Contemporary History and a coeditor of the Journal of Contemporary History. *He is the author of numerous books and articles on twentieth-century Europe, the diplomacy of the Middle East, and world affairs. In this selection from his most recent book,* A History of Zionism, *Laqueur explores the complicated and increasingly hostile relationship which evolved between Zionists and Palestinian Arabs prior to 1918.*

Zionism and the Arab Problem

Among the Jewish workers who demonstrated in Tel Aviv on May 1, 1921, the day of international working-class solidarity, there was a small group of Communists who distributed leaflets in Arabic calling the down-trodden and exploited masses to rise against British imperialism. Expelled from the ranks of the parade, they were last seen disappearing with their leaflets into the small streets between Tel Aviv and Jaffa. A few hours later a wave of Arab attacks on Jews in Jaffa started, triggered off, the Arabs claimed, by the provocation of the godless Bolsheviks, whose propaganda had aroused great indignation among the local population. In the course of these riots and of the subsequent military operations, 95 persons were killed and 219 seriously wounded.

The disturbances of May 1921, following the riots in Jerusalem and the attacks in Galilee the previous year, shocked and confused the Zionists.[1] Many of them became aware for the first time of the danger of a major conflict between the two peoples. It was asserted that Zionist ignorance and ineptitude were to blame, for at the time of the Balfour Declaration the Muslims had been well disposed towards the Jews, but had not found among them understanding and a willingness to compromise. Consequently they had made common cause with the Christian Arab leaders against the "Zionist peril."

From *A History of Zionism* by Walter Laqueur, pp. 209–222, 226–234. Copyright © 1972 by Walter Laqueur. Reprinted by permission of Holt, Rinehart and Winston, Inc. and George Weidenfeld and Nicolson Ltd.

[1] Jakob Klatzkin, in *Die Araberfrage in Palästina* (Heidelberg, 1921), p. 21; Dr. M. Lewite, "Zur Orientierung in der arabischen Frage," *Jüdische Rundschau,* 5 August 1921.

Whatever the cause of the 1921 riots, whatever the explanations offered and accepted, from then on the Arab question began to figure increasingly in the discussions at Zionist congresses, in internal controversies, and of course in Zionist diplomacy.

Yet fifteen years later, when the Arab question had become the most important issue in Zionist politics, critics were once again to argue in almost identical terms that the movement was now paying the price for having so long ignored the existence of the Arabs, their interests, and their national aspirations. It was also said that but for this neglect a conflict between the peoples could have been prevented. The Zionists, the critics claimed, had acted as though Palestine was an empty country: "Herzl visits Palestine but seems to find nobody there but his fellow Jews; Arabs apparently vanish before him as in their own Arabian nights."[2] "If you look at prewar Zionist literature," Dr. Weizmann said in a speech in 1931, "you will find hardly a word about the Arabs."[3] This implied that the Zionist leaders had been half aware of the existence of the Arabs but for reasons of their own had acted as if they did not exist. Or had it been a case of real, if astonishing blindness?

The issue was in fact considerably more complex. The Zionists certainly paid little attention to the first stirrings of the Arab national movement and few envisaged the possibility of a clash of national interests. But they did of course know that several hundred thousand Arabs lived in Palestine and that these constituted the majority of the local population. Even the pre-Herzlian Zionists were aware of the fact that Palestine was not quite empty. Rabbi Kalischer, who had never been anywhere near the Holy Land, wrote in 1862 about the danger of Arab banditry, anticipating the question whether Jewish settlers would be safe in such a country. The Russian Zionists in their writings in the early 1880s expressed confidence that Jews and Arabs could live together in peace. Lilienblum noted the existence of an Arab population, but said that it was small and backward, and that if a hundred thousand Jewish families were to settle over a period of twenty years, the Jews would no longer be strangers to the Arabs. Levanda argued that both Arabs and Jews would profit from Jewish settlement. When Ahad Haam went to Palestine in 1891 he reported that the country was not empty, that the Arabs,

2 J. N. Jeffries, *Palestine: The Reality* (London, 1939), p. 40.
3 *Jüdische Rundschau,* 27 November 1931.

and above all the town dwellers among them, were quite aware of Jewish activities and desires, but pretended not to notice them so long as they seemed to constitute no real danger. But if one day the Jews were to become stronger and threaten Arab predominance, they would hardly take this quietly.[4]

In Herzl's mind the Arabs certainly did not figure prominently, though he did not ignore them altogether. He met individual Arabs and corresponded with a few of them. He was aware of the rising national movement in Egypt and on various occasions stressed the close relationship between Jews and Muslims. In *Altneuland,* his Zionist utopia, Reshid Bey, personifying the Arabs, says that Jewish immigration had brought tremendous benefits to the Arabs: the export of oranges had increased tenfold. When asked by a non-Jewish visitor whether Jewish immigration had not ruined the Arabs and forced them to leave, he replies: "What a question! It was a blessing for all of us," adding however that the landowners benefited more than others because they had sold land to the Jews at a great profit.[5] Herzl's vision seemed to Ahad Haam too good to be true. How could millions of Jews live in a country which barely provided a poor living for a few hundred thousand Arabs? Max Nordau replied that he and Herzl were thinking in terms of modern methods of cultivation which would make mass settlement possible without any need for the Arabs to leave. They envisaged the spread of European civilization and the growth of an open European society in which there would be room for everyone. They were opposed, he said, counterattacking his East European critics, to a narrow, introspective, religious nationalism concerned primarily with rebuilding the Temple of Jerusalem.[6] Nordau, however, was not always so optimistic about the future of Arab-Jewish relations. On at least one occasion he considered the possibility of a Turkish-Zionist alliance against the danger of an Arab separatist movement.[7] Or perhaps this was only a political move to remind the Arabs, who were then anxious to enlist Turkish assistance against Jewish immigration, that the Zionists too had some bargaining power.

From the early days of Jewish immigration there were in fact

---

[4] "Truth from Eretz Israel," *Hamelitz,* June 1891.
[5] *Altneuland,* p. 133.
[6] *Die Welt,* 13 March 1903.
[7] Max Nordau, *Zionistische Schriften* (Berlin, 1909), p. 172.

clashes, often bloody, between the new settlers and their Arab neighbors. The annals of the settlements are full of stories of theft, robbery, and even murder. In a report on his trip to Palestine in 1898 Leo Motzkin stated that in recent years there had been "countless fights between Jews and Arabs who had been incited against them."[8] But such accounts have to be viewed in the context of time and place. Clashes like these were not uncommon in other parts of the world. They occurred not only between Arabs and Jews, but equally between one Arab village and another.

Moreover, the state of security in the outlying districts of the Ottoman empire was not up to the standards of Western Europe.[9] On the other hand it cannot be maintained that these incidents totally lacked political undertones, that, in other words, Jews and Arabs were living peacefully together before political Zionism appeared on the scene, and, more specifically, before the Balfour Declaration confronted the Palestinian Arabs with the danger of losing their country.[10]

As early as 1891 a group of Arab notables from Jerusalem sent a petition to Constantinople signed by 500 supporters complaining that the Jews were depriving the Arabs of all lands, were taking over their trade, and were bringing arms to the country.[11] Anti-Jewish feeling was spread by the churches in Palestine. Eliyahu Sapir wrote in 1899 that the main blame was with the Catholic church, and in particular the Jesuits, but he also mentioned the impact of the French anti-Semitic publicist Drumont on certain Arab newspapers.[12] It was commonly accepted at the time that the poor Muslim sections of the population who had benefited from Jewish settlement were on the whole well disposed towards the Jews whereas the Christian Arabs were hostile. This appraisal was correct to the extent that many Arab nationalist newspapers published before the First World War were in Christian hands and that, generally speaking, the percentage of Christian Arabs among the intelligentsia, and thus among the

---

8 *Stenographisches Protokoll der Verhandlungen des II. Zionisten-Kongresses* (Vienna, 1899), p. 125.

9 H. M. Kalvarisky, in *She'ifotenu* 2, no. 2: 50.

10 N. Mandel, "Turks, Arabs and Jewish Immigration into Palestine 1882–1914," in Albert Hourani, ed., *Middle Eastern Affairs* 4 (London, 1965): 84–6. See also Mandel's dissertation (same title), Oxford, 1965.

11 Quoted in *Sefer Toldot Hahagana* (Tel Aviv, 1954) 1: 66.

12 E. Sapir, "Hatred of Israel in Arab literature," *Hashiloah* (1899), p. 222 *et seq.*

founders of the Arab national movement in Syria and Palestine, was disproportionately high. But the attitude of the Muslim upper and middle classes was not basically different, whereas early Zionist emissaries encountered outside Palestine much more sympathy among Christian Arabs fearful of Muslim domination. Sami Hochberg, the Jewish editor of a Constantinople newspaper, was told by Lebanese Christians in 1913 that they hoped the Jews would soon become the majority in Palestine and achieve autonomous status to counterbalance Muslim power.[13] The idea that the Christian Arabs were fundamentally anti-Zionist, while the Muslims were potential friends, lingered on nevertheless for a long time after the First World War, despite the fact that Ruppin and other members of the Zionist Executive in Palestine frequently tried to explain to their colleagues that the real state of affairs was vastly more complicated.[14]

The total population of Palestine before the outbreak of the First World War was almost 700,000. The number of Jews had risen from 23,000 in 1882 to about 85,000 in 1914. More than 100,000 Jews had entered Palestine during the years between, but approximately half of them did not stay. Many moved on to America; one of these wanderers between several worlds was the author of *Hatikvah,* the Zionist national anthem.

Jaffa around 1905 was a city of about 30,000 inhabitants, of whom two-thirds were Muslim Arabs. Haifa, with its 12,000 residents, was hardly bigger than neighboring Acre. Jerusalem was by far the biggest city in the country. Of its population of 60,000, 40,000 were Jews and the rest Muslim and Christian Arabs. A contemporary guide book reports that the situation of the Jews had somewhat improved in recent years. They were no longer concentrated in the dirty Jewish quarter in the old city, many having moved to the residential quarters outside the city wall. On the Sabbath the market was almost empty and public transport came more or less to a standstill.[15] The majority of the Jews still belonged to the old preimmigration community, either taking no interest in Zionism or actively opposed to

[13] Hochberg to Jacobson, Zionist Archives, Cologne AII, quoted in P. A. Alsberg, "The Arab Question in the Policy of the Zionist Executive before the First World War," in *Shivat Zion* 4: 189. See also, N. Mandel, "Attempts at an Arab-Zionist Entente 1913–14," *Middle Eastern Studies* 1, April 1965.
[14] In a report to the Zionist executive in 1912, quoted in Yaacov Ro'i, "Attempts of the Zionist Organisation to Influence the Arab Press in Palestine between 1908–14," *Zion* 3–4 (1967): 205.
[15] Meyers Reisebücher, *Palästina und Syrien* (Leipzig, 1907), p. 128.

it. These were pious men and women, dependent on alms given by their coreligionists abroad. They lived in a ghetto viewed with shame and horror by the new immigrants, the very existence of which reminded them of a milieu from which they had just escaped. The living conditions of the Sephardic Jews, most of them Arabic-speaking, were quite different, as there were many merchants as well as professional men and artisans among them.

The Zionist immigrants, as distinct from the established Jewish community, numbered no more than 35,000–40,000 in 1914, of whom only one-third lived in agricultural settlements. While Arab spokesmen protested against Jewish immigration, Jewish observers noted with concern that the annual natural increase of the Arab population was about as big as the total number of Jews who had settled with so much effort and sacrifice on the land over a period of forty years. Leading Zionists used to say: "Unless we hurry, others will take Palestine." A German Zionist physician who had settled in Haifa around the turn of the century noted dryly: "No one will take it, the Arabs have it and they will stay the leading force by a great margin."[16] Twenty years later, Dr. Auerbach wrote that it had been the most fateful mistake of Zionist policy to pay insufficient attention to the Arabs in the early days. But he was not at all certain that more attention would have solved the problem, for "the Arabs are hostile and will always be hostile," even if the Jews were paragons of modesty and self-denial.[17]

Relations between the Jewish settlers and their Arab neighbors were, then, from the very beginning not untroubled. The land of the early Jewish settlements had formerly belonged to Arab villagers in the neighborhood who had been heavily in debt and had been forced to sell. There was bitterness against the newcomers, and sporadic armed attacks, and the situation was aggravated by the refusal of the Jewish settlers to share the pasture land with the Arabs as had been the custom before.[18] In Galilee the problem was even more acute because the Arab peasants were poorer than in southern Palestine, as were the Jewish colonies, which could not offer employment to the Arabs who had lost their land. The Jewish settlers tried to assist the nearby Arab villages by lending out on occasion agricultural ma-

---

16 Elias Auerbach, in *Die Welt* (1910), p. 1101.
17 *Jüdische Rundschau*, 13 January 1931.
18 Belkind, quoted in A. Cohen, *Israel vehaolam ha'aravi* (Merhavia, 1964), p. 68.

chinery, while Jewish physicians were treating Arab patients often free of charge. But not all the new settlers were willing to accept the local customs, nor was it to be expected that those who had lost their land would not feel anger and resentment against the new owners.[19]

A short note in a Hebrew journal published in 1909 tells the story of an Arab woman working at Wadi Hanin, a stretch of land recently acquired by the Jews. Suddenly she started weeping, and when asked by those working with her why she was crying she answered that she had recalled that only a few years earlier this very plot had belonged to her family.[20]

Before the fall of Abdul Hamid in 1908 the Arab nationalist mood had found no organized political expression, since no political activity was permitted within the Ottoman Empire. The sultan's representatives ruled with an iron hand, and no one dared openly to express sympathy with the ideas of Arab nationalism. A sudden and dramatic change came when the Young Turks overthrew the sultan and announced that the Ottoman Empire would in future be ruled constitutionally. New Arab newspapers were founded, voicing radical demands in a language unheard before. Elections were held for the new parliament and the atmosphere was charged with political tension. With this national upsurge the struggle against Zionism became almost overnight one of the central issues in Palestinian Arab policy. Leaflets were widely distributed calling on the Arabs not to sell any more land to the Jews, and demanding that the authorities should stop Jewish immigration altogether. The Haifa newspaper *Al Karmel* was established with the express purpose of combating Zionism. Even before, in 1905, Neguib Azoury, a Christian Arab and previously an assistant to the Turkish pasha of Jerusalem, had written that it was the fate of the Arab and the Jewish national movements to fight until one or the other prevailed.[21] There was a sharp increase in armed attacks on Jewish settlements and on individual Jews. The newspaper campaign, as a contemporary observer noted, reached even the felahin in their mud huts and the Bedouin in their tents.

---

[19] *Ibid.*, pp. 65–9 and *Sefer Toldot hahagana* 1: 73–7.
[20] *Hashiloah,* 1909, p. 466.
[21] Neguib Azoury, *Le Réveil de la Nation Arabe* (Paris, 1905), p. v; *Sefer Toldot Hahagana*, p. 185; Mandel, *Middle Eastern Affairs,* p. 94.

Christian Arabs were again said to be in the forefront of the struggle, inciting the Muslim masses to carry out a full-scale pogrom to destroy not only the whole Zionist colonization but also the Jewish population in the cities.[22] These fears were exaggerated, as soon appeared, but the alarmist reports received from Jaffa and Jerusalem induced the Zionist leaders for the first time to pay more than cursory attention to the Arabs of Palestine.

What could be done to establish friendly relations with them? It was easier to pose the question than to answer it. There had been some lonely warning voices. Yitzhak Epstein, a teacher and an agriculturist, had said in a closed meeting at the time of the seventh Zionist Congress (1905) that the Arab question was the most important of all the problems facing Zionism, and that Zionism should enter into an alliance with the Arabs. The Jews who returned to their country should do so not as conquerors; they should not encroach upon the rights of a proud and independent people such as the Arabs, whose hatred, once aroused, would have the most dangerous consequences. Epstein's views, and the arguments used by his critics to refute them, are of considerable interest and deserve to be carefully studied. They anticipated in almost every detail the debates which have continued since inside the Zionist movement, and between the Zionists and their critics.[23]

Epstein maintained that there had been not a few cases in which Arab and Druze smallholders had lost their livelihood as the result of Zionist land purchases. In law the Jews were right, but the political and moral aspect was more complicated and they had a clear obligation to the felahin. It was easy to make enemies among the Arabs and very difficult to gain friends. Every step had therefore to be carefully considered. Only such land should be bought that others were not already cultivating. At the same time the Jews had to give full support to the national aspirations of the Arabs. While Herzl had aimed at a Turkish-Zionist entente, Epstein envisaged a charter between Jews and Arabs ("those two old Semitic peoples") which would be of great benefit to both sides and to all mankind. The Arabs had a great many gifts, but they needed the Jews to help them to

[22] Professor A. S. Yehuda in a report to Professor O. Warburg of the Zionist executive, dated 31 August 1911, cited by Ro'i, "Attempts of the Zionist Organisation . . . ," p. 212.
[23] His speech was subsequently published under the title "She'ela ne'elma," in *Hashiloah*, 1907, pp. 193–206.

make economic and cultural progress. The Jews should enter into such an agreement with pure, altruistic motives, without any intention of subjugating the neighboring people. There ought to be no rivalry between them; the two peoples should assist each other. Hitherto in their political activities the Zionists had not been in contact with the right people. They had talked to the Ottoman government and to everyone else who had anything to do with Palestine. But they had not spoken to the Arab people, the real owners of the country. The Zionists had behaved like a matchmaker who had consulted every member of the family with the exception of the bridegroom. Epstein concluded with several recommendations for improving relations with the Arab neighbors: the most important task was to help raise the living standard of the peasants. Jewish hospitals, schools, kindergartens, and reading rooms should be open to them. The Jewish schools should move away from a narrow nationalist spirit. The intention should be not to proselytize the Arabs but to help them find their own identity. The Jews should take account of the psychological situation of the Arabs, something which had been utterly neglected in the past. Once established, high-level educational institutions would attract thousands of students from neighboring Arab countries, and this too would strengthen the fraternal alliance between the two peoples.

Epstein's thesis provoked a reply from a colleague[24] who argued that the Arab peasant had been exploited not by the Jews but by Arab effendis and moneylenders. Everyone agreed that the Arab had benefited from the presence of the Jews. If nevertheless one day he were to turn against the Jews, the reason would not be Jewish land purchases but the "eternal enmity towards a people which had been exiled from its country." To buy the friendship of the Arabs was exceedingly difficult, as Epstein himself had admitted. Why then try so hard? History was full of examples showing that the more the Jews tried to ingratiate themselves with other peoples, the more they had been hated. Had not the time come for the Jews to concern themselves at long last with their own existence and survival? But these considerations quite apart, Epstein's suggestions were said to be quite unrealistic for the simple reason that the Jews did not have the money to carry out such grandiose projects. They

---

[24] Nehama Puchachevski, in *Hashiloah,* 1908, pp. 67–9.

were facing the gravest difficulties in establishing their own elementary school system. It was therefore absurd to dream about universities for the Arabs. They themselves hardly knew how to cultivate the soil—how could they teach others? It was all very well to talk about the blessings of modern civilization which Zionism could bring to the Arabs, but for the time being the Jews had next to nothing to offer. The Arabs had never ceased to be a people, and unlike the Jews, everywhere hated and persecuted, they needed no national revival. It was therefore quite unconvincing to maintain that they needed Jewish friendship. Epstein had argued that what the Jews could give the Arabs they could get nowhere else, and it was at this point that his critic finally lost her temper: "To give—always to give, to the one our body, to the other, our soul, and to yet another the remnant of the hope ever to live as a free people in its historical homeland."

The debate I have briefly summarized contained in essence all the main arguments among Zionists on the Arab question: "healthy national egoism" being urged on the one side and on the other the demand that Jewish settlement in Palestine should be based on the highest moral principles and proceed only in agreement with the Arabs. Epstein's criticism was justified inasmuch as quite a few European Zionists tended to ignore the presence of the Arabs. Some Zionist reference works published before the First World War characteristically do not even refer to what Epstein in a most striking and meaningful phrase called the "hidden question." When the German Zionists produced a propaganda brochure in 1910, Elias Auerbach, who wrote on the prospects for future development, found it necessary to stress at the very beginning of his article the obvious fact that Palestine was not an empty country and that its character was shaped by the strongest ethnic element in its population.[25]

Some of the new arrivals looked down on the Arabs. One observer wrote that on a few occasions he had detected an attitude towards the Arabs which reminded him of the way Europeans treated the blacks.[26] But no one could fairly charge with lack of political caution and moral obtuseness the men who represented the Zionist Executive in Palestine at the time, and who were responsible inter alia for purchasing land. It is certainly no coincidence that these

[25] Elias Auerbach, in *Palästina* (Cologne, 1910), p. 121.
[26] Hugo Bergmann, *Jawne und Jerusalem* (Prague, 1919), p. 60.

very people (Arthur Ruppin, Y. Thon, R. Benyamin) were among the founding members twenty years later of the *Brit Shalom*, the highly unpopular group which regarded an Arab-Jewish rapprochement as the main task of the Zionist movement. Undeniably the Zionist Executive in Europe is open to criticism for concentrating most of its efforts on Constantinople and the various European capitals, showing little foresight in its relations with the Arabs, though from time to time it did press resolutions stressing the importance of making efforts to gain the sympathy of Palestine's Arab population. Sokolow wrote after his visit to the Near East in 1914 that "the question of our relations with the Arab population has become more acute."[27] But there was no follow-up, no consistent policy. After the First World War no congress passed without solemn declarations stressing Zionist sympathies for the national movement in the Orient and the Arab national movement in particular. But, as Ussishkin said, the Zionists had no power in Palestine, and such declarations were therefore meaningless. Nor was it quite clear to whom they should have talked. There were individual Arab notables, but there was no Arab political leadership in Palestine, certainly not before 1908. The political parties which then emerged were small, consisting of a few dozen members, and not very representative.

The Zionist leaders simply would not consider the presence of half a million non-Jews an insurmountable obstacle, formidable enough to make them give up their cherished dreams about the return of the Jewish people to their homeland. They had tried to carry out some of Epstein's ideas; they had drained swamps and irrigated desert lands. But the budget of the Zionist Executive was small and those responsible for the promotion of agricultural settlement knew that restricting their purchases to poor land would doom the whole enterprise. If the Arabs believed in Herzl's hints about the many millions at his disposal, the members of the Zionist Executive knew better.

Jewish workers, it was thought, should have played a decisive role in improving relations with the Arab population. But it was precisely the influx of Jewish workers into Palestine with the second *Aliyah* which aggravated the conflict. After a clash between Arab and Jewish workers in Jaffa in the spring of 1908, Levontin, director

---

[27] Quoted in Yaacov Ro'i, "The Zionist Attitude to the Arabs, 1908–14," in *Middle Eastern Studies,* April 1968, pp. 210, 216.

of the local Anglo-Palestine Bank, wrote to Wolffsohn, the head of the World Zionist Executive, that the young men from the *Poalei Zion* were largely responsible for the growing tension. They had been walking around armed with big sticks and some of them with knives and rifles, behaving towards the Arabs with arrogance and contempt.[28] On another occasion in the same year Levontin wrote to Wolffsohn that the Zionist labor leaders were sowing hatred against Zionism in the heart of the local population by speaking and writing against giving jobs to the Arabs. Arthur Ruppin, who certainly did not lack sympathy for the Jewish workers, reported to Wolffsohn in 1911 that he too was continually trying to impress on them the need to refrain from any act of hostility in their relations with the Arabs.[29]

What made the *Moskub* (as the Arabs called the pioneers from Russia) an especially disturbing factor in Arab-Jewish relations? For they were influenced by the Russian populists and by Leo Tolstoy; they did not come to Palestine as conquerors, but believed with A. D. Gordon that only a return to the soil, to productive labor, would redeem the Jewish people. But when they arrived in Palestine they realized that the great majority of those employed in the existing Jewish settlements were Arabs. This they regarded as a cancer in the body politic of the *Yishuv.* It had not been the aim of Zionism to establish a class of landowners in Palestine whose vineyards and orchards and orange groves were worked by Arab plantation workers. From the outset the pioneers and their trade unions fought for the replacement of Arab by Jewish labor wherever feasible in the face of strong opposition from the Jewish farmers, who naturally preferred cheaper and more experienced Arab laborers. Moreover the young men and women of *Poalei Zion* had left czarist Russia with the memory of the pogroms still with them, and the issue of Jewish self-defense figured high among their priorities. They were Socialists and internationalists, and the lowliest Arab peasant had as much human dignity in their eyes as any prominent Turkish pasha. But they did not take kindly to attacks and molestations, and they were sometimes liable to overreact in their response. These members of *Poalei Zion* were not like the liberals of our day—they had no feelings of guilt about the Arabs. Their socialism was largely (though not exclusively)

[28] Quoted in Alsberg, "The Arab Question in the Policy of the Zionist Executive before the First World War," in *Shivat Zion* 4: 163.
[29] *Ibid.*, p. 184.

in the Marxist tradition. Following Marx, they regarded the spread of Western ideas and techniques in the East as a priori progressive, needing no further ideological justification. They believed in working-class solidarity, but this extended only to workers already established in jobs in industry, not necessarily to those who were competing against organized labor. Since under the centuries of Muslim rule Palestine had remained a desolate, underdeveloped country, they had no compunction about ousting a few landowners and peasants whom they held responsible for its backwardness and neglect. There was nothing in Socialist doctrine, as they interpreted it, which dictated that East European Jewry should remain poor and unproductive and that Palestine should stay backward and infertile.[30]

It is one of the tragic ironies of the history of Zionism that those who wanted close relations with the Arabs contributed, albeit unwittingly, to the sharpening of the conflict. Between the two world wars no one strove more actively for a reconciliation between Jews and Arabs than Haim Margalit Kalvarisky. Born in Russia in 1868, he was trained as an agronomist and came to Palestine in 1895. For many years he worked for Baron Hirsch's colonization society and had a great many influential Arab friends. He was firmly convinced that Arab-Jewish agreement was the *conditio sine qua non* of a successful Zionist policy. Yet it was precisely Kalvarisky's activities around the turn of the century—the land purchases in the Tiberias district—which first provoked Arab resistance on a major scale. During the years 1899–1902 about one-half of this district was acquired by Jewish land companies and it was then for the first time that the danger of denationalization became a political slogan among the Arabs.[31] Under the impact of these events Nagib Nasser, later editor of the Haifa newspaper *Al Karmel,* was converted to anti-Zionism and decided to devote his efforts to the enlightenment of his fellow citizens with regard to the "Jewish peril."[32]

Among the Jewish workers no group was more pacifist and anti-militarist in character than *Hapoel Hatzair.* A. D. Gordon, their chief

[30] After the First World War they showed more awareness. At the fourteenth Zionist Congress in Vienna (1925) no one was more emphatic than Ben-Gurion on the necessity "to find the way to the heart of the Arab people." Empty phrases about peace and fraternity, he insisted, were not sufficient; what was wanted was a genuine alliance between Jewish and Arab workers. He was thereupon attacked by the revisionists as a cosmopolitan and doctrinaire Socialist theoretician.

[31] See Kalvarisky's own account in *Ha'olam* 7 (1914); and in *She'ifotenu,* p. 54.

[32] Mandel, St. Antony's Papers, pp. 93–4.

ideologist, was opposed in principle to the use of violence and justified self-defense only in extreme circumstances. But he and his comrades wanted every tree and every bush in the Jewish homeland to be planted by the pioneers. It was in this group that the idea of Jewish agricultural communal settlements found its most fervent adherents. They were shocked, as has been already mentioned, when they found that the settlers of the first *Aliyah* had become plantation owners, and that among the permanent residents of these colonies there were actually more Arabs than Jews. According to a contemporary account, every Jewish farmer in Zichron Yaakov provided for three or four Arab families, and the situation elsewhere was hardly different.[33] Ahad Haam called Zichron "not a colony but a disgrace." Few Jewish peasants engaged any longer in manual labor. This state of affairs was not, of course, in keeping with the original aims of Zionism, let alone of Socialism. Yet, paradoxically, as far as Arab-Jewish relations were concerned it was a stabilizing factor, whereas the activities of the Socialists, with their fanatical insistence on manual labor ("redemption through toil"), seemed to confirm Arab suspicions about Jewish separatism and the displacement of Arab peasants and workers.

General security deteriorated sharply in Palestine after the revolution of 1908 against the sultanate. Jewish settlements in lower Galilee were frequently attacked, and there were clashes between Jews and Arabs in Haifa, Jaffa, and Jerusalem. The situation was even more critical in Galilee. Much of this, however, was part of the general lawlessness which spread as a result of events in Constantinople and the general weakening of Turkish authority. The Jews were not the only victims. The German settlements also came in for many attacks until Berlin intervened and dispatched a warship to Haifa.[34] But the way in which the Arab newspapers commented on these attacks showed that there was reason for concern. The Zionists had at first regarded the activities of Nagib Nasser as an isolated phenomenon. But *Al Karmel* was joined by other newspapers of a similar character, such as *Falestin* in Jaffa (founded in 1911), and *Al Muntada* in Jerusalem, which began to appear in 1912. Virulent pamphlets and books were published and the Arab press outside Palestine began to open its pages to articles about the Zi-

[33] Menahem Sheinkin, quoted in *Sefer Toldot Hahagana* 1: 135.
[34] *Sefer Toldot Hahagana,* p. 191.

onist danger.[35] Leading Jewish citizens such as David Yellin expressed apprehension: "Fifteen years ago the Muslims hated the Christians, while their attitude towards the Jews had been one of contempt. Now their attitude towards the Christians has changed for the better and to the Jews for the worse." A group of leading citizens wrote to Ruppin from Haifa that "we are alarmed to see with what speed the poison sown by our enemies is spreading among all layers of the population. We must fear all possible calamities. It would be criminal to continue preserving the attitude of placid onlookers."[36]

In part, the deterioration was the fault of the new immigrants, who did not know the language of the Arabs and made no effort to understand and respect their customs. There is no doubt that their communal living, their radical political and social ideas, and the ostentatious equality they observed between the sexes among the new immigrants, shocked and dismayed most Arabs. Their ways must have appeared to them indecent and immoral. There were other complaints: in their new settlements the Jews refused to employ Arab guards but tried to defend themselves against the incursions of thieves and robbers. In the past, Palestinian Jews had tried to cope with such emergencies by invoking the help of the foreign consuls, or by paying *baksheesh* to the local Turkish authorities or to the headmen of the neighboring Arab villages. The new guardians and their association, the *Hashomer,* made many mistakes, partly because few of them had mastered the Arab language, partly because they were appalled by the cowardice of the old *Yishuv* when it came to standing up to the Arabs. They wanted to impress on their neighbors that they belonged to a different breed: if they erred, they preferred to err on the side of toughness. They did not regard themselves as a race of supermen; they did not want to be feared; they did not despise the Arabs; they simply wished to be respected. They expressly excluded from their ranks those who claimed that "the Arab understands only the language of the whip."[37]

*   *   *

[35] Mandel, *Middle Eastern Affairs,* p. 97.
[36] Quoted in Ro'i, "The Zionist Attitude . . . ," p. 227.
[37] *Sefer Toldot Hahagana,* p. 308. This refers to Josef Lishanski, born in Metulla, who spoke the language and knew the customs of the Arabs much better than the newcomers. He was one of the most famous *shomrim* of the early period. During the First World War he played a leading part in the *Nili* conspiracy.

The conflict had various causes, although the one most frequently mentioned at the time was not in fact the most important. The number of *felahin* dispossessed was small. Only a tiny percentage of the land acquired by the Zionists was bought from small peasants; most of it came from the large landowners. One-quarter of all Jewish land in Palestine (the Esdraelon valley) was in fact acquired from one single absentee landlord, the Christian Arab Sursuq family which lived in Beirut. Various British committees of enquiry (such as the Shaw and Simpson committees) discovered in the 1920s that a large landless class was developing in the Arab sector and that more and more land was coming into a few hands. But this was not mainly the result of Jewish immigration. A similar tendency could also be observed in Egypt, and in other countries which were gradually coming into the orbit of the modern capitalist economy.

During the early years of Zionist settlement the Jewish land buyers showed no more concern than the Arab effendis for the fate of the *felahin* who were evicted. Only gradually did it dawn on them that, moral considerations quite apart, they were facing a potentially explosive political issue. Later on, greater care was taken to pay compensation or to find alternative employment for those who lost their land. But the effects of Jewish settlement on the Arab economy were minimal, as a statistical comparison shows: urbanization in Palestine did not proceed at a faster rate than in the neighboring Arab countries; Arab immigration into Palestine exceeded emigration from that country; and the birth rate rose more quickly than in the neighboring countries, as did the living standards of the Arabs in the neighborhood of the new Jewish settlements. These facts have frequently been quoted by Zionist authors, and they are irrefutable, as far as they go, both for the prewar period and the 1920s. If some Arabs suffered as a result of Jewish settlement, the number of those who benefited directly or indirectly was certainly greater. True, if Arab living standards improved, the Jewish settlers were still much better off, and the emergence of prosperous colonies must have caused considerable envy.

From a purely economic point of view, Arab resistance to Jewish immigration and settlement was inexplicable and unjustified. But then the economic aspect of the conflict was hardly ever of decisive importance. For that reason the Zionist hope, shared by Marxists and non-Marxists alike, that economic collaboration would act as a powerful stimulus towards political reconciliation, was quite un-realistic. The conflict was, of course, basically political in character, a clash between two national movements. The Arabs objected to Jewish immigration not so much because they feared proletarian-ization, as because they anticipated that the Jews intended one day to become masters of the country and that as a result they would be reduced to the status of a minority.

Only a handful of Zionists dreamed at the time of a Jewish state. The Turks had not the slightest intention of granting even a modest measure of independence to any part of the Ottoman Empire. But it is quite immaterial in this context whether Zionism at the time really had plans for conquest—perhaps the Arabs were better judges of the capacity of the Jews and their ambitions than the Zionists themselves. The idea of a Jewish state had had a few protagonists from the very beginning. Zeev Dubnow, for instance, one of the early *Bilu* settlers, in 1882 wrote to his more famous brother, the historian, that the final aim was to restore one day the independence of Eretz Yisrael. To this end settlements were to be established, the land and industry were to pass into Jewish hands, and the rising generation was to be taught the use of arms.[38] Michael Halpern, also, one of the early *shomrim,* used to talk occasionally about the conquest of the country by legions of Jewish soldiers. But these were flights of fancy indulged in by a few individuals, and no one took them seri-ously at the time.

At the other extreme, and equally unrepresentative, there were a few advocates of cultural assimilation; with their return to the East the Jews were to shed their European influences and reacquire Eastern customs and mental habits. The idea of the common Semitic origin of Jews and Arabs as a basis for close collaboration between the two peoples appeared early in the history of the Zionist move-ment. It figures in the writings of Epstein and of R. Benyamin (who worked in Ruppin's office in Jaffa). Sokolow, in an interview with the Cairo newspaper *Al Ahram* in 1914, said that he hoped the Jews would draw near to Arab culture in every respect, to build up together a great Palestinian civilization.[39] After the First World War, when the wisdom of the East was enjoying a fashionable success in Europe, M. Ben Gavriel (Eugen Hoeflich), a Viennese writer who settled in

---

[38] *Ktavim letoldot Chibat Zion* 3: 495.
[39] Ro'i, "The Zionist Attitude . . . ," pp. 217–18.

Jerusalem, propagated this same idea in a series of books and articles.[40] Even a radical Socialist such as Fritz Sternberg, who subsequently became better known as a Marxist theoretician, attributed decisive importance to the common Semitic origins of the two peoples and to the spiritual affinity felt by the Jews for the Arabs: "The east European Jews are still almost orientals," he wrote.[41] Even after the Second World War the concept of a Semitic federation in the Middle East still had some enthusiastic supporters in Israel.

It was not readily obvious what these ideologists were trying to prove, for even if a common racial or ethnic origin could have been demonstrated, they were overoptimistic in suggesting that it would have a strong political impact. Consanguinity is not necessarily a synonym for friendship, and the bitterest quarrels are traditionally those between members of one family. Most Zionist leaders of the day subscribed to the idea of Arab-Jewish brotherhood, or at any rate paid lip service to it, but they did so more often than not, it would appear, because of their inability to find any other ideological justification or a more tangible practical approach to improve relations with the Arabs. One of the dissidents was Richard Lichtheim, a leading German Zionist, who together with Jacobson represented the Zionist Executive in Constantinople. In his reports to his superiors he agreed that it was vital to make every effort to win the goodwill of the Arabs, and to organize Jewish settlement in such a way as to serve Arab interests as well. But he had no illusions about the outcome of such a policy:

> The Arabs are and will remain our natural opponents. They do not care a straw for the "joint semitic spirit." I can only warn urgently against a historical or cultural chimera. They want orderly government, just taxes and political independence. The east of today aspires to no marvels other than American machinery and the Paris toilet. Of course the Arabs want to preserve their nation and cultivate their culture. What they need for this, however, is specifically European: money, organization, machinery.

---

[40] Beginning with *Die Pforte des Ostens* (Vienna, 1924), in which he also advocated a binational state. Jabotinsky, on the other hand, had no patience with such theories. When he approached Nordau during the war about the establishment of a Jewish Legion which was to fight against the Turks, he was told, "But you cannot do that, the Muslims are kin to the Jews, Ishmael was our uncle." "Ishmael is not our uncle," Jabotinsky replied. "We belong, thank God, to Europe and for two thousand years have helped to create the culture of the west."

[41] "Die Bedeutung der Araberfrage fuer den Zionismus," in *Der Jude*, 1918, p. 150.

The Jew for them is a competitor who threatens their predominance in Palestine. . . .[42]

Writing many years later, Lichtheim stated that it had been clear to him even before 1914 that the national aspirations of the Zionists and the Palestinian Arabs were irreconcilable.[43]

Ruppin, on the other hand, continued to believe in a binational state. He would despair of the possibility of ever realizing the Zionist idea, he still declared at the Zionist Congress in Vienna in 1925, if there were no possibility of doing justice to the national interests of both Jews and Arabs. But soon after doubts set in. He realized that all Palestinian Arabs were opposed to Zionism, and if any solution of the Palestinian problem were made contingent on the agreement of the Arabs it would imply the cessation of immigration and of Jewish economic development. In December 1931 he sadly wrote to Victor Jacobson, his old friend from the Constantinople days: "What we can get today from the Arabs—we don't need. What we need—we can't get. What the Arabs are willing to give us is at most minority rights as in eastern Europe. But we have already had enough experience of the situation in eastern Europe. . . ."[44]

Politics apart, relations between Jews and Arabs were not too bad in pre-1914 Palestine, considering the great cultural and social differences between the communities. They were neighbors, and as among neighbors all over the world there was cooperation as well as conflict. Among the old residents, notably the Sephardic community, Arabic was for many the native language. Children grew up in the same street, Jews were in business together with Arabs, some wrote poems in Arabic or articles for the Arab press. There were even, at a limited level, social contacts. Among the new immigrants, too, there was considerable interest in things Arab. The Jewish watchmen, the *shomrim,* often adopted the Arab headgear (*kefiya*), and went out of their way to make friends in the neighboring villages. Arab colloquialisms entered the Hebrew language, though not usually on the highest literary level. With Moshe Smi-

---

[42] Reports dated October and November 1913, quoted in Ro'i, "The Zionist Attitude . . . ," pp. 214–15.
[43] Lichtheim, *Rückkehr,* p. 228.
[44] A. Ruppin, *Pirke Khayai* (Tel Aviv, 1968), 3: 203.

lansky's *Hawadja Musa,* the Arab theme entered Hebrew literature
well before the First World War. His short stories about the *felahin*
and their world, written with great feeling and sympathy, often ideal-
ized their way of life. The Zionists respected the Arabs as human
beings, regarding them as distant, if rather backward and ineffectual,
cousins. There was certainly no hatred on their part. But being totally
absorbed in their own national government, they did not recognize
that their cousins, too, were undergoing a national revival, and they
sometimes seemed to deny them the right to do so.

In the deliberations of the Zionist Executive various aspects of
the Arab question were discussed from time to time. Ruppin, in his
report to the eleventh Zionist Congress, noted that the Zionists had
to make up for a great deal they had neglected, and to correct the
errors they had committed. "It is of course quite useless to content
ourselves with merely assuring the Arabs that we are coming into
the country as their friends. We must prove this by our deeds."[45]
At the previous congress, Shlomo Kaplanski, one of the leaders of
the Labor Zionists, had stressed the necessity of a rapprochement
with the Arabs. He did not believe in a lasting conflict between the
Zionists and the *felahin* and was confident that an understanding with
the democratic forces in the Arab world—though not perhaps with
the effendis—could be reached.[46]

But Ruppin had no recipe for making friends among the Arabs
and had to resort to the old arguments: Zionist colonization had
brought great material benefits to the Arabs, they had learned
modern agricultural methods from the Jews, Jewish doctors had
helped to stamp out epidemics among them. Ruppin was aware that
the utmost tact and caution had to be used when buying Arab land
so that no harsh results would follow. At one stage, in May 1911,
he suggested in a memorandum to the Zionist Executive a limited
population transfer. The Zionists would buy land near Aleppo and
Homs in northern Syria for the resettlement of the Arab peasants who had been dispossessed in Palestine. But this was vetoed
because it was bound to increase Arab suspicions about Zionist
intentions.[47]

[45] Arthur Ruppin, *Building Israel* (New York, 1949), p. 63.
[46] *Stenographisches Protokoll* . . . (Berlin, 1911), pp. 81–2. Wolffsohn, president of
the Zionist Organisation, replied: "Don't forget to tell this to your friends in Palestine!" *Ibid.*
[47] The correspondence is quoted in Alsberg, "The Arab Question . . . ," p. 175.

Although Dr. Ruppin's scheme was rejected, the idea of a population transfer preoccupied other members of the Zionist executive. In 1912 Leo Motzkin, dissenting from the views of Ahad Haam (who had by that time reached deeply pessimistic conclusions about the Arab attitude, based on the belief that they would never accept a Jewish majority), suggested that the Arab-Jewish problem should be considered in a wider framework: there were extensive uncultivated lands around Palestine belonging to Arabs; perhaps they would be willing to settle there with the money realized from selling their land to the Zionists?[48] Again in 1914 Motzkin and Sokolow seem to have played with the idea of a population transfer. Its most consistent advocate was Israel Zangwill, the Anglo-Jewish writer, who in a series of speeches and articles during and after the First World War criticized the Zionists (with whom he had parted company at the time of the Uganda conflict) for ignoring the fact that Palestine was not empty. The concept of an "Arab trek" to their own Arabian state played a central part in his scheme. Of course, the Arabs would not be compelled to do so, it would all be agreed upon in a friendly and amicable spirit. Zangwill pointed to many such migrations which had taken place in history, including the migration of the Boers to the Transvaal: why should not the Arabs realize that it was in their best interests? They would be fully compensated by the Zionists. Zangwill later explained to a friend that he expected that in the postwar world, reconstituted on a basis of love and reason, the Arab inhabitants of Palestine, for whose kinsmen, after years of oppression, a new state would be set up in Arabia, would naturally sympathize with the ideal of the still more unfortunate nation of Israel and would be magnanimous enough to leave these few thousand square miles to the race which had preserved its dream of them for 2,000 years. Zangwill foresaw two states rising side by side; "Otherwise, he did not see that a Jewish state could arise at all, but only a state of friction."[49]

But the idea of a population transfer was never official Zionist policy. Ben-Gurion emphatically rejected it, saying that even if the Jews were given the right to evict the Arabs they would not make

[48] In his speech at the annual conference of German Zionists at Posen, *Jüdische Rundschau*, 12 July 1912.

[49] Redcliffe N. Salaman, *Palestine Reclaimed* (London, 1920), pp. 175–6.

use of it.[50] Most thought at that time that there would be sufficient room in Palestine for both Jews and Arabs following the industrialization of the country and the introduction of intensive methods of agriculture. Since no one before 1914 expected the disintegration of the Turkish Empire in the foreseeable future, the question of political autonomy did not figure in their thoughts. They were genuinely aggrieved that the Arabs were not more grateful for the economic benefits they had come to enjoy as the result of Jewish immigration and settlement. They thought that the growth of Arab nationalism and anti-Zionist attacks were the result of the activities of individual villains, the effendis (who were annoyed because the Jews had spoiled the *felahin* by paying them higher wages), and the Christian Arabs (who had to demonstrate that they were as good patriots as their Muslim fellow citizens).

When an Arab national movement developed in Palestine after 1908, the Zionists did not at first attach much importance to it because it consisted of very few people who, moreover, were divided into several factions and parties. It is not difficult to draw up a substantial list of Zionist sins of omission and commission before 1914. They should have devoted far more attention to the Arab question, and been more cautious in land purchases. Many more should have learned Arabic and the customs of their neighbors, and they should have taken greater care not to offend their feelings. They should have accepted Ottoman citizenship and have tried to make friends with Arabs on a personal level, following the example of Kalvarisky. There were possibilities of influencing Arab public opinion, of explaining that the Jews were not coming to dominate the Arabs. But the means put at the disposal of Dr. Ruppin and his colleagues in Jaffa for this purpose were woefully insufficient. Much more publicity should have been given, for instance, to Wolffsohn's statement at the eleventh Zionist Congress that the Jews were not looking for a state of their own in Palestine but merely for a *Heimstätte.* Whether this would have dispelled Arab fears is less certain, for they worried not so much about the Zionist presence as about their future plans. In this respect Arab apprehension was not unfounded. The Zionists, on the other hand, did not foresee that as a result of growing prosperity the number of Palestinian Arabs would rapidly grow. They did

---

[50] D. Ben-Gurion, in an article published in 1918 included in *Anakhnu veshekhnenu* (Tel Aviv, 1931), p. 41.

not face the fact that the Palestinian Arabs belonged to a people of many millions which was by no means indifferent to the future of the Holy Land.

The Palestinian Arabs who had tolerated (and despised) the local Jews[51] were genuinely afraid of the aggressive new immigrants who seemed to belong to an altogether different breed. They resented them for the same reasons that substantial mass immigration has always and everywhere produced tension: peasants were afraid of change, shopkeepers and professional men feared competition, religious dignitaries, whether Christian or Muslim, were anything but friendly towards the Jews for traditional, doctrinal reasons. Arab anti-Zionist propaganda after 1908 was, of course, highly exaggerated. The economic situation of the Arabs had certainly not deteriorated as a result of the influx of these strangers, and they overrated the Zionist potential. The Jews had neither the money nor the intention to buy up all the land (as Arab propaganda claimed), to dispossess and proletarianize all Arab peasants. Their political ambitions certainly did not extend to the Nile and the Euphrates.

But the Arabs were correct in the essential point, namely that the Jews wanted to establish a position of strength in Palestine, through their superior organization and economic power, and that they intended to become eventually a majority. They sensed this logic of events more correctly than the Zionists themselves, who did not think in terms of political power and lacked the instinct for it. The early Zionists were all basically pacifists. The idea that it might be impossible to establish a state without bloodshed seems never to have occurred to them. The first to raise the question was a non-Zionist, the sociologist Gumplowicz, in a letter to Herzl: "You want to found a state without bloodshed? Where did you ever see that? Without violence and without guile, simply by selling and buying shares?"[52]

But even the most exemplary behavior on the part of the Zionists would not have affected the real source of the conflict, namely, that the Jews were looking in Palestine for more than a cultural center. However effective their propaganda, however substantial the material

---

[51] Eliezer Ben-Yehudah, who emigrated to Palestine from Russia in 1882, wrote in his autobiography that he found that the Arabs did not hate the Jews but despised them for their cowardice. *Kitve Ben Yehuda* (Jerusalem, 1941), p. 37.
[52] W. Cahnmann, in *Herzl Yearbook* (New York, 1958), p. 165.

benefits that would have accrued to the Arabs from the Jewish settlement, it would still have left unanswered the decisive question—to
whom was the country eventually to belong? It was more than a
little naive to put the blame for Arab anti-Zionism on professional
inciters, frustrated Arab notables, and the notorious urban riff-raff,
for there was a basic clash between two national movements. Full
identification on the part of the Zionists with the aims of pan-
Arabism from an early date would perhaps have helped to blunt the
sharpness of the conflict. But this was of course not in accordance
with the aims of the Jewish national revival. Nor would it have induced the Arabs to receive the Zionist immigrants with open arms.
The Arab world was already plagued by the presence of religious
and ethnic minorities and the conflicts between them. Any further
increase in their number and strength would have only added to
its anxieties. Given the character of the Zionist movement, with its
basic demands (immigration and settlement), and given also the
natural fears of the Palestinian Arabs, it is impossible even with
the benefit of hindsight to point with any degree of conviction to
an alternative Zionist policy, even before the Balfour Declaration,
which might have prevented conflict.[53]

[53] Mandel, St. Antony's Papers, p. 108 and dissertation.

J. L. Talmon
ISRAEL AMONG THE NATIONS

In this second selection from Israel among the Nations, *J. L. Talmon seeks with compassion, but also with pride in the Zionist achievement, to view the origins of the Arab-Israeli conflict in the broadest context—the place of world Jewry in modern history.*

One does not have to be a committed Zionist to recognize that the establishment of the State of Israel has been the most remarkable and most constructive achievement of the Jewish people as a corporate entity for the last 2,000 years, and one of the great feats of universal history. Since this essay is written in anything but a mood of self-congratulation, it is only fair to begin by highlighting the outstanding features, familiar though they be, of this vast and inspiring panorama.

In no time at all, relatively speaking, the Zionist movement succeeded in focusing the interest, the emotions, the passions, and the will of members of widely dispersed and very heterogeneous Jewish communities throughout the world upon what had for very long been nothing more than a mere vision. It was able to set up on a completely voluntary basis a whole network of institutions—a government, a national assembly, an administrative apparatus, and an army—long before Jews had even settled in the territory over which they would ultimately achieve political sovereignty. The movement won the Platonic and sometimes even ardent sympathy of wide sections of Gentile public opinion in many countries, and then, through a masterly exploitation of propitious circumstances in a fluid historical situation, obtained formal pledges of assistance from great powers and recognition of its claims by the highest international bodies. It undertook and triumphantly accomplished the task of building, without resort to force, a national-territorial community out of immigrants who came from different climates, cultural traditions, and economic conditions; it established self-governing towns and villages, agriculture and industry, and local organs of self-defense—

Reprinted with permission of Macmillan Publishing Co., Inc. and George Weidenfeld and Nicolson Ltd. from *Israel among the Nations* by J. L. Talmon, pp. 130–134, 142–147. Copyright © 1970 by J. L. Talmon. Footnotes omitted.

all this in the teeth of obstruction of all kinds, culminating in determined chicanery and armed resistance by the indigenous Arab population. It laid the foundations for a new civilization, based on an artificially revived language, and on an endeavor to throw a bridge across the centuries into the remotest past. It undertook at the same time social experiments requiring the most strenuous idealism and avant-garde daring.

Faced at last with the ineluctable necessity of marshaling all the moral and material resources for a national liberation struggle, the Zionist movement was able to organize civil disobedience, underground activity, terrorist and guerrilla operations, while simultaneously conducting an intensive diplomatic campaign on the world stage. It was then called upon to go through the supreme test of fighting the invading armies of half a dozen states. Notwithstanding the permanent armed siege under which the new state has since had to live for all the twenty years of its existence Israel has remained a genuine and effective democracy, the only one within a radius of thousands of miles, and strong enough to sustain itself in spite of deep internal divisions. Its record in education and culture, without being spectacular, has been quite respectable, and its success in transforming a motley of what could almost be called races into a coherent modern nation has been highly impressive. Finally, there is the incredible feat of arms—the famous victory of June 1967 over four combined Arab armies.

The historian looks to other movements of national liberation for terms of reference and points of comparison. The national aspiration of a normal people struggling for independence turns on a relatively simple issue, aggravated and complicated as it may be by practical circumstances: the expulsion of foreign rulers. In such instances the moral case is so self-evident as to need no proof or elaboration. Not so Zionism. I am not only referring to the obvious fact that the Jews had neither territory nor nationhood in the conventional sense when they embarked on the Zionist venture. I have in mind the moral dilemmas which the very Jewishness of the Zionists could not but make extremely acute. Believers themselves in the right of national self-determination, they could pursue it only at the cost of conflict with Arabs claiming the same simple right. In analogous fashion, though fundamentally anti-imperialist and passionately democratic, the Zionists had no choice but to look for help to imperial powers.

Many a Jewish youth stood bewildered in the cross-fires of those days—between the demands of the religious conscience and those of secular power-politics; between messianic nationalism on the one side, and messianic revolutionary universalism on the other.

The failures or sins of which Zionism has been guilty in this respect call—I wish to submit—not for censure alone, but also for compassion as unavoidable tragedies. This sustained, strenuous effort—awe-inspiring in its single-mindedness, astonishing in its global strategies, and often heart-rending in the moral dilemmas it was called upon to confront—was carried out in the midst of the greatest calamity that has ever befallen a people, and brought to fruition on the morrow of the most horrible blood-letting that any group has ever experienced. Dull must be the man, Jew or Gentile, who would fail to respond with a thrill to this most powerful assertion of the will to live in the shadows and the agonies of death; to this triumph of the human spirit over the deepest degradation and wretchedness.

On the strength of a long and close familiarity with the history of national movements, admittedly restricted to Europe, I would venture to claim that Zionism was the richest of them all. In Zionism we find all the salient features of each rolled into one: the aura of ancient myth and the vision of renovation which constituted the unique appeal of the Greek war of independence; the theoretical, not to say metaphysical, elaboration of national ideology in nineteenth-century Germany; the missionary idealism of the Italian risorgimento, coupled with consummate diplomatic skill and finesse; the dogged romantic desperation of the Irish and the Poles; the cultural and literary renaissance of the Slav peoples; the social radicalism of many a national liberation movement in Asia and Africa. The wonderful gallery of great and colorful personalities thrown up by Zionism will stand comparison with any of the finest and ablest national leaders among the nations: Herzl with Mazzini, Weizmann with Cavour or Masaryk, Ben-Gurion with Bismarck or Pilsudski, Jabotinsky with Nehru, Buber with Fichte, Bialik with Mickiewicz and Petofi, Aharon David Gordon with Gandhi. Israel has also exploded many of the most rooted and widely held fallacies about Jews. The great Theodor Mommsen was sure that the Jew lacked all talent for politics, just as Ernest Renan had little hesitation in lending his immense authority as a Semitic scholar to the idea that Jews possessed no aptitude for philosophy, science, and the arts. Which Gentile only half a century ago had any doubt that the Jews could not fight, were all cowards, and knew nothing of military honor? Israel has changed all that to the point where a French shopkeeper in June 1967 could express his surprise that Poland could have been so quickly and so completely beaten by the Germans in 1939, "when there were so many Jews in Poland in those days."

Israel has been seen as the fulfillment and ultimate dénouement of Jewish history, but it has also been seen as the greatest deviation from the course of that history. It may be altogether too metaphysical a pursuit for the scholarly historian to try to define the "true essence," the "authentic spirit," or the "preordained direction" of a millennial history spun over such diverse epochs, civilizations, and regions, and to describe developments which do not conform to that "authentic core" as deviations, false starts, perversions, heresies, or culs-de-sac. We all know that these speculations are so often the fuel of political ideologies. All of us are by now also sufficiently dialectical in our thinking to view revolution as both the coming to a climax of the old, and the transmutation of that longstanding reality into an opposite state of affairs.

There is nothing absurd or illegitimate in the view that the establishment of a political and warrior state in some way constitutes a repudiation of a long Jewish tradition. According to this philosophy, preexilic Jewish statehood was a tribal phase to be outgrown, and outgrown it was, with the result that the Jews came into their own for the next 2,000 years as a strictly religious confraternity, an entirely apolitical civilization. Continuing this trend of thought, one would conclude that Zionism was an assimilationist movement par excellence. Its inspiration was the envious desire to emulate the example of "all the nations," to be like them, and the modes of action to which it resorted were alien to a tradition of nearly 2,000 years.

*   *   *

The Jewish movement of national liberation derived from a thoroughly liberal-humanitarian impulse. It was at the same time driven on by intensely antiliberal forces. The climate in which it was destined to realize its aspiration was nothing short of apocalyptic. Above all, it was condemned to come into conflict with another national aspiration, which clash—let us have the courage to face the brutal truth—was incapable of resolution in any spirit of democratic liberalism.

It was the misfortune of Zionism to have arrived late, and to have achieved its aim in the nick of time, if not, indeed, again too late. The very close early association with the Russian revolutionary ideology imbued Zionism, especially its left wing, with Mazzinian notions of a united front of all oppressed nationalities struggling for liberation against a common oppressor. Yet by the time Zionism arrived, nationalism everywhere in Europe had developed into a cult of sacred egoism. Zionism expressed and represented a yearning for a home for the oppressed and for those who wished to be themselves—has there ever been a nobler aspiration? Yet the planet had by then been divided, and there were no longer any empty spaces. The home to which Zionism naturally aspired was inhabited by another people, the Arabs, and ruled by a third nation, the Turks. All of mankind's history has been a history of invasion, conquest of nation by nation, deportation of populations or their absorption by others, not to speak of extermination. At the turn of the century such things had become both objectively and subjectively impossible, most of all to Jews. They were destined to become possible and horribly inevitable again half a century later. Herzl saw the Jewish problem as an international problem, as a matter of general concern to all nations. What he would have liked best was an international agreement and international machinery, with money provided by Jews and, if possible, also by European governments, for the resettlement of Jewish immigrants. There was no escape in practice from an association with some great power, which might have been, in this sinful world of ours, suspected of being more mindful of imperial interests than of humanitarian challenges. When Herzl began his rounds in quest for a powerful ally, finding access to Wilhelm II, Joseph Chamberlain, Abdul Hamid, and others, imperialism seemed at its zenith. The rule of the white man over all the colored races had seemed a preordained and blessed fulfillment—the more so for the fact that such imperial powers as Great Britain and France represented advanced political regimes and progressive social systems. But white hegemony and European self-assurance received a strong jolt in the form of the resounding victory of Japan over imperial Russia in 1904 (which was the year of Herzl's death). For the first time in modern history, a colored race had succeeded in defeating one of the great white powers. In retrospect we can see that event as the beginning of the end of Western imperialism. The Japanese victory triggered a series of momentous explosions in Asia and Africa: the Young Turk revolution, the revolution in Persia, a little later the Chinese revolution, the radicalization of the Congress party in India, and the first rumblings of Arab nationalism in the Levant.

Nothing was calculated to please the Zionists more than the spreading of the League of Nations umbrella over the Balfour Declaration and British rule in Palestine. Representing, as it did, an international decision to help the homeless Jews, it seemed to do away with the specter of Jews having to fight, and ultimately to displace, Arabs. Palestine was put under a League of Nations mandate after World War I, and it was in response to the growth of Arab nationalism that Iraq and Syria and the Lebanon found themselves in the same status. The Zionists would say that the latter mandates were established to prepare the local Arabs for independence and the Palestine Mandate to facilitate the upbuilding of the Jewish national home as promised in the Balfour Declaration: could a fairer and most just procedure be imagined? The Arabs, however, would interpret matters differently: if Iraq, Syria, and Lebanon were entitled to independence, so too were the Palestinian Arabs.

The State of Israel came into being some twenty years later at a time when the process of decolonization was already in full swing (in fact, the withdrawal of the British from Palestine in 1948 was modeled on their withdrawal from India a year earlier). It is more than doubtful whether a few years later the majority necessary for the UN resolution on the partition of Palestine could have been obtained at all. Few, if any, of the new Asian and African states, which were due to be admitted to the UN soon after, and which now maintain friendly relations with Israel, would have been prepared to vote for the establishment of a Jewish state before having had an opportunity to see Israel at work not as a society of colonial planters, but as a society of workers and producers, and to derive benefit from its services and example.

The exit of the white man from Asia and Africa and the arrival of the Jews into that nodal point where the two continents touch is a coincidence with tremendous symbolic overtones. Its significance for Israel is further deepened by the fact that the reemergence of vast ancient civilizations like China, Japan, and India, and the rise of a large number of new nations, are bound to make for a relative decline in the weight of the Jewish ingredient in the sum total of human civilization. The races of Asia and Africa were not brought up on the Bible. They cannot be expected to respond to the magic names of Zion and Jerusalem in the way Bible readers do. They have never been preoccupied or obsessed with the Jewish phenomenon: they have never admired, feared, or persecuted the Jews. Their record is clean of anti-Semitism, but it is also empty of Jews. Hence their proneness to equate Israeli Jews with white intruders.

The Zionist-British relationship bears the mark of "too little and too late," and of an ambiguity which burdened the Jews with guilt without at the same time granting them the sweets of sin. It is no mean irony that while the Balfour Declaration may have looked like a deal between imperial Britain and the Jews, disguised on Britain's part by high-sounding idealistic formulae, the entire history of the Anglo-Zionist partnership was one of a sustained effort on England's part to escape the obligations and the logic of that solemn pledge. There has never been agreement on what that pledge really contained. Nor, for that matter, do we really know, in spite of the innumerable reasons given by or attributed to the British government, why the Balfour Declaration was even issued—as Christopher Sykes, the son of Sir Mark Sykes, one of the architects of British policies in the Middle East during World War I, points out in his perceptive *Crossroads to Israel.* The late British Empire was acquired, it is said, in a fit of absent-mindedness; so, too, the Balfour Declaration seems to have been issued by a group of men who did not know what they were doing.

The statesmen of 1917 may have been confused, inattentive, muddled, idealistic, or shrewd; they may have been moved by humanitarian sentiment, by strategic considerations, by the wish to gain the sympathy of American Jewry for the Allied war effort, or to wean the Russian Jews away from Bolshevism, by the desire, finally, to cut the French out of Palestine. It is difficult, perhaps impossible, to know. But certainly no one gave precise thought to the ways in which the Balfour Declaration should be implemented. And in any case, contrary to popular belief, surprisingly little attention seems to have been paid to the idea of turning Palestine into a bastion for Suez.

Very soon after 1917 and throughout the thirty years of British administration that followed, there was little disagreement among the British, least of all among the men called upon to implement the mandate in Whitehall and in Palestine, that the association with Zionism was at best a terrible embarrassment and liability. Few, even among those who supported Zionism,—or, more accurately, among those who from time to time could be alerted by the Zionists to prevent another attempt at whittling away the provisions of the Balfour Declaration—did so out of a sense of conviction or a disposition to give a helping hand to something good and desirable. Instead they acted out of a sense of obligation to a pledged word, in a resigned attempt to make the best of a bad job. Lloyd George seems to have been speaking for most of his colleagues when, in 1919, he tried to still objections to Zionism with the confident assertion that Britain's age-long experience of empire would enable her to take on all parties concerned—Jews, Arabs, Christians, the pope, and the caliph—and (he did not use the expression, though he implied it) muddle through somehow. Why should the Arabs, who were about to get so much, when for centuries under the Turks they had had nothing, "begrudge the Jews that little notch"? And, indeed, who were the Arabs? Before 1914, they had hardly impinged upon the consciousness of Europe, except perhaps as another native population with colorful nomadic Bedouins, etc., etc.

One man saw the dilemma clearly, and that was Balfour himself:

> The contradiction between the letter of the Covenant and the policy of the Allies is even more flagrant in the case of the independent nation of Palestine than in that of the independent nation of Syria. For in Palestine we do not propose even to go through the form of consulting the wishes of the present inhabitants of the country. . . . The four great powers are committed to Zionism, and Zionism, be it right or wrong, good or bad, is rooted in age-long tradition, in present needs, in future hopes, of far profounder importance than the desires and prejudices of the seven hundred thousand Arabs who now inhabit that ancient land. . . .

With all this, Balfour was most reluctant for Britain to assume the mandate, and very anxious to hand it over to the United States. England was tired and disillusioned in the wake of the bloodiest of wars the world had seen till then; the imperial urge and the sense of mission were by then too enfeebled for her to take up the kind of challenge Balfour may have had in mind: to plan and execute with the cooperation of Jews and various international agencies a scheme of colonization and settlement within a fixed number of years. It may well be that had such an approach been seriously attempted, the Arabs, dazed and weak as they still were, would have been placed before a fait accompli without any injury to their economic interests. They might then have accepted the accomplished fact, and the long drawn-out agony would have been avoided. But all this is plausible only within the theoretical sphere. As a matter of historical fact, such Keynesian methods as Five Year programs, Marshall plans, Four Point proposals, etc., were still beyond the ken of most people in the West. The British administration in Palestine had not been intended and was not equipped for such undertakings. Its greatest ambition was to keep the peace somehow and to get the essential services running, harassed as it was by the opposing claims of the Jews—impatient, arrogant, intent on forging ahead—and the Arabs—sulky, riotous, and aggrieved.

Was the Arab-Jewish conflict inevitable? Can one put one's finger on sins of commission or omission, on points of no return, and say that had this or that happened or not happened, been done or not been done, things would have taken a radically different course? The more I ponder these questions, the more confirmed I become in the grim conclusion that although in detail, in style and tone, the Jews might have acted more wisely or more tactfully, it would not have made much difference in the final analysis. The same cannot be said about the Arabs. On very many occasions they could, by making concessions, have arrested or very significantly slowed down the growth of the Jewish national home so as to prevent its transformation into a Jewish state. By adopting an attitude of absolute and total intransigence, they reduced the *Yishuv*'s alternatives either to giving up Zionism or to carrying out its program to the full extent in the teeth of Arab opposition. Since no give and take was possible, since even such modest forms of Zionism as a measure of immigration and settlement encountered maximum resistance, there seemed no choice but to aim at maximum strength. God had hardened the heart of Pharaoh.

Suggestions for Additional Reading

Two general bibliographies, which may be consulted on all the topics introduced in this collection, can be found in Muriel Emanuel, ed., *Israel: A Survey and Bibliography* (New York, 1971); and Raphael Patai, ed., *Encyclopedia of Zionism and Israel*, 2 vols. (New York, 1971).

For further studies of European anti-Semitism in the late nineteenth century and the Jewish response to it see Hannah Arendt, *The Origins of Totalitarianism* (Cleveland, 1958); Robert F. Byrnes, *Antisemitism in Modern France* (New Brunswick, 1950); Louis Greenberg, *The Jews in Russia,* 2 vols. (New Haven, 1951); Michael R. Marrus, *The Politics of Assimilation: A Study of the French Jewish Community at the Time of the Dreyfus Affair* (London, 1971); Paul W. Massing, *Rehearsal for Destruction: A Study of Political Anti-Semitism in Imperial Germany* (New York, 1949); Joseph Nedava, *Trotsky and the Jews* (Phila., 1971); G. J. Pulzer, *The Rise of Political Anti-Semitism in Germany and Austria* (New York, 1964); Howard M. Sachar, *The Course of Modern Jewish History* (New York, 1958); Ismar Schorsch, *Jewish Reactions to German Anti-Semitism, 1870–1914* (New York, 1972); J. L. Talmon, *The Unique and the Universal* (New York, 1965); and Henry J. Tobias, *The Jewish Bund in Russia: From its Origins to 1905* (Stanford, 1972).

Several studies of the rise of Zionism are most useful. These include Alex Bein, *Theodore Herzl: A Biography* (New York, 1970); Ben Halpern, *The Idea of the Jewish State,* 2nd ed. (Cambridge, Mass., 1969); Arthur Hertzberg, ed., *The Zionist Idea: A Historical Analysis and Reader* (New York, 1971); Hans Kohn, ed., *Nationalism and the Jewish Ethic: Basic Writings of Ahad Ha'Am* (New York, 1962); Norman Kotker, *Herzl the King* (New York, 1972); Walter Laqueur, *A History of Zionism* (New York, 1972); Rufus Learsi, *Fulfillment: The Epic Story of Zionism* (New York, 1972); Ludwig Lewisohn, ed., *Theodore Herzl: A Portrait for This Age* (New York, 1955); Marvin Lowenthal, ed., *The Diaries of Theodore Herzl* (New York, 1962); Nathan Rotenstreich, *Tradition and Reality: The Impact of History on Modern Jewish Thought* (New York, 1972); Leon Simon, *Ahad Ha-Am, Asher Ginzberg* (New York, 1960); J. L. Talmon, *Israel among the Nations* (New York, 1970); Robert G. Weisbord, *African Zion: The Attempt to Establish a*

Jewish Colony in the East Africa Protectorate 1903–1905 (Phila., 1968); Meyer W. Weisgal and Joel Carmichael, eds., *Chaim Weizmann: A Biography by Several Hands* (London, 1962); Chaim Weizmann, *Trial and Error* (New York, 1949); and *The Letters and Papers of Chaim Weizmann,* vols. 1 and 2 (London, 1968, 1971).

Zionist activities in Palestine before 1918 are dealt with in Alex Bein, ed., *Arthur Ruppin: Memoirs, Diaries, Letters* (New York, 1971); Amos Elon, *The Israelis: Founders and Sons* (New York, 1971); Esco Foundation for Palestine, *Palestine: A Study of Jewish, Arab and British Policies,* 2 vols. (New Haven, 1947); Ben Halpern, *The Idea of the Jewish State*; Arthur Hertzberg, ed., *The Zionist Idea*; Walter Laqueur, *A History of Zionism*; V. D. Segre, *Israel: A Society in Transition* (London, 1971); and Chaim Weizmann, *Trial and Error.*

The origins of the Balfour Declaration are explored in John Bowle, *Viscount Samuel* (London, 1957); Elie Kedourie, *England and the Middle East: The Destruction of the Ottoman Empire 1914–1921* (London, 1956); Jon Kimche, *The Unromantics, the Great Powers and the Balfour Declaration* (London, 1968); Aaron S. Klieman, *Foundations of British Policy in the Arab World: The Cairo Conference of 1921* (Baltimore, 1970); Walter Laqueur, *A History of Zionism*; Jukka Nevakivi, *Britain, France and the Arab Middle East 1914–1920* (London, 1969); Howard M. Sachar, *The Emergence of the Middle East 1914–1924* (New York, 1969); Herbert Samuel, *Memoirs* (London, 1945); Leonard Stein, *The Balfour Declaration* (London, 1961); and Chaim Weizmann, *Trial and Error.*

For further studies of the origins of the Arab-Israeli conflict in the period before 1918 see Ibrahim Abu-Lughod, ed., *The Transformation of Palestine: Essays on the Origin and Development of the Arab-Israeli Conflict* (Evanston, 1971); George Antonius, *The Arab Awakening* (New York, 1965); Aharon Cohen, *Israel and the Arab World* (New York, 1970); Amos Elon, *The Israelis: Founders and Sons*; Rony E. Gabbay, *A Political Study of the Arab-Jewish Conflict* (New York, 1959); J. M. N. Jeffries, *Palestine: The Reality* (London, 1939); Walid Khalidi, ed., *From Haven to Conquest: Readings in Zionism and the Palestine Problem until 1948* (Beirut, 1971); Walter Laqueur, *A History of Zionism*; Neville Mandel, "Attempts at an Arab-Zionist Entente, 1913–1914," *Middle Eastern Studies,* April 1965; Neville Mandel, "Turks, Arabs and Jewish Immigration into Palestine 1882–1914," in Albert Hourani, ed., *Middle Eastern Affairs, St. Antony's Papers,* 4

(London, 1965); William R. Polk, David H. Stamler, and Edmund Asfour, *Backdrop to Tragedy: The Struggle for Palestine* (Boston, 1957); Yaacov Ro'i, "The Zionist Attitude to the Arabs, 1908–14," *Middle Eastern Studies,* April 1968; and J. L. Talmon, *Israel among the Nations.*

1 2 3 4 5 6 7 8 9 10

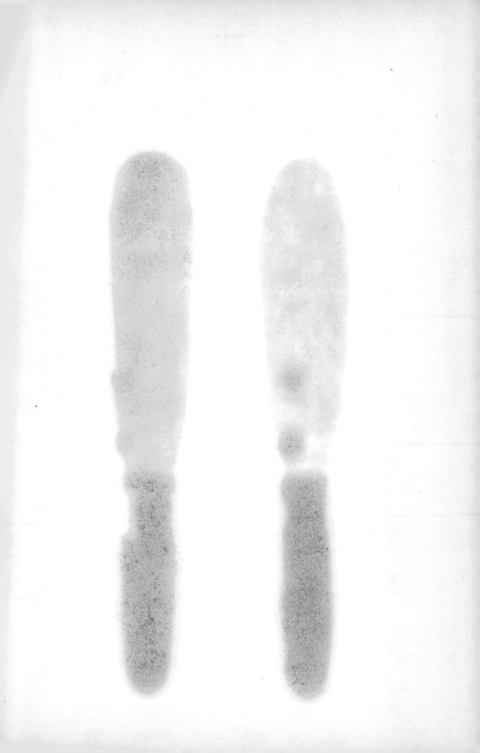

DATE DUE